Frommer's®

French Phrasebook & Culture Guide

1st Edition

WILEY

Wiley Publishing, Inc.

Published by:

Wiley Publishing, Inc.

111 River St.
Hoboken, NJ 07030-5774

Copyright © 2010 Wiley Publishing, Inc., Hoboken, New Jersey. All rights reserved.
No part of this publication may be reproduced, stored in a retrieval system, or
transmitted in any form or by any means, electronic, mechanical, photocopying,
recording, scanning, or otherwise, except as permitted under Sections 107 or 108
of the 1976 United States Copyright Act, without either the prior written permission
of the Publisher, or authorization through payment of the appropriate per-copy fee
to the Copyright Clearance Center, 222 Rosewood Drive, Danvers, MA 01923,
978/750-8400, fax 978/646-8600. Requests to the Publisher for permission should
be addressed to the Legal Department, Wiley Publishing, Inc., 10475 Crosspoint
Blvd., Indianapolis, IN 46256, 317/572-3447, fax 317/572-4355, or online at
http://www.wiley.com/go/permissions.

Wiley and the Wiley Publishing logo are trademarks or registered trademarks of
John Wiley & Sons, Inc. and/or its affiliates. Frommer's is a trademark or registered
trademark of Arthur Frommer. Used under license. All other trademarks are the
property of their respective owners. Wiley Publishing, Inc. is not associated with
any product or vendor mentioned in this book.

ISBN-13: 978-0-471-79299-4
ISBN-10: 0-471-79299-3

Series Editor: Maureen Clarke
French Editor: Marc Nadeau
Travel Tips and Culture Guide: David Applefield
Travel Content Editor: Michael Spring
Editorial Assistant: Melinda Quintero
Photo Editor: Richard H. Fox
Cover design by Fritz Metsch

With special thanks to Jennifer Reilly.

Interior Design, Content Development, Translation, Copyediting, Proofreading,
Production, and Layout by:
Publication Services, Inc., 1802 South Duncan Road, Champaign, IL 61822
Linguists: Frederique Vincent-Goodall, John Garvey, Aimee Ehrs

For information on our other products and services or to obtain technical support,
please contact our Customer Care Department within the U.S. at 800/762-2974, out
side the U.S. at 317/572-3993 or fax 317/572-4002.

Wiley also publishes its books in a variety of electronic formats. Some content that
appears in print may not be available in electronic formats.

Manufactured in the United States of America

9 8 7 6 5 4

Contents

An Invitation to the Reader

In researching this book, we discovered many wonderful sayings and terms useful to travelers in France. We're sure you'll find others. Please tell us about them, so we can share the information with your fellow travelers in upcoming editions. If you were disappointed with an aspect of this book, we'd like to know that, too. Please write to:

Frommer's French Phrasebook & Culture Guide, 2nd Edition
Wiley Publishing, Inc.
111 River St. • Hoboken, NJ 07030-5774

An Additional Note

The packager, editors, and publisher cannot be held responsible for the experiences of readers while traveling. Your safety is important to us, however, so we encourage you to stay alert and be aware of your surroundings. Keep a close eye on cameras, purses, and wallets, all favorite targets of thieves and pickpockets.

Frommers.com

Frommer's travel resources don't end with this guide. Frommer's website, **www.frommers.com**, has travel information on more than 4,000 destinations. We update features regularly, giving you access to the most current trip-planning information and the best airfare, lodging, and car-rental bargains. You can also listen to podcasts, connect with other Frommers.com members through our active-reader forums, share your travel photos, read blogs from guidebook editors and fellow travelers, and much more.

INTRODUCTION: HOW TO USE THIS BOOK

As a Romance language, French is closely related to Latin, Spanish, Italian, Portuguese, and Romanian. The most widely taught second language after English, French is spoken by more than 75 million people in countries throughout the world including France, Belgium, parts of Switzerland, Algeria, Tunisia, and Morocco, many nations of West Africa, Tahiti, several Caribbean islands, and Canada. French was also the official language of the English courts for centuries—from the Middle Ages until 1731—and its effect on English is extensive and indelible; roughly 45 percent of modern English vocabulary is of French origin.

Our intention is not to teach you French; we figure you'll find an audio program for that. Our aim is to provide a portable travel tool that's easy to use. The problem we noticed with most phrasebooks is that you practically have to memorize the contents before you know where to look for a term you might need on the spot. This phrasebook is designed for fingertip referencing, so you can whip it out and find the words you need fast.

Like most phrasebooks, part of this book organizes terms by chapters, like the chapters in a Frommer's guide—getting a room, getting a good meal, and so on. And within those sections, we tried to organize phrases intuitively, according to how frequently most readers are likely to use them. But let's say you're in a cab and you've received the wrong change, and you forget which chapter covers money. With Frommer's PhraseFinder, you can quickly look up "change" in the dictionary, and learn how to say "Sorry, but this isn't the right change." Then you can follow the cross reference for numbers, and quickly learn how to specify how much you're missing.

What will make this book most practical? What will make it easiest to use? These are the questions we asked ourselves constantly as we assembled these travel terms.

Our immediate goal was to create a phrasebook as indispensable as your passport. Our far-ranging goal, of course, is to enrich your experience of travel. And with that, we offer the following wish: *Bon voyage!*

CHAPTER ONE

SURVIVAL FRENCH

If you tire of toting around this phrasebook, tear out this section. With the right hand gestures, you'll get a lot of mileage from the terms in the next 43 pages.

BASIC GREETINGS

For a full list of greetings and introductions, see p135.

Hello.	**Bonjour!**
	boh~-zhoohr
How are you?	**Comment allez-vous?**
	koh-maw~-tah-lay-voo
I'm fine, thanks.	**Bien, merci.**
	bee-yeh~ mayhr-see
And you?	**Et vous?**
	ay voo
My name is ____.	**Je m'appelle ____.**
	zhuh mah-pehl
And yours?	**Et vous?**
	ay voo
It's a pleasure to meet you.	**Ravi(e) de faire votre connaissance.**
	rah-vee duh fayhr voh-truh koh-nay-sans
Please.	**S'il vous plaît.**
	seel voo play
Thank you.	**Merci.**
	mayhr-see
Yes.	**Oui.**
	wee
No.	**Non.**
	noh~

1

OK.	**D'accord.** *dah-kohr*
No problem.	**Pas de problème.** *pah duh proh-blehm*
I'm sorry, I don't understand.	**Je suis désolé(e), je ne comprends pas.** *zhuh swee day-zoh-lay zhuh nuh koh~-praw~ pah*
Would you speak slower, please?	**Pouvez-vous parler plus lentement, s'il vous plaît?** *poo-vay-voo pahr-lay plue law~t-maw~ seel voo play*
Would you speak louder, please?	**Pouvez-vous parler plus fort, s'il vous plaît?** *poo-vay-voo pahr-lay plue fohr seel voo play*
Do you speak English?	**Parlez-vous anglais?** *pahr-lay-voo-zaw~-glay*
Do you speak any other languages?	**Parlez-vous d'autres langues?** *pahr-lay-voo doh-truh law~g*
I speak ____ better than French.	**Je parle ____ mieux que le français.** *zhuh pahrl ____ mee-yeuh kuh luh fraw~-say*

For languages, see English / French dictionary.

Would you spell that, please?	**Pouvez-vous épeler cela?** *poo-vay-voo-zay-play suh-lah*
Would you please repeat that?	**Pouvez-vous répéter cela, s'il vous plaît?** *poo-vay-voo ray-pay-tay suh-lah, seel voo play*
Would you point that out in this dictionary?	**Pouvez-vous me le montrer dans ce dictionnaire?** *poo-vay-voo muh luh moh~-tray daw~ suh deek-see-oh~-ayhr*

THE KEY QUESTIONS

With the right hand gestures, you can get a lot of mileage from the following list of single-word questions and answers.

Who?	**Qui?**
	kee
What?	**Quoi?**
	kwah
When?	**Quand?**
	kaw~
Where?	**Où?**
	oo
Why?	**Pourquoi?**
	poohr-kwah
How?	**Comment?**
	koh-maw~
Which?	**Quel / Quelle?**
	kehl
How many / much?	**Combien?**
	koh~-bee-yeh~

THE ANSWERS: WHO

For full coverage of pronouns, see p22.

him	**lui**
	lwee
her	**elle**
	ehl
them	**eux / elles**
	euh / ehl
I	**moi**
	mwah
you (singular)	**toi / vous**
	twah / voo
you (plural)	**vous**
	voo
us	**nous**
	noo

THE ANSWERS: WHEN

now	**maintenant**
	maw~t-naw~
later	**plus tard**
	plue tahr
in a minute	**dans une minute**
	daw~-zoon mee-noot
today	**aujourd'hui**
	oh-zhoohr-dwee
tomorrow	**demain**
	duh-meh~
yesterday	**hier**
	yayhr
in a week	**dans une semaine**
	daw~-zoon smehn
next week	**la semaine prochaine**
	lah smehn proh-shen
last week	**la semaine dernière**
	lah smen dayhr-nyayhr
next month	**le mois prochain**
	luh mwah proh-sheh~
At ___	**À ___**
	ah
ten o'clock this morning.	**dix heures ce matin,**
	dee-zoehr suh mah-teh~
two o'clock this afternoon.	**deux heures cet après-midi,**
	doeh-zoehr seh-tah-pray-mee-dee
seven o'clock this evening.	**sept heures ce soir,**
	seh-toehr suh swahr

For a full list of numbers, see p7.

THE ANSWERS: WHERE

here	**ici**	
	ee-see	
there	**là**	
	lah	
near	**près**	
	pray	
closer	**plus près**	
	plue pray	
closest	**le plus près**	
	luh plue pray	
far	**loin**	
	lweh~	
farther	**plus loin**	
	plue lweh~	
farthest	**le plus loin**	
	luh plue lweh~	
across from	**de l'autre côté de**	
	duh lo-truh koh-tay duh	
next to	**à côté de**	
	ah koh-tay duh	
behind	**derrière**	
	day-ree-yayhr	
straight ahead	**tout droit**	
	too dwah	
left	**à gauche**	
	ah gohsh	
right	**à droite**	
	ah dwaht	
up	**en haut**	
	aw~-noh	
down	**en bas**	
	aw~ bah	
lower	**plus bas**	
	plue bah	

higher	**plus haut**
	plue-zoh
forward	**en avant**
	aw~-nah-vaw~
back	**en arrière**
	aw~-nah-ree-yayhr
around	**autour**
	oh-toohr
across the street	**l'autre côté de la rue**
	loh-truh koh-tay duh lah roo
down the street	**bas de la rue**
	bah duh lah roo
on the corner	**au coin de la rue**
	oh kweh~ duh lah roo
kitty-corner	**à l'opposé**
	ah loh-poh-zay
____ blocks from here	**à ____ rues d'ici**
	ah ____ roo dee-see

For a full list of numbers, see the following page.

THE ANSWERS: WHICH

this one	**celui-ci / celle-ci**
	suh-lwee see / sehl see
that one	**celui-là / celle-là**
	suh-lwee lah / sehl lah
this (here)	**ceci**
	suh-see
that (there)	**cela**
	suh-lah
these ones (here)	**ceux-ci / celles-ci**
	soeh-see / sehl see
those ones (there)	**ceux-là / celles-là**
	soeh-lah / sehl lah

NUMBERS & COUNTING

one	**un** *uh~*	eighteen	**dix-huit** *dee-zhweet*
two	**deux** *deuh*	nineteen	**dix-neuf** *deez-noehf*
three	**trois** *twah*	twenty	**vingt** *veh~t*
four	**quatre** *kah-truh*	twenty-one	**vingt-et-un** *veh~-tay-uh~*
five	**cinq** *saw~k*	twenty-two	**vingt-deux** *veh~t-deuh*
six	**six** *sees*	thirty	**trente** *traw~t*
seven	**sept** *seht*	forty	**quarante** *kah-raw~t*
eight	**huit** *hweet*	fifty	**cinquante** *seh~kaw~t*
nine	**neuf** *noehf*	sixty	**soixante** *swah-saw~t*
ten	**dix** *dees*	seventy	**soixante-dix** *swah-saw~t-dees*
eleven	**onze** *oh~z*	seventy-one	**soixante-et-onze** *swah-saw~-tay-oh~z*
twelve	**douze** *dooz*	seventy-two	**soixante-douze** *swah-sa~t-dooz*
thirteen	**treize** *trehz*	eighty	**quatre-vingt** *kah-truh-vaw~*
fourteen	**quatorze** *kah-tohrz*	eighty-one	**quatre-vingt-un** *kah-truh-vaw~-tuh~*
fifteen	**quinze** *keh~z*	ninety	**quatre-vingt-dix** *kah-truh-vaw~-dees*
sixteen	**seize** *sehz*	ninety-one	**quatre-vingt-onze** *kah-ruh-vaw~-toh~z*
seventeen	**dix-sept** *dee-seht*	one hundred	**cent** *saw~*

two hundred	**deux cents**	one thousand	**mille**
	doeh saw~		*meel*
two hundred	**deux cent un**	two thousand	**deux mille**
and one	*doeh saw~-*		*doeh meel*
	tuh~		

FRACTIONS & DECIMALS

one-eighth	**un huitième**
	uh~ hwee-tee-ehm
one-quarter	**un quart**
	uh~ kahr
one-third	**un tiers**
	uh~ tee-yayhr
one-half	**un demi / une demie**
	uh~ duh-mee / oon duh-mee
two-thirds	**deux tiers**
	doeh tee-yayhr
three-quarters	**trois quarts**
	twah kahr
double	**double**
	doo-bluh
triple	**triple**
	tree-pluh
one-tenth	**un dixième**
	uh~ dee-zyehm
one-hundredth	**un centième**
	uh~ saw~-tyehm
one-thousandth	**un millième**
	uh~ meel-yehm

MATH

addition	**l'addition**
	lah-dee-see-yoh~
$2 + 1$	**deux plus un**
	doeh plue-zuh~

subtraction	**la soustraction**
	lah soo-strahk-see-yoh~
2 – 1	**deux moins un**
	doeh mweh~ uh~
multiplication	**la multiplication**
	lah muel-tee-plee-kah-see-yoh~
2 × 3	**deux fois trois**
	doeh fwah twah
division	**la division**
	lah dee-vee-zee-yoh~
6 ÷ 3	**six divisé par trois**
	sees dee-vee-say pahr twah

ORDINAL NUMBERS

first	**premier / première**
	preh-mee-ay / preh-mee-yayhr
second	**deuxième**
	doeh-zee-yehm
third	**troisième**
	twah-zee-yehm
fourth	**quatrième**
	kah-tree-yehm
fifth	**cinquième**
	saw~-kee-yehm
sixth	**sixième**
	see-zee-yehm
seventh	**septième**
	seh-tee-yehm
eighth	**huitème**
	hwee-tee-yehm
ninth	**neuvième**
	noeh-vee-yehm
tenth	**dixième**
	dee-zee-yehm
last	**dernier / dernière**
	dayhr-nyay / dayhr-nee-yayhr

MEASUREMENTS

Measurements will usually be metric, though you may need a
few American measurement terms.

inch	**pouce**
	poos
foot	**pied**
	pee-yay
mile	**mile**
	meel
millimeter	**millimètre**
	mee-lee-meh-truh
centimeter	**centimètre**
	saw~-tee-meh-truh
meter	**mètre**
	meh-truh
kilometer	**kilomètre**
	kee-loh-meh-truh
hectare	**hectare**
	ehk-tahr
squared	**carrés**
	kah-ray
short	**court / courte**
	koohr / koohrt
long	**long / longue**
	loh~ / loh~g

VOLUME

milliliter	**millilitre**
	mee-lee-lee-truh
liter	**litre**
	lee-truh
kilo	**kilo**
	kee-loh

ounce	**once**
	oh~s
cup	**tasse**
	tahs
pint	**pinte**
	peh~t
quart	**quart**
	kahr
gallon	**gallon**
	gah-luhn

QUANTITY

some	**quelques**
	kehl-kuh
none	**aucun / aucune**
	oh-kuh~ / oh-kuen
all	**tous / toutes**
	too / toot
many / much	**beaucoup**
	boh-koo
a little bit (can be used	**un peu**
for quantity or for time)	*uh~ pueh*
dozen	**une douzaine**
	oon doo-zeh~n

SIZE

small	**petit / petite**
	puh-tee / puh-teet
the smallest (literally	**le plus petit / la plus petite**
"the most small")	*luh plue ptee / lah plue peh-teet*
medium	**moyen / moyenne**
	mwah-yaw~ / mwah-yaw~n
a little medium	**un moyen de taille petit**
	uhn mwah-yaw~ duh tie ptee

big	**grand / grande** *graw~ / graw~d*
fat	**gros / grosse** *groh / grohs*
really fat	**très gros / très grosse** *tray groh / tray grohs*
the biggest	**le plus grand / la plus grande** *luh plue graw~ / lah plue graw~d*
wide	**large** *lahrzh*
narrow	**étroit / étroite** *ay-twah / ay-twaht*
too	**trop** *troh*
not enough	**pas assez** *pah-zah-say*

TIME

Remember that civilians in Europe and French-speaking Canada make use of the 24-hour clock. After 12 noon, hours continue upward, so that 1:00 PM is the 13th hour, 2:00 PM is the 14th hour, and so on. The French also write time differently: Instead of separating hours from minutes with a colon, they use a lowercase "h." For example: 11:30 AM is 11h30; 11:30 PM is 23h30.

For full coverage of numbers, see p7.

HOURS OF THE DAY

What time is it?	**Quelle heure est-il?** *keh-loehr ey-teel*
At what time?	**À quelle heure?** *ah keh-loehr*
For how long?	**Pendant combien de temps?** *paw~-daw~ koh~-bee-yeh~ duh taw~*

It's one o'clock.	**Il est une heure.**
	eel ayt-oon oehr
It's two o'clock.	**Il est deux heures.**
	eel ay doeh-zoehr
It's two thirty.	**Il est deux heures trente.**
	eel ay doeh-zoehr traw~t
It's two fifteen.	**Il est deux heures et quart.**
	eel ay doeh-zoehr ay kahr
It's a quarter to three.	**Il est trois heures moins quart.**
	eel ay twah-zoehr mwah kahr
It's noon.	**C'est midi.**
	say mee-dee
It's midnight.	**C'est minuit.**
	say mee-nwee
It's early.	**Il est tôt.**
	eel ay toh
It's late.	**Il est tard.**
	eel ay tahr
in the morning	**au matin**
	oh mah-taw~
in the afternoon	**dans l'après-midi**
	daw~ lah-pray mee-dee
at night	**dans le soir**
	daw~ luh swahr
at dawn	**à l'aube**
	ah lohb

DAYS OF THE WEEK

Monday	**lundi**
	luh~-dee
Tuesday	**mardi**
	mahr-dee
Wednesday	**mercredi**
	mehr-kruh-dee

Thursday	**jeudi**
	zhoeh-dee
Friday	**vendredi**
	vaw~druh-dee
Saturday	**samedi**
	sahm-dee
Sunday	**dimanche**
	dee-maw~sh
today	**aujourd'hui**
	oh-zhohr-dwee
tomorrow	**demain**
	duh-maw~
yesterday	**hier**
	ee-yayhr
the day before yesterday	**avant-hier**
	ah-vaw~-tee-yayhr
one week	**une semaine**
	oon seh-meh~n
next week	**la semaine prochaine**
	lah smeh~n pro-sheh~n
last week	**la semaine dernière**
	lah smeh~n dayhr-nayhr

MONTHS OF THE YEAR

January	**janvier**
	zhaw~-vee-yay
February	**février**
	fay-vree-yay
March	**mars**
	mahrs
April	**avril**
	ah-vreel

May	**mai**
	may
June	**juin**
	zhweh~
July	**juillet**
	zhoo-ee-ay
August	**août**
	oot
September	**septembre**
	seh-taw-bruh
October	**octobre**
	ohk-toh-bruh
November	**novembre**
	noh-vaw-bruh
December	**décembre**
	day-saw-bruh
next month	**le mois prochain**
	luh mwah proh-shaw~
last month	**le mois dernier**
	luh mwah dayhr~nyay

SEASONS OF THE YEAR

spring	**le printemps**
	luh preh~-taw~
summer	**l'eté**
	lay-tay
autumn	**l'automne**
	loh-tuhn
winter	**l'hiver**
	lee-vayhr

Faux Amis

If you try winging it with "Frenglish," beware of false cognates, known as faux amis, "false friends"— French words that sound like English ones, but with different meanings. Here are some of the most commonly confused terms.

gros(se)	fat
dégoutant(e)	gross
bras	arm
soutien-gorge	bra
main	hand
principal(e)	main
raisin	grape
raisin sec	raisin
pain	bread
douleur	pain
boulette	small ball (like a meatball)
balle	bullet
vacances	holiday
chambres libres	vacancies
injurer	to insult
blesser	to injure
résumé	synopsis
curriculum vitae	résumé
manger	to eat
mangeoire	manger
robe	dress
peignoir	robe
assister	to attend an event
aider	to help
attendre	to wait
librairie	bookstore
bibliothèque	library

FRENCH GRAMMAR BASICS

ALPHABET & PRONUNCIATION

French uses the same alphabet as English, with the addition of the ligature **œ**, used in words like **sœur** (sister) and **œil** (eye). French pronunciation can seem quite difficult. There are several **"nasal vowels"** that are sometimes used when **m** or **n** follows a vowel. Only the nasal is pronounced, not the **m** or **n**, unless another vowel comes along afterward.

The **nasal** will be represented with a **~**. Try this example by tightening your throat as if to whine, snort, or hum:

a good white wine **un bon vin blanc**
uh~ boh~ veh~ blaw~

Another tricky bit is the guttural French **r**. It's sounded in the back of the throat, somewhere near a German "ach." Because the French **r** is all but impossible without practice or prior experience, we'll help you hint at it by adding *hr* to pronunciations.

Letter	Name	Pronunciation
a	*ah*	**ah** as in *father*
		au: oh as in *so*
		ai, aie: ay as in *paid*
		ail: ie as in *tie*
		an: aw~ as in *long*
b	*bay*	**b** as in *bay*
c	*say*	**ca, co, cu:** hard **k** sound as in *car*
		ce, ci: s sound before **i, e,** as in *cent*
d	*day*	**d** as in *day*
		d at end of word is usually silent
e	*uh*	**uh** as in *women,* unstressed, but with lips more pursed
		e at end of word is usually silent
		ein: eh~ as in *men*
		en, em: aw~ as in *long*
		ent: at end of word is usually silent
		er: at end of word, **ay** as in *face*

Letter	Name	Pronunciation
		es at end of word is usually silent
		et, ez: at end of word, **ay** as in *face*
		eu, eue: oeh like German **oe**, **oeh**
e stressed	*eh*	**eh** as in *vet*
e stressed (é)	*ay*	**ay** as in *say*
f	*ehf*	**f** as in *father*
g	*zhay*	**ga, go, gu:** hard **g** sound as in *gold*
		ge, gi: zh as **g** in *massage* or **s** in *vision*
h	*ahsh*	silent
i	*ee*	**ee** as in *machine*
		il: at end of word, **ee** as in *see*
		in, im: eh~ as in *men*
j	*zhee*	**zh** as **g** in *massage* or **s** in *vision*
k	*kah*	hard **k** sound as in *kitten*
l	*ehl*	**l** as in *million*
m	*ehm*	**m** as in *money*
n	*ehn*	**n** as in *nothing*
		n, nd, nt: at end of word, ~ nasalizes preceding vowel
		ne: at end of word, as in *phone*
o	*oh*	**o:** inside word, at end of word, or before silent final letter, **oh** as in *so*
		o: before nonsilent final letter, **uh** as in *come*
		oe, œ: uh like German but lower
		oi: wah as in *bourgeois*
		on: oh~ as in *phone*
		ou: oo as in *routine*
p	*pay*	**p** as in *pay*
q	*koeh*	**qu:** hard **k** sound as in *liquor*
r	*ehr*	**r, hr: r** as in *argument*, usually far back in throat

Letter	Name	Pronunciation
s	*ehs*	**s** as in *sister*
		s: between vowels, including final silent e, **z** as in *misery*
		s at end of word is usually silent
t	*tay*	**t** as in *tea*
		t at end of word is usually silent
		tre, ttre: at end of word, as in *bet*
u	*ueh*	**ue, ueh** as in *due*, but shorter
		un, um: uh~ as in *under*
v	*vay*	**v** as in *volt*
w	*doo-bluh-vay*	**v** as in *volt*
x	*eeks*	**x:** before unstressed vowel, **ks** as in *fixed*
		x: before stressed vowel, **gz** as in *examine*
		x at end of word is usually silent
y	*ee-grehk*	**ee** as in *mighty*
		y: before vowel, **y** as in *yank*
z	*zehd*	**z** as in *zip*
		z at end of word is usually silent

GENDER & ADJECTIVE AGREEMENT

All nouns in French are assigned a masculine or feminine gender, most often accompanied by a masculine or feminine definite article (**le** or **la**). Definite articles (the), indefinite articles (a), and related adjectives must also be masculine or feminine and singular or plural, depending on the noun they're modifying (see the examples in the following boxes).

Unlike English adjectives, French adjectives generally follow the noun, and they must agree in number and gender with the nouns they modify. Some common adjectives do come before the noun, however. These generally have to do with beauty, age, number, goodness, and size.

Quirks of Gender

A group of people always takes the masculine form unless the group is completely composed of females.

John and his sisters are blonds.

Jean et ses sœurs sont blonds.
zhah~-nay say soehr soh~ bloh~

The Definite Article ("The")

	Singular	Plural
Masculine	*le* petit magasin cher (the small, expensive store)	*les* petits magasins chers (the small, expensive stores)
Feminine	*la* petite chambre chère (the small, expensive room)	*les* petites chambres chères (the small, expensive rooms)

When a singular definite article appears directly in front of a noun that begins with a vowel, it is contracted with an apostrophe:

	Singular	Plural
Masculine	l'amour (love)	les amours (loves)
Feminine	l'église (the church)	*les* églises (the churches)

The Indefinite and Partitive Articles ("A", "An," and "Any" / "Some")

	Singular	Plural
Masculine	un grand magasin intéressant (a big, interesting store)	des grandes magasins intéressants (some / any big, interesting stores)
Feminine	une grande chambre intéressante (a big, interesting room)	des grandes chambres intéressantes (some / any big, interesting rooms)

How Much Do You Really Want? (The "Partitive")

French often uses what's called "the partitive" to express
some of a larger whole; the words "some" or "any" are
never implied, as in English. In other words, if you went
to the store for "milk" (rather than for "some" milk), it
would suggest all the milk in the world to a French speaker.
In French, the words "some" or "any" must always be
explicit, as in the examples below.

de + la = de la glace *duh lah glas*	some ice
de + le = du lait *doo lay*	some milk (or some ice cream)
de + l' + vowel (f) **= de l'essence** *duh leh-saw~s*	some gasoline
de + l' + vowel (m) **= de l'eau** *duh loh*	some water
de + les (f) **= des aubergines** *day-zoh-bayhr-zheen*	some eggplant(s)
de + les (m) **= des haricots verts** *day-zay-ree-koh vayhr*	some green beans

THIS / THESE / THAT / THOSE

When modifying nouns, "this," "that," "these," and "those" must
agree with the noun in gender and number.

	This / That	These / Those
Masculine	**ce château** (this / that castle) **cet immeuble** (this / that building)	**ces châteaux** (these / those castles) **ces immeubles** (these / those buildings)
Feminine	**cette maison** (this / that house) **cette usine** (this / that factory)	**ces maisons** (these / those houses) **ces usines** (these / those factories)

French does not usually make a distinction between "this and "that" or between "these" and "those." If necessary, the endings **-ci** (here, nearby) and **-là** (over there) can be added for emphasis:

I'd like this ring here, not that necklace there.	**Je voudrais cette bague-ci, pas ce collier-là.** *zhuh voo-dray seht bahg-see pah suh kohl-yay-lah*
You take these taxis right here, not those coaches over there.	**On prend ces taxis-ci, pas ces cars-là.** *oh~ praw~ say tahk-see-see pah say kahr-lah*

When **ce** is used with **être** (to be) to mean "this is," it makes a contraction. The plural form of "these are" also uses **ce**, not **ces**:

That's his widow.	**C'est sa veuve.** *say sah voehv*
These are our husbands.	**Ce sont nos maris.** *say soh~ noh mah-ree*

PERSONAL PRONOUNS

English	French	Pronunciation
I	Je	zhuh
You (singular, familiar)	Tu	tueh
He / She / It	Il / Elle	eel / ehl
We	Nous	noo
You (plural / singular formal)	Vous	voo
They (*m* / *f*)	Ils / Elles	eel / ehl

Hey, You!

French has two words for "you": *tu*, spoken among friends and familiars when addressing only one person, and *vous*, used among strangers or as a sign of respect for elders and authority figures, and to address more than one person—even if you're speaking to a group of your family members or close friends. When speaking with a stranger, expect to use *vous* unless you are invited to use *tu*.

When a verb begins with a vowel, if the subject appears directly in front of it, **je** (I) forms a contraction. The plural subjects change in pronunciation, though:

English	French	Pronunciation
I like.	J'aime.	zhehm
You (singular, familiar) like.	Tu aimes.	tueh ehm
He / She / It likes.	Il / Elle aime.	ee-lehm / eh-lehm
We like.	Nous aimons.	noo-zeh-moh~
You (plural / singular, formal) like.	Vous aimez.	voo-zeh-may
They (*m* / *f*) like.	Ils / Elles aiment.	ee-lehm / eh-lehm

REGULAR VERB CONJUGATIONS

French verb infinitives end in **ER** (**parler**, to speak), **IR** (**choisir**, to choose), and **RE** (**vendre**, to sell). Most verbs (known as "regular verbs") are conjugated according to the rules for those endings. These are the present-tense conjugations for regular verbs.

Present Tense

ER Verbs	PARLER "To Speak"	
I speak.	Je parle.	zhuh pahrl
You (singular, familiar) speak.	Tu parles.	tueh pahrl
He / She / It speaks.	Il / Elle parle.	eel / ehl pahrl
We speak.	Nous parlons.	noo pahr-loh~
You (plural / singular, formal) speak.	Vous parlez.	voo pahr-lay
They speak.	Ils / Elles parlent.	eel / ehl pahrl

IR Verbs	CHOISIR "To Choose"	
I choose.	Je choisis.	zhuh shwah-zee
You (singular, familiar) choose.	Tu choisis.	tueh shwah-zee
He / She / It chooses.	Il / Elle choisit.	eel / ehl shwah-zee
We choose.	Nous choisissons.	noo shwah-zee-soh~
You (plural / singular, formal) choose.	Vous choisissez.	voo shwah-zee-say
They choose.	Ils / Elles choisissent.	eel / ehl shwah-zees

RE Verbs	VENDRE "To Sell"	
I sell.	Je vend**s**.	zhuh vaw~
You (singular, familiar) sell.	Tu vend**s**.	tueh vaw~
He / She / It sells.	Il / Elle vend. (no ending)	eel / ehl vaw~
We sell.	Nous vend**ons**.	noo vaw~-doh~
You (plural / singular, formal) sell.	Vous vend**ez**.	voo vaw~-day
They sell.	Ils / Elles vend**ent**.	eel / ehl vaw~d

Past Tense

One way of expressing past tense in French is the **passé composé**. The passé composé is formed like the construction "I have walked," in English—with a helping verb (the present tense of **avoir**, to have; or in rare cases, **être**, to be), plus the past participle of the action verb. For the verb "to walk," for example, it's equivalent to "I walked," "I did walk," or "I have walked" in English.

The past participle has a standard form for each type of regular verbs. The following boxes demonstrate how to conjugate **avoir** and then combine it with the past participle of regular **ER**, **IR**, and **RE** verbs to form the past tense.

Passé Composé / Past with Avoir

Present Tense	AVOIR "To Have"	
I have.	J'**ai**.	zhay
You (singular, familiar) have.	Tu **as**.	tueh ah
He / She / It has.	Il / Elle **a**.	eel / ehl ah
We have.	Nous av**ons**.	noo-zah-voh~
You (plural / singular, formal) have.	Vous av**ez**.	voo-zah-vay
They have.	Ils / Elles **ont**.	eel-zoh~ / ehl-zoh~

ER Verbs	AVOIR + PARLER "To Speak"	
I spoke.	J'*ai* parlé.	zhay pahr-lay
You (singular familiar) **spoke.**	Tu *as* parlé.	tueh ah pahr-lay
He / She / It spoke.	Il / Elle *a* parlé.	eel / ehl ah pahr-lay
We spoke.	Nous av*ons* parlé.	noo-zah-voh~pahr-lay
You (plural / singular, formal) **spoke.**	Vous av*ez* parlé.	voo-zah-vay pahr-lay
They spoke.	Ils / Elles *ont* parlé.	eel-zoh~ / ehl-zoh~ pahr-lay
Past Participle:	parlé.	pahr-lay

IR Verbs	AVOIR + CHOISIR "To Choose"	
I chose.	J'*ai* chois*i*.	zhay shwah-zee
You (singular, familiar) **chose.**	Tu *as* chois*i*.	tueh ah shwah-zee
He / She / It chose.	Il / Elle *a* chois*i*.	eel / ehl ah shwah-zee
We chose.	Nous av*ons* chois*i*.	noo-zah-voh~shwah-zee
You (plural / singular, formal) **chose.**	Vous av*ez* chois*i*.	voo-zah-vay shwah-zee
They chose.	Ils / Elles *ont* chois*i*.	eel-zoh~ / ehl-zoh~ shwah-zee
Past participle:	chois*i*	shwah-zee

RE Verbs	AVOIR + VENDRE "To Sell"	
I sold.	J'*ai* vend*u*.	zhay vaw~-doo
You (singular, familiar) sold.	Tu *as* vend*u*.	tueh ah vaw~-doo
He / She / It sold.	Il / Elle *a* vend*u*.	eel / ehl ah vaw~-doo
We sold.	Nous av*ons* vend*u*.	noo-zah-voh~ vaw~-doo
You (plural / singular, formal) sold.	Vous av*ez* vend*u*.	voo-zah-vay vaw~-doo
They sold.	Ils / Elles *ont* vend*u*.	eel-zoh~ / ehl-zoh~ vaw~-doo
Past participle:	vend*u*	vaw~-doo

Passé Composé / Past with Être

A few exceptional verbs—mostly involving verbs of motion—use **être** (to be) instead of **avoir** to form the **passé composé**. Like adjectives, past participles with **être** must agree with the subject in number and gender. Note that the pronunciation of the past participle never changes.

Present Tense	ÊTRE "To Be"	
I am.	Je *suis*.	zhuh swee
You (singular, familiar) are.	Tu *es*.	tueh ay
He / She / It is.	Il / Elle *est*.	eel / ehl ay
We are.	Nous *sommes*.	noo-suhm
You (plural / singular, formal) are.	Vous *êtes*.	voo-zeht
They are.	Ils / Elles *sont*.	eel soh~ / ehl soh~

IR Verbs	ÊTRE + PARTIR "To Leave"	
I left.	Je *suis* part*i(e)*.	zhuh swee pahr-tee
You (singular, familiar) left.	Tu *es* part*i(e)*.	tueh ay pahr-tee
He / She / It left.	Il *est* part*i*. / Elle *est* part*ie*.	eel / ehl ay pahr-tee
We left.	Nous *sommes* part*i(e)*s.	noo-suhm pahr-tee
You (plural / singular, formal) left.	Vous *êtes* part*i(e)*s.	voo-zeht pahr-tee
They left.	Ils *sont* part*is*. / Elles *sont* part*ies*.	eel soh~ / ehl soh~ pahr-tee

The following verbs use **être** as the helping verb for the **passé composé**:

aller (to go)	Je suis allé*(e)*. (I went.)	zhuh swee-zah-lay
arriver (to arrive)	Je suis arrivé*(e)*. (I arrived.)	zhuh swee-zah-ree-vay
descendre (to go down)	Je suis descend*u(e)*. (I went down.)	zhuh swee day-saw~-doo
devenir (to become)	Je suis deven*u(e)*. (I became.)	zhuh swee dehv-nueh
entrer (to come in)	Je suis entré*(e)*. (I came in.)	zhuh swee-zaw~-tray
monter (to go up)	Je suis monté*(e)*. (I went up.)	zhuh swee moh~-tay
mourir (to die)	Je suis mort*(e)*. (I died.)	zhuh swee mohr / mohrt
naître (to be born)	Je suis né*(e)*. (I was born.)	zhuh swee nay

partir (to leave)	Je suis parti*(e)*. (I left.)	zhuh swee pahr-tee
rentrer (to come / go home)	Je suis rentré*(e)*. (I went home.)	zhuh swee raw~-tray
rester (to stay)	Je suis resté*(e)*. (I stayed.)	zhuh swee res-tay
retourner (to go back)	Je suis retourné*(e)*. (I went back.)	zhuh swee ray-toohr-nay
revenir (to come back)	Je suis revenu*(e)*. (I came back.)	zhuh swee reh-vnueh
sortir (to go out)	Je suis sorti*(e)*. (I went out.)	zhuh swee sohr-tee
tomber (to fall)	Je suis tombé*(e)*. (I fell.)	zhuh swee toh~-bay
venir (to come)	Je suis venu*(e)*. (I came.)	zhuh swee vnueh

Having It All

Avoir means "to have," but it's also used to describe conditions, such as hunger or thirst, body pain, and age:

I'm hungry.	**J'ai faim.**	*zhay feh~*
I have a headache.	**J'ai mal à la tête.**	*zhay mah-lah lah teht*
I am ten years old.	**J'ai dix ans.**	*zhay dee-zah~*

Avoir is also used in the two common fixed expressions, *avoir besoin de*, "to need," and *il y a*, "there is," "there are":

I need a pillow.
    J'ai besoin d'un oreiller.
    zhay beh-zwah~ duh~-noh-ray-ay

There are two seats available.
    Il y a deux places libres.
    eel-yah doeh plas lee-bruh

The Future

For novice French speakers, the easiest way to express the future is to use the present tense of the irregular verb **aller** (to go) as a helping verb plus the infinitive. We use the same structure in English when we say things like "I'm going to eat."

Present Tense	ALLER "To Go"	
I go.	Je *vais*.	zhuh vay
You (singular, familiar) **go.**	Tu *vas*.	tueh vah
He / She / It goes.	Il / Elle *va*.	eel / ehl vah
We go.	Nous *allons*.	noo-zah-loh~
You (plural / singular, formal) **go.**	Vous *allez*.	voo-zah-lay
They go.	Ils / Elles *vont*.	eel / ehl voh~

ER Verbs	ALLER + PARLER "To Talk"	
I'm going to talk.	Je *vais* parler.	zhuh vay pahr-lay
You're (singular, familiar) **going to talk.**	Tu *vas* parler.	tueh vah pahr-lay
He / She / It is going to talk.	Il / Elle *va* parler.	eel / ehl vah pahr-lay
We're going to talk.	Nous *allons* parler.	noo-zah-loh~ pahr-lay
You're (plural / singular, formal) **going to talk.**	Vous *allez* parler.	voo-zah-lay pahr-lay
They're going to talk.	Ils / Elles *vont* parler.	eel / ehl voh~ pahr-lay

IRREGULAR VERBS

French has numerous irregular verbs that stray from the standard
ER, **IR**, and **RE** conjugations. Rather than bog you down with too
much grammar, we're providing the present tense conjugations
for some of the most commonly used irregular verbs.

BOIRE "To Drink"

I drink.	Je b*ois*.	zhuh bwah
You (singular, familiar) **drink.**	Tu b*ois*.	tueh bwah
He / She / It drinks.	Il / Elle b*oit*.	eel / ehl bwah
We drink.	Nous b*uvons*.	noo bueh-voh~
You (plural / singular, formal) **drink.**	Vous b*uvez*.	voo bueh-vay
They drink.	Ils / Elles b*oivent*.	eel / ehl bwahv
Past participle:	b*u*	bueh

CONNAÎTRE "To Know" (a person / place)

I know Marc.	Je connais Marc.	zhuh koh-nay mahrk
You (singular, familiar) **know Nice.**	Tu conn*ais* Nice.	tueh koh-nay nees
He / She / It knows my parents.	Il / Elle conn*aît* mes parents.	eel / ehl koh-nay
We know your (girl)friends.	Nous conn*aissons* vos amies.	noo koh-nay-soh~ voh-zah-mee
You (plural / singular, formal) **know this hostel.**	Vous conn*aissez* cet auberge.	voo koh-nay-say seh-toh-bayrzh
They know our children.	Ils / Elles conn*aissent* nos enfants.	eel / ehl koh-nehs noh-zaw~-faw~
Past participle:	conn*u*	koh-nueh

DIRE "To Say", "To Tell"

I say.	Je dis.	zhuh dee
You (singular, familiar) say.	Tu dis.	tueh dee
He / She / It says.	Il / Elle dit.	eel / ehl dee
We say.	Nous disons.	noo dee-zoh~
You (plural / singular, formal) say.	Vous dites.	voo deet
They sat.	Ils / Elles disent.	eel / ehl deez
Past participle:	dit	dee

ÉCRIRE "To Write"

I write.	J'écris.	zheh-kree
You (singular, familiar) write.	Tu écris.	tueh eh-kree
He / She / It writes.	Il / Elle écrit.	eel / ehl eh-kree
We write.	Nous écrivons.	noo-zeh-kree-voh~
You (plural / singular, formal) write.	Vous écrivez.	voo-zeh-kree-vay
They write.	Ils / Elles écrivent.	eel-zeh-kreev / ehl-zeh-kreev
Past participle:	écrit	eh-kree

"Faire" Weather

The verb *faire* (to do, to make) is also used impersonally to describe the weather:

It's hot / cold out.	**Il fait chaud / froid.** eel fay shoh / fwah
The weather's nice / bad today.	**Il fait beau / mauvais aujourd'hui.** eel fay boh / moh-vay oh-zhoohr dwee

FAIRE "To Do," "To Make"

I do.	Je fais.	zhuh fay
You (singular, familiar) do.	Tu fais.	tueh fay
He / She / It does.	Il / Elle fait.	eel / ehl fay
We do.	Nous faisons.	noo feh-zoh~
You (plural / singular, formal) do.	Vous faites.	voo feht
They do.	Ils / Elles font.	eel / ehl foh~
Past participle:	fait	fay

OUVRIR "To Open"

I open.	J'ouvre.	zhoovhr
You (singular, familiar) open.	Tu ouvres.	tueh oovhr
He / She / It opens.	Il / Elle ouvre.	eel / ehl oovhr
We open.	Nous ouvrons.	noo-zoo-vroh~
You (plural / singular, formal) open.	Vous ouvrez.	voo-zoo-vray
They open.	Ils / Elles ouvrent.	eel-zoovhr / ehl-zoovhr
Past participle:	ouvert	oo-vayhr

PARTIR "To Leave"

I leave.	Je par*s*.	zhuh pahr
You (singular, familiar) leave.	Tu par*s*.	tueh pahr
He / She / It leaves.	Il / Elle par*t*.	eel / ehl pahr
We leave.	Nous part*ons*.	noo pahr-toh~
You (plural / singular, formal) leave.	Vous part*ez*.	voo pahr-tay
They leave.	Ils / Elles part*ent*.	eel / ehl pahrt
Past participle:	part*i* (with **être**; agrees with subject)	pahr-tee

POUVOIR "Can," "To Be Able"

I can.	Je p*eux*.	zhuh poeh
You (singular, familiar) can.	Tu p*eux*.	tueh poeh
He / She / It can.	Il / Elle p*eut*.	eel / ehl poeh
We can.	Nous pouv*ons*.	noo poo-voh~
You (plural / singular, formal) can.	Vous pouv*ez*.	voo poo-vay
They can.	Ils / Elles p*euvent*.	eel / ehl poehv
Past participle:	p*u*	pue

PRENDRE "To Take"

I take.	Je prend**s**.	zhuh praw~
You (singular, familiar) take.	Tu prend**s**.	tueh praw~
He / She / It takes.	Il / Elle pren**d**.	eel / ehl praw~
We take.	Nous pre**n**ons.	noo pruh-noh~
You (plural / singular, formal) take.	Vous pre**n**ez.	voo pruh-nay
They take.	Ils / Elles pren**n**ent.	eel / ehl prehn
Past participle:	pr**i**s	pree

SAVOIR "To Know" (a fact)

I know how to drive.	Je s**ai**s conduire.	zhuh say koh~-dweer
You (singular, familiar) know the route.	Tu s**ai**s la route.	tueh say lah root
He / She / It knows where.	Il / Elle s**ai**t où.	eel / ehl say oo
We know the answer.	Nous sav**on**s la réponse.	noo sah-voh~ lah ray-poh~s
You (plural / singular, formal) know his / her problem.	Vous sav**ez** son problème.	voo sah-vay soh~ praw-blehm
They know the truth.	Ils / Elles sav**ent** la vérité.	eel / ehl sahv lah vay-ree-tay
Past participle:	s**u**	sue

SORTIR "To Go Out," "To Exit"

I go out.	Je sor**s**.	zhuh sohr
You (singular, familiar) **go out.**	Tu sor**s**.	tueh sohr
He / She / It goes out.	Il / Elle sor**t**.	eel / ehl sohr
We go out.	Nous sort**ons**.	noo sohr-toh~
You (plural / singular, formal) **go out.**	Vous sort**ez**.	voo sohr-tay
They go out.	Ils / Elles sort**ent**.	eel / ehl sohrt
Past participle:	sort**i** (with **être**; agrees with subject)	sohr-tee

VENIR "To Come"

I come.	Je v**iens**.	zhuh vee-yeh~
You (singular, familiar) **come.**	Tu v**iens**.	tueh vee-yeh~
He / She / It comes.	Il / Elle v**ient**.	eel / ehl vee-yeh~
We come.	Nous ven**ons**.	noo vnoh~
You (plural / singular, formal) **come.**	Vous ven**ez**.	voo vnay
They come.	Ils / Elles v**iennent**.	eel / ehl vee-yehn
Past participle:	ven**u** (with **être**; agrees with subject)	vnueh

VOIR "To See"

I see.	Je vois.	zhuh vwah
You (singular, familiar) see.	Tu vois.	tueh vwah
He / She / It sees.	Il / Elle voit.	eel / ehl vwah
We see.	Nous voyons.	noo vwah-yoh~
You (plural / singular, formal) see.	Vous voyez.	voo vwah-yay
They see.	Ils / Elles voient.	eel / ehl vwah
Past participle:	vu	vue

You can say "I want" to make a request, but it's much more polite, just like in English, to say "I would like"—**je voudrais**. Therefore, we will provide this conditional tense rather than the present tense for this verb.

VOULOIR "To Want"

I would like to eat.	Je voudrais manger.	zhuh voo-dray mah~-zhay
You (singular, familiar) would like a beer.	Tu voudrais une bière.	tueh voo-dray oon bee-ayhr
He / She / It would like a knife.	Il / Elle voudrait un couteau.	eel / ehl voo-dray uh~ koo-toh
We would like some ketchup.	Nous voulions du ketchup.	noo voo-lee-oh~ doo keht-shup
You (plural / singular, formal) would like some books.	Vous vouliez des livres.	voo voo-lee-ay day lee-vruh
They would like to stay.	Ils / Elles voudraient rester.	eel / ehl voo-dray ruh-stay

REFLEXIVE VERBS

French uses more reflexive verbs than English. A verb is reflexive when its subject and object both refer to the same person or thing:

Marie looks at herself in the mirror.	**Marie se regard dans le miroir.**	*mah-ree suh ruh-gahr daw~ luh meer-wahr*

The following common verbs are often used reflexively: **s'habiller** (to get dressed, literally to dress oneself), **s'appeler** (to be named, literally to call oneself), **se baigner** (to bathe oneself), and **se lever** (to wake up, literally to raise oneself).

To indicate that a verb is reflexive, French attaches a reflexive pronoun to the verb according to the subject:

SE LEVER "To Get Up"

I get up.	Je *me* lève.	zhuh muh lehv
You (singular, familiar) **get up.**	Tu *te* lève*s*.	tueh tuh lehv
He / She / It gets up.	Il / Elle *se* lève.	eel / ehl suh lehv
We get up.	Nous *nous* lev*ons*.	noo noo leh-voh~
You (plural / singular, formal) **get up.**	Vous *vous* levez.	voo voo leh-vay
They get up.	Ils / Elles *se* lèv*ent*.	eel / ehl suh lehv

When a reflexive pronoun ending with a vowel comes before a verb that starts with a vowel, all but the **nous** and **vous** forms make contractions. Note the contractions and pronunciation changes for the following verb.

Reflexive verbs use **être** in the **passé composé** (remember to make the verbs agree). The reflexive pronoun goes directly before the helping verb.

She woke up.	**Elle s'est levée.**	*ehl say luh-vay*
They (a group of females) woke up.	**Elles se sont levées.**	*ehl suh soh~ luh-vay*

An impersonal usage of a reflexive verb appears in two common, useful phrases:

What's happening?	**Qu'est-ce qui se passe?**
	kehs kee suh pahs
What happened?	**Qu'est-ce qui s'est passé?**
	kehs kee say pah-say

S'AMUSER "To Have a Good Time"

I am having a good time.	Je m'amuse.	zhuh mah-muehz
You (singular, familiar) are having a good time.	Tu t'amuses.	tueh tah-muehz
He / She / It is having a good time.	Il / Elle s'amuse.	eel / ehl sah-muehz
We are having a good time.	Nous nous amusons.	noo noo-zah-mueh-zoh~
You (plural / singular, formal) are having a good time.	Vous vous amusez.	voo voo-zah-meuh-zay
They are having a good time.	Ils / Elles s'amusent.	eel / ehl sah-muehz

---

Who's Calling, Please?

Many reflexive verbs can also be used in a nonreflexive sense. The reflexive pronoun makes all the difference between *j'appelle Jean* (I'm calling John) and *je m'appelle Jean* (my name is John, literally I call myself John).

NEGATIVES

To render a statement negative, bracket the verb with **ne . . . pas**, as in the examples below. **Ne** contracts to **n'** in front of a vowel. (In spoken French, the **ne** is often omitted, so you'll need to listen for the **pas**.)

	ALLER "To Go"	
I am not going.	Je *ne* vais *pas*.	zhuh nuh vay pah
You (singular, familiar) are not going.	Tu *ne* vas *pas*.	tueh nuh vah pah
He / She / It is not going.	Il / Elle *ne* vas *pas*.	eel / ehl nuh vah pah
We are not going.	Nous *n'*allons *pas*.	noo nah-loh~ pah
You (plural / singular, formal) **are not going.**	Vous *n'*allez *pas*.	voo nah-lay pah
They are not going.	Ils / Elles *ne* vont *pas*.	eel / ehl nuh voh~ pah

Other Negatives

Here are some other negative expressions that follow a similar pattern.

NEVER: ne . . . jamais

I never like dancing.	Je *n'*aime *jamais* danser.	zhuh neyhm zhah-mey dah~-say

NO LONGER: ne . . . plus

I no longer like this.	Je *n'*aime *plus* ça.	zhuh neyhm plue sah

NO ONE: ne . . . personne

I like no one.	Je *n'*aime *personne*.	zhuh neyhm payhr-suhn

NOTHING / ANYTHING: ne . . . rien

| I don't like anything. | Je n'aime *rien*. | zhuh neyhm ree-yaw~ |

ONLY: ne . . . que

| I only like you. | Je n'aime *que* toi. | zhuh neyhm kuh twah |

QUESTIONS

There are several ways to ask a question in French: The very simplest is just to use the tone of your voice. Just like in English, a sentence that drops in pitch at the end is a statement, but a sentence that rises in pitch is instantly a question.

You have (some) soap.   **Vous avez du savon.**
                         voo-zah-vay due sah-voh~

Do you have (any) soap? **Vous avez du savon?**
                         voo-zah-vay due sah-voh~

Another easy and useful way to ask a question is to stick the fixed phrase **Est-ce que** onto the beginning of the sentence. There's no literal translation for **Est-ce que** that makes much sense; word-for-word it means "Is it that . . .?"

Do you have (any) soap? **Est-ce que vous avez du savon?**
                         ehs kuh voo-zah-vay doo sah-voh~

For other kinds of questions, see p3.

POSSESSIVES

French has no **'s** shorthand to show ownership. If you want to talk about "the girl's name," you have to say **le nom de la fille** (the name of the girl). The preposition de changes depending on which definite article follows it.

de + la = de la	la bouchon *de la* bouteille (the bottle's cork)	lah boo-shoh~ duh lah boo-tayh
de + le = du	les portes *du* restaurant (the restaurant's doors)	lay pohrt doo ruh-stoh-raw~
de + l' = de l'	la main *de l'*actrice (the actress's hand) le fil *de l'*ordinateur (the computer's cord)	lah meh~ duh lahk-trees luh fee duh lohr-dee-nah-toehr
de + les = des	la chanson *des* sœurs (the sisters' song) les valises *des* passagers (the passengers' suitcases)	lah shaw~-soh~ day soehrs lay vah-lees day pah-sah-zhay

Possessive Adjectives
Masculine Noun

My dog is black.
Mon chien est noir.
moh~ shee-yeh~-nay nwahr

Your dog is pretty.
Ton chien est beau.
toh~ shee-yeh~-nay boh

His / Her / Its dog is small.
Son chien est petit.
soh~ shee-yeh~-nay ptee

Our dog is lost.
Notre chien est perdu.
nohtr shee-yeh~-nay pehr-due

Your dog is dirty.
Votre chien est sale.
vohtr shee-yeh~-nay sahl

Their dog is new.
Leur chien est nouveau.
loehr shee-yeh~-nay noo-voh

Feminine Noun

My car is black.
Ma voiture est noire.
mah vwah-tuehr ay nwahr

Your car is pretty.
Ta voiture est belle.
tah vwah-tuehr ay behl

His / Her / Its car is small.
Sa voiture est petite.
sah vwah-tuehr at puh-teet

Our car is lost.	**Notre voiture est perdue.**
	nohtr vwah-tuehr ay pehr-due
Your car is dirty.	**Votre voiture est sale.**
	vohtr vwah-tuehr ay sahl
Their car is new.	**Leur voiture est nouvelle.**
	loehr vwah-tuehr ay noo-vehl

Plural Noun (Masculine or Feminine)

My luggage is black.	**Mes bagages sont noir.**
	may bah-gahzh soh~ nwahr
Your luggage is pretty.	**Tes bagages sont beaux.**
	tay bah-gahzh soh~ boh
His / Her / Its luggage is small.	**Ses bagages sont petits.**
	say bah-gahzh soh~ ptee
Our luggage is lost.	**Nos bagages sont perdus.**
	noh bah-gahzh soh~ pehr-due
Your luggage is dirty.	**Vos bagages sont sales.**
	voh bah-gahzh soh~ sahl
Their luggage is new.	**Leurs bagages sont nouveaux.**
	loehr bah-gahzh soh~ noo-voh

DIRECTIONS

Although they have many other uses, the prepositions **à** and **de** have a variety of translations—such as "to," "from," "at," "for," or "of"—when people talk about places. See the rules for using **de**, **du**, **de l'**, and **des** on p42. **À** changes very similarly to **de**.

à + la = à la	Tu reste *à la* gare. (You're staying at the train station.)	tueh rehst ah lah gahr
à + l' = à l'	Elle est *à l'*hôtel. (She's at the hotel.)	ehl ay-tah loh-tehl
à + le = au	Nous partons *au* théâtre. (We're leaving for the theatre.)	noo pahr-toh~ oh tay-ahtr
à + les = aux	Ils vont aller *aux* musées. (They're going to go to the museums.)	eel voh~-tah-lay oh mueh-zay

FRENCH ETIQUETTE

Remember that the French love form and style. It's not so much what you do, it's how you do it. So when in France, pay attention to detail. Think elegance before efficiency or speed. This is not only true with regard to the way you dress or dine, but in your gestures, your way of speaking, the time you take for doing things. Be deliberate.

It's better to be overly formal and rigorously polite than slightly too casual or too quickly familiar. Anger is never a solution in France. The bittersweet end of diplomacy is called seduction, and it's the key to obtaining results in France—with everything from upgrading a hotel room to talking your way out of a traffic ticket. Be elegant and self-deprecating. Once you've mastered this, even routine experiences in France may prove delightful.

If you speak French, you're kilometers ahead of the crowd of visitors. If you don't, master at least the verbal keys to the French heart: *bonjour, merci,* and *excusez-moi.* When in doubt use the *vous* form of "you" until the French person you're speaking with invites you to use the *tu* form. (This won't happen quickly.) Note that in the workplace, employees will often call each other by their first names but will still maintain the *vous* form. Don't think that you can jump into the *tu* form after a few minutes, even if the person you're talking to is friendly or young or otherwise casual.

Greetings & Farewells   These are important in France. *Bonjour, Madame* or *Bonjour, Monsieur* should become second nature to you. Young people may use the more casual greeting of *salut,* but you should begin with a full *Bonjour, Madame* or *Bonjour, Monsieur* when greeting people. Of course, this becomes *Bonsoir, Madame* or *Bonsoir, Monsieur* after about 6pm. A slight acknowledgment or nod of the head often accompanies the words. You are honoring the other person's presence. Remember the form even when you really want to yell or complain or if you feel completely indifferent. This is not hypocrisy; it's protocol, it's international diplomacy, and it's essential. Plus, it's fun.

The common greeting of *Ca va?* Or *Comment ca va?* is only used when you already know the person you're greeting. Otherwise, you'll be perceived as a lunatic or dangerous person. In general, French people don't talk to people they don't know. If they do, it is with great reserve and caution, almost with a tone of apology. In fact, any question that may be perceived as even slightly personal (regarding where you live, what you do, what you think, how you feel) is often preceded with the very standard French apology: *Je ne veut pas vous deranger, mais* . . . ("I don't mean to disturb you, but . . ."), followed by the question. Or, *Excusez moi si c'est indiscret mais* . . . ("Excuse me if it's indiscreet, but . . ."), followed by the question. This is often amusing to English-speakers, but it's important to understand. Respect and protect the personal space and intimacy of *l'autre* (the other) in France.

Breaking the Ice   Think of each French person as having a picket fence or wall (*cloison*) around him or herself. The French often appreciate the Anglo-Saxon ability to ignore that fence or at least to knock on it. They'll marvel at your ability to be casual but often have a hard time breaking the ice in social encounters themselves. Once you've penetrated the barrier, though, you must be prepared for some genuine exchange. Beyond the protocol, the French are ready for real content and serious dialogue. They're also confused by our Anglo-Saxon tendency to readily share everything about ourselves, from our annual income or apartment rent to our family problems and personal hang-ups, and just as readily forget we ever met them.

Kissing *(Les Bises)*   When greeting someone they know, the French shake hands and/or give a quick succession of impersonal kisses on alternating cheeks called *les bises* (from *bisou*, or kiss). There are lots of nuances—often based on regional differences—that only experience can sort out. Some people give two kisses, some three, and others four. If there are six people in the room and you give four *bises* each, that calls for a lot of kissing. Remember, this is just a form of saying *bonjour*. The French are used to and comfortable with close personal contact. They are not bothered by human proximity or touching (though they don't often touch another's arm or shoulder to add emphasis, as North Americans tend to). In general, they don't require the same distance Anglo-Saxons insist upon when talking. So get used to *les bises*. Even French people have cute little moments when two people are unsure if it'll be two, three, or four bises. Two is the most common; four is more classical; three is for those who want to be a bit different without abandoning tradition.

People from the south of France and the younger generation tend to kiss more. *Les bises* are usually for men and women or women and women, but good male friends practice *les bises* also. Start on the left cheek and don't really kiss; just touch cheeks and steer your lips away.

In the work place, handshakes are required when people greet each other, whether for the first time or the zillionth time. When you arrive at work, for example, you shake hands with coworkers and say *bonjour*. It may seem highly repetitive, but it's a very pleasant way for people to acknowledge each other. The handshake or *les bises* are repeated when leaving. Every time you enter and exit a room you greet everyone present. Failure to say hello and goodbye is perceived as rude.

Gestures   Even nonverbal language in France is expressive and poetic and particularly French. French facial gestures—especially with the pursing of lips and flaring of nostrils, combined with suggestive and smartly critical smirks—are a form of communication in themselves. The French thought-process seems to begin in the upper lip. The shrug is also a culturally distinct part of French conversation. It is often accompanied by a half-swallowed form of *je ne sais pas* ("I don't know") or the very, very French *temp-pis*, which simply means, "That's the way it is, so what? Live with it, accept it!" It's actually fun having an expression that becomes the catch-all for everything you can't control; at the very least, it's a great way of dealing with less-than-perfect service.

BASIC FACTS

Form of government   Republic
Capital   Paris
Official Currency   Euro
Official Language   French
Regional Languages   Basque, Breton, Catalan, Corsican, Provencal, Alsatian
Surface Area   211,209 sq. mi. (547,030 sq. km)
Population   64 million
Population Density in Paris   50,000 inhabitants per square mile, making Paris one of Europe's most densely populated cities.
Average Family Size   1.8 children
Average Age of Population   39
Average Life Expectancy   79.6 (83 for women; 76 for men)

THE MOST POPULAR NAMES IN FRANCE

Girls   Lea, Manon, Emma, Chloe, Camille, Oceane, Clara, Marie, Sarah, Ines
Boys   Lucas, Theo, Thomas, Hugo, Maxime, Enzo, Clement, Alexandre, Quentin

CHAPTER TWO

GETTING THERE & GETTING AROUND

This section deals with every form of automated transportation. Whether you've just reached your destination by plane or you're renting a car to tour the countryside, you'll find the phrase you need in the next 30 pages.

AT THE AIRPORT

I am looking for ____	**Je cherche ____**
	zhuh shayhrsh
a porter.	**un porteur.**
	uh~ pohr-toehr
the check-in counter.	**l'enregistrement.**
	law~-ruh-zhee-struh-maw~
the ticket counter.	**les guichets.**
	lay gee-shay
arrivals.	**les arrivées.**
	lay-zah-ree-vay
departures.	**les départs.**
	lay day-pahrt
gate number ____.	**la porte numéro ____.**
	lah pohrt nue-may-roh

For a full list of numbers, see p7.

the waiting area.	**la salle d'attente.**
	lah sahl dah-taw~t
the men's restroom.	**les WC pour hommes.**
	lay vay-say poo-ruhm
the women's restroom.	**les WC pour femmes.**
	lay vay-say pour fahm
the police station.	**le bureau de police.**
	luh bue-roh duh poh-lees
a security guard.	**un agent de la sécurité.**
	uh~-nah-zhaw~ duh lah say-kue-ree-tay

the smoking area.	**la salle fumeur.**
	lah sahl fue-moehr
the information booth.	**le guichet d'information.**
	luh gee-shay daw~-fohr-mah-see-yoh~
a public telephone.	**un téléphone public.**
	uh~ tay-lay-fohn pue-bleek
an ATM.	**une billeterie automatique.**
	oon bee-yeh-tree oh-toh-mah-teek
baggage claim.	**la zone de récupération des bagages.**
	lah zohn duh ray-kue-pay-rah-see-yoh~ day bah-gahzh
a luggage cart.	**un caddie.**
	uh~ kah-dee
a currency exchange.	**un bureau de change.**
	uh~ bue-roh duh shaw~zh
a café.	**un café.**
	uh~ kah-fay
a restaurant.	**un restaurant.**
	uh~ reh-stoh-raw~
a bar.	**un bar.**
	uh~ bahr
a bookstore or newsstand.	**une librairie ou un kiosque à journaux.**
	oon lee-brey-ree oo uh~ kee-yohsk ah zhoohr-noh
a duty-free shop.	**une boutique hors taxe.**
	oon boo-teek ohr tahks
Is there Internet access here?	**Est-il possible d'accéder à l'Internet d'ici?**
	ey-teel poh-see-bluh dahk-say-day ah leh~-tayhr-neht dee-see

May I have someone paged, please?	**Pourriez-vous appeler quelqu'un par haut-parleur, s'il vous plaît?** *poo-ree-yay-voo ah-play kehl-kuh~ pahr oh pahr-loehr seel voo play*
Do you accept credit cards?	**Acceptez-vous les cartes de crédit?** *ahk-sehp-tay-voo lay kahrt duh kray-dee*

CHECKING IN

I would like a one-way ticket to ____.	**Je voudrais un aller simple pour ____.** *zhuh voo-dray uh~-nah-lay seh~- pluh poohr*
I would like a round-trip ticket to ____.	**Je voudrais un aller-retour pour ____.** *zhuh voo-dray uh~-nah-lay ruh- toohr poohr*
How much are the tickets?	**Combien coûtent les billets?** *koh~-bee-yeh~ koot lay bee-yay*
Do you have anything less expensive?	**Avez-vous quelque chose de moins cher?** *ah-vay-voo kehl-kuh shohz duh mwaw~ shayhr*
What time does flight ____ leave?	**À quelle heure le vol ____ part-il?** *ah keh-loehr luh vohl ____ pahr- teel*
What time does flight ____ arrive?	**À quelle heure le vol ____ arrive-t-il?** *ah keh-loehr luh vohl ____ ah- reev-teel*
How long is the flight?	**Combien de temps le vol dure-t-il?** *koh~-bee-yeh~ duh taw~ luh vohl duehr-teel*
Do I have a connecting flight?	**Y a-t-il une correspondance?** *yah-tee-loon koh-ray-spoh~-daw~s*

Common Airport Signs

Arrivées	Arrivals
Départs	Departures
Terminal	Terminal
Porte	Gate
Guichets	Ticketing
Douane	Customs
Récupération des bagages	Baggage Claim
Pousser	Push
Tirer	Pull
Interdit de fumer	No Smoking
Entrée	Entrance
Sortie	Exit
Hommes	Men's
Femmes	Women's
Navettes	Shuttle Buses
Taxis	Taxis

Do I need to change planes?	**Dois-je changer d'avion?** *dwah-zhuh shaw~-zhay dah-vee-yoh~*
My flight leaves at __:__ (time).	**Mon vol part à ____ heures ____.** *moh~ vohl pahr ah ____ oehr*
What time will the flight arrive?	**A quelle heure le vol va-t-il arriver?** *ah keh-loehr luh vohl vah teel ah-ree-vay*
Is the flight on time?	**Le vol est-il à l'heure?** *luh vohl ey-teel ah-loehr*
Is the flight delayed?	**Le vol est-il en retard?** *luh vohl ey-teel aw~ ruh-tahr*

For full coverage of numbers, see p7.
For full coverage of time, see p12.

From which terminal is flight ____ leaving?

De quel terminal le vol ____ part-il?
duh kehl tayhr-mee-nahl luh vohl ____ pahr-teel

From which gate is flight ____ leaving?

De quelle porte le vol ____ part-il?
duh kehl pohrt luh vohl ____ pahr-teel

How much time do I need for check-in?

De combien de temps ai-je besoin pour l'enregistrement?
duh koh~-bee-yeh~ duh taw~ ay-zhuh buh-zweh~ poohr law~-reh-zhee-struh-maw~

Is there an express check-in line?

Y a-t-il une file d'enregistrement express?
yah-teel oon feel daw~-reh-zhee-struh-maw~ ehk-spray

Do you have electronic check-in?

Y a-t-il un point d'enregistrement électronique?
yah-teel uh~ pwah daw~-rehzh-ee-strumaw~ ay-lehk-troh~-ik

Seat Preferences

I would like ____ ticket(s) in ____	**Je voudrais ____ billet(s) de ____** *zhuh voo-dray ____ bee-yay duh*
first class.	**première classe.** *preh-mee-yayhr klahs*
business class.	**classe affaire.** *klahs ah-fayhr*
economy class.	**classe économique.** *klahs ay-koh~-noh-meek*
I would like ____	**Je voudrais ____** *zhuh voo-dray*
Please don't give me ____	**S'il vous plaît, ne me donnez pas de place ____** *seel voo play nuh muh doh-nay pah duh plahs*
a window seat.	**une place côté hublot.** *oon plahs koh-tay oo-bloh*
an aisle seat.	**une place côté couloir.** *oon plahs koh-tay kool-wahr*
an emergency exit row seat.	**une place côté issue de secours.** *oon plahs koh-tay ee-sue duh suh-koohr*
a bulkhead seat.	**une place au premier rang.** *oon plahs pruh-mee-yay raw~*
a seat by the restroom.	**une place près des toilettes.** *oon plahs pray day twah-leht*
a seat near the front.	**une place à l'avant de l'avion.** *oon plahs ah lah-vaw~ duh lah-vee-yoh~*
a seat near the middle.	**une place au milieu de l'avion.** *oon plahs oh meel-yoeh duh lah-vee-yoh~*
a seat near the back.	**une place à l'arrière de l'avion.** *oon plahs ah lah-ree-yayhr duh lah-vee-yoh~*

GETTING THERE

Is there a meal on the flight?	**Un repas sera-t-il servi durant le vol?**
	uh~ ruh-pah suh-rah-teel sayhr-vee due-raw~ luh vohl
I'd like to order ____	**Je voudrais commander ____**
	zhuh voo-dray koh-maw~-day
a vegetarian meal.	**un repas végétarien.**
	uh~ ruh-pah vay-zhay-tah-ree-yeh~
a kosher meal.	**un repas kasher.**
	uh~ ruh-pah kah-shayhr
a diabetic meal.	**un repas spécial diabétique.**
	uh~ ruh-pah spay-see-yahl dee-ah-bay-teek
I am traveling to ____.	**Je vais à ____.**
	zhuh vay ah
I am coming from ____.	**Je viens de ____.**
	zhuh vee-yeh~ duh
I arrived from ____.	**Je suis arrive(e) de ____.**
	zhuh sweez-ah-ree-vay duh

For full coverage of countries, see English / French dictionary.

May I ____ my reservation?	**Puis-je ____ ma réservation?**
	Pwee-zhuh ____ mah ray-suhr-vah-see-yoh~
change	**changer**
	shaw~-zhay
cancel	**annuler**
	aw~-nue-lay
confirm	**confirmer**
	koh~-feer-may
I have ____ bags / suitcases to check.	**J'ai ____ sacs / valises à enregistrer.**
	zhay ____ sahk / vah-leez ah aw~-reh-zhee-stray

For a full list of numbers, see p7.

Passengers with Special Needs

Is that handicapped accessible?

Ce vol est-il accessible aux personnes à mobilité réduite?

suh vohl ey-teel ahk-suhs-see-bluh oh payhr-suh-nah moh-bee-lee-tay ray-dweet

May I have a wheelchair / walker, please?

Puis-je avoir une chaise roulante / un déambulateur, s'il vous plaît?

Pwee-je ah-vwahr oon shehz roo-law~t / uh~ day-aw~-bue-lah-toehr seel voo play

I need some assistance boarding.

J'ai besoin d'assistance à l'embarquement.

zhay buh-zweh~ dah-sees-taw~s ah law~-bahrk-maw~

I need to bring my service dog.

J'ai besoin d'emmener avec moi mon chien aidant.

zhay buh-zweh~ daw~-m-nay ah-vek mwah moh~ shee-yeh~-nay-daw~

Do you have services for the deaf?

Offrez-vous des services spéciaux aux malentendants?

oh-fray-voo day sayhr-vees spay-see-yoh oh mah-law~-taw~-daw~

Do you have services for the blind?

Offrez-vous des services spéciaux aux malvoyants?

oh-fray-voo day sayhr-vees spay-see-yoh oh mahl-vwah-yaw~

Trouble at Check-In

How long is the delay?

Le retard est de combien de temps?

luh ruh-tahr ay duh koh~-bee-yeh~ duh taw~

My flight was late.

Mon vol avait du retard.

moh~ voh-lah-vay due ruh-tahr

I missed my flight.

J'ai manqué mon vol.

zhay maw~-kay moh~ vohl

When is the next flight?	**À quelle heure part le prochain vol?**
	ah keh-loehr pahr luh pro-shaw~ vohl
May I have a meal voucher?	**Puis-je avoir un chèque-repas?**
	pwee-zhuh ah-vwahr uh~ shek-ruh-pah
May I have a room voucher?	**Puis-je avoir un bon de chambre?**
	pwee-zhuh ah-vwahr uh~ boh~ duh shaw~-bruh

AT CUSTOMS / SECURITY CHECKPOINTS

I'm traveling with a group.	**Je voyage avec un groupe.**
	zhuh vwah-yahzh ah-vek uh~ groop
I'm on my own.	**Je voyage seul(e).**
	zhuh vwah-yahzh soehl
I'm traveling on business.	**Je voyage pour affaires.**
	zhuh vwah-yahzh pooh-rah-fayhr
I'm on vacation.	**Je suis en vacances.**
	zhuh swee-zaw~ vah-kaw~s
I have nothing to declare.	**Je n'ai rien à déclarer.**
	zhuh nay ree-yeh~-nah day-klah-ray
I would like to declare ____.	**Je voudrais déclarer ____.**
	zhuh voo-dray day-klah-ray
I have some liquor.	**J'ai de l'alcool.**
	zhay duh lahl-kool
I have some cigars.	**J'ai des cigares.**
	zhay day see-gahr
They are gifts.	**Il s'agit de cadeaux.**
	eel sah-zee duh kah-doh
They are for personal use.	**Ils sont pour mon usage personnel.**
	eel soh~ poohr moh~-nue-sahzh payhr-suh-nehl

Listen Up: Security Lingo

Veuillez enlever vos chaussures / bijoux.	Please remove your shoes / jewelry.
Veuillez enlever votre blouson / pull.	Please remove your jacket / sweater.
Veuillez placer vos bagages sur le tapis roulant.	Please place your bags on the conveyor belt.
Veuillez vous mettre de côté.	Please step to the side.
Nous désirons vous fouiller.	We have to do a hand search.

That is my medicine.

Ce médicament est à moi.
suh may-dee-ka-maw~ ey-tah mwah

I have my prescription.

J'ai l'ordonnance qui va avec.
zhay lohr-doh~-naw~s kee vah ah-vek

My children are traveling on the same passport.

Mes enfants figurent sur le même passeport.
may-zaw~-faw~ fee-guehr suehr luh mehm pahs-pohr

May I have a male / female officer conduct the search?

Puis-je être fouillé(e) par un officier du sexe masculin / féminin?
pwee-zhuh eh-truh foo-wee-yay pahr uh~-noh-fee-see-yay due sehks mah-skue-law~ / fay-mee-naw~

Trouble at Security

Help me. I've lost _____	**Veuillez m'aider. J'ai perdu _____** *voeh-yay may-day; zhay payhr-due*
my passport.	**mon passeport.** *moh~ pahs-pohr*
my boarding pass.	**mon bordereau d'embarque-ment.** *moh~ bohr-droh daw~-bahrk-maw~*
my identification.	**ma pièce d'identité.** *mah pee-yehs dee-daw~-tee-tay*
my wallet.	**mon portefeuille.** *moh~ pohr-tuh-foeh-yuh*
my purse.	**mon sac à main.** *moh~ sah-kah meh~*
Someone stole my purse / wallet!	**On a volé mon sac à main / mon portefeuille.** *oh~-nah voh-lay moh~ sah-kah meh~ / moh~ pohr-tuh-foeh-yuh*

IN-FLIGHT

It's unlikely you'll need much French on the plane, but these phrases will help if a bilingual flight attendant is unavailable or if you need to talk to a French-speaking neighbor.

I think that's my seat.	**Je pense que c'est ma place.** *zhuh paw~s kuh say mah plahs*
May I have _____	**Puis-je avoir _____** *pwee-zhuh ah-vwahr*
mineral water?	**de l'eau minérale?** *duh loh-mee-ney-rahl*
water (plain)?	**de l'eau non-gazeuse?** *duh loh due noh~-gah-zoehz*
sparkling water?	**de l'eau petillante / de l'eau mousseuse?** *duh loh peh-tee-yaw~t / duh loh moo-soehz*

orange juice?	**un jus d'orange?**
	uh~ zhue doh-raw~zh
a soda pop?	**un coca?**
	uh~ koh-kah
a diet soda?	**un coca allegé / un coca light?**
	uh~ koh-kah ah-lay-zhay / uh~ koh-kah liet
a beer?	**une bière?**
	oon bee-yahr
some wine?	**du vin?**
	due veh~

For a full list of drinks, see p108.

a pillow?	**un oreiller?**
	uh~-noh-ray-yay
a blanket?	**une couverture?**
	oon koo-vayhr-tuehr
headphones?	**un casque?**
	uh~ kahsk
a magazine or newspaper?	**un magazine ou un journal?**
	uh~ mah-gah-zeen oo uh~ zhoohr-nahl
When will the meal be served?	**Quand le repas sera-t-il servi?**
	kaw~ luh ruh-pah suh-rah-teel sayhr-vee
How long until we land?	**Dans combien de temps allons-nous atterrir?**
	daw~ koh~-bee-yeh~ duh taw~ ah-loh~-noo ah-teh-reehr
May I move to another seat?	**Puis-je changer de place?**
	pwee-zhuh shaw~-zhay duh plahs
How do I turn the light on / off?	**Comment éteint-on / allume-t-on les lumières?**
	koh-moh ay-teh~-toh~ / ah-luem-toh~ lay lue-mee-yayhr

Trouble In-Flight

These headphones are broken.	**Mon casque ne marche pas.** *moh~ kask nuh mahrsh pah*
Excuse me, I spilled something.	**Pardon, je me suis renversé quelque chose dessus.** *pahr-doh~ zhuh muh swee raw~-vayhr-say kehl-kuh shohz duh-sue*
My child spilled something.	**Mon enfant s'est renversé quelque chose dessus.** *moh~-naw~-faw~ say raw~-vayhr-say kehl-kuh shohz duh-sue*
My child is sick.	**Mon enfant est malade.** *moh~-naw~faw~-tay mah-lahd*
I need an airsickness bag.	**J'ai besoin d'un sac pour le mal de l'air.** *zhay buh-zweh~ duh~ sahk poohr luh mahl duh layhr*
I smell something strange.	**Je sent quelque chose bizarre.** *zhuh saw~ kehl-kuh shohz bee-zahr*
That passenger is behaving suspiciously.	**Ce passager se comporte bizzarement.** *suh pah-sah-zhay suh koh~-pohrt bee-zahr-maw~*

BAGGAGE CLAIM

Where is baggage claim for flight ____?	**Où est la zone de récupération des bagages pour le vol ____?** *oo ay lah zohn duh ray-kue-pay-rah-see-yoh~ day bah-gazh poohr luh vohl*
Would you please help me with my bags?	**Pouvez-vous m'aider à trouver mes bagages, s'il vous plaît?** *poo-vay-voo may-day ah troo-vay may bah-gazh seel voo play*
I am missing ____ bags / suitcases.	**Il me manque ____ sacs / valises.** *eel muh maw~k ____ sahk / vah-leez*

For a full list of numbers, see p7.

My bag is / was ____	**Mon sac est / était ____**
	moh~ sah-kay / sah-kay-tay
lost.	**perdu.**
	payhr-due
damaged.	**abîmé.**
	ah-bee-may
stolen.	**volé.**
	voh-lay
a suitcase.	**une valise.**
	oon vah-leez
a briefcase.	**un porte-documents.**
	uh~ pohrt-doh-kue-maw~
a carry-on.	**un bagage à main.**
	uh~ bah-gah-zhah meh~
a suit bag.	**un porte-costume.**
	uh~ pohrt-koh-stuem
a trunk.	**une malle.**
	oon mahl
golf clubs.	**des clubs de golf.**
	day klueb duh gohlf
hard.	**á coques dures.**
	ah kohk duehr
made out of ____	**en ____**
	aw~
canvas.	**toile.**
	twahl
vinyl.	**vinyle.**
	vee-neel
leather.	**cuir.**
	kweer
hard plastic.	**plastique dur.**
	plah-steek duehr
aluminum.	**aluminium.**
	ah-lue-mee-nee-uhm

For a full list of colors, see the English / French dictionary.

RENTING A VEHICLE

Is there a car rental agency in the airport?	**Y a-t-il une agence de location de voitures dans cet aéroport?** *yah-teel oo-nah-zhaw~s duh loh-kah-see-yoh~ duh vwah-tuehr daw~ seh-tay-roh-pohr*
I have a reservation.	**J'ai une réservation.** *zhay oon ray-zayhr-vah-see-yoh~*

VEHICLE PREFERENCES

I would like to rent ____	**Je voudrais louer ____** *zhuh voo-dray loo-ay*
an economy car.	**une voiture économie.** *oon vwah-tuehr ay-koh-noh-mee*
a midsize car.	**une voiture intermédiaire.** *oon vwah-tuehr aw~-tayhr-may-dee-yayhr*
a sedan.	**une berline.** *oon bayhr-leen*
a convertible.	**une décapotable.** *oon day-kah-poh-tah-bluh*
a van.	**un fourgon.** *uh~ foohr-goh~*
a sports car.	**une voiture de sport.** *oon vwah-tuehr duh spohr*
a 4-wheel-drive vehicle.	**un véhicule à quatre roues motrices.** *uh~ vay-ee-kue-lah ka-truh roo moh-trees*
a motorcycle.	**une moto.** *oon moh-toh*
a scooter.	**un scooter.** *uh~ skoo-tayhr*

Do you have one with ____

En avez-vous une avec ____
aw~-nah-vay-voo oon ah-vek

air conditioning?

la climatisation?
lah klee-mah-tee-zah-see-yoh~

a sunroof?

un toit ouvrant?
uh~ twah oov-raw~

a CD player?

un lecteur de CD?
uh~ lek-toehr duh say-day

satellite radio?

la radio par satellite?
lah rah-dee-oh pahr sah-tuh-leet

satellite tracking?

la télédétection?
lah tay-lay-day-tek-see-yoh~

an onboard map?

un système de navigation?
uh~ sees-tehm duh nah-vee-gah-see-yoh~

a DVD player?

un lecteur de DVD?
uh~ lek-toehr duh day-vay-day

child seats?

des sièges pour enfant?
day see-yehz poohr aw~faw~

Do you have ____

Avez-vous ____
ah-vay-voo

a smaller car?

une voiture plus petite?
oon vwah-tuehr plue puh-teet

a bigger car?

une voiture plus grande?
oon vwah-tuehr plue graw~d

a cheaper car?

une voiture moins chère?
oon vwah-tuehr mweh~ shayhr

Do you have a nonsmoking car?

Avez-vous une voiture non fumeur?
ah-vay-voo oon vwah-tuehr noh~ fue-moehr

I need an automatic transmission.

J'ai besoin d'une voiture à transmission automatique.
zhay buh-zweh~ doon vwah-tuehr ah traw~z-mee-shee-yoh~ ohtoh-mah-teek

GETTING THERE

A standard transmission is okay.	**D'accord pour une boîte de vitesses** *dah-kohr poohr oon bwaht duh vee-tess*
May I have an upgrade?	**Puis-je bénéficier de la classe supérieure?** *pwee-zhuh bay-nay-fee-see-yay duh lah klahs sue-pay-ree-yoehr*

MONEY MATTERS

What's the daily / weekly / monthly rate?	**Quel est le tarif journalier / hebdomadaire / mensuel?** *keh-lay luh tah-reef zhoohr-nah-lee-yay / ehb-doh-mah-dayhr / maw~-swehl*
What is the mileage rate?	**Quel est le prix au kilomètre?** *keh-lay luh pree oh kee-loh-meh-truh*
How much is insurance?	**Combien coûte l'assurance?** *koh~-bee-yeh~ koot lah-sue-raw~s*
Are there other fees?	**Y a-t-il d'autres coûts?** *yah-teel doh-truhs koo*
Is there a weekend rate?	**Y a-t-il un tarif spécial pour le week-end?** *yah-teel uh~ tah-reef spay-see-yahl poohr luh wee-kend*

TECHNICAL QUESTIONS

What kind of gas does it take?	**Quel type d'essence consomme-t-elle?** *kehl teep day-saw~s koh~-som-tehl*
Do you have the manual in English?	**Avez-vous un manuel en anglais?** *ah-vay-voo uh~ maw~-nwehl aw~-naw~-glay*
Do you have an English booklet with the local traffic laws?	**Avez-vous une brochure en anglais sur le code de la route local?** *ah-vay-voo oon broh-shuehr aw~-naw~-glay suehr luh kohd duh lah root loh-kahl*

Road Signs

Vitesse limitée	Speed Limit
Stop	Stop
Céder le passage	Yield
Danger	Danger
Voie sans issue	No Exit
Voie unique	One Way
Entrée interdite	Do Not Enter
Route fermée	Road Closed
Péage	Toll
Espèces uniquement	Cash Only
Parking interdit	No Parking
Parking payant	Parking Fee
Garage couvert	Parking Garage

CAR TROUBLES

The _____ doesn't work.
_____ ne marche pas.
_____ nuh mahrsh pah

See diagram on p66 for car parts.

It is already dented.
La carrosserie est déjà abîmée.
lah kah-roh-seh-ree ay day-zhah ah-bee-may

It is scratched.
La carrosserie est rayée.
lah kah-roh-seh-ree ay ray-ay

The windshield is cracked.
Le pare-brise est fendu.
luh pahr-breez ay faw~-due

The tires look low.
Les pneus ont l'air de manquer d'air.
lay puh-noeh oh~ layhr duh maw~-kay dayhr

It has a flat tire.
L'un des pneus est à plat.
luh~ day puh-noeh ay-tah plah

Whom do I call for service?
Qui dois-je appeler pour me faire dépanner?
kee dwah-zhuh ah-play poohr muh fayhr day-pah-nay

1. la porte du réservoir
2. le coffre
3. le butoir de pare-chocs
4. la glace
5. le pare-brise
6. les essuie-glaces
7. le lave-glace
8. la serrure
9. la serrure automatique
10. le pneu
11. la roue
12. l'allumage
13. les feux de détresse
14. la jauge d'essence
15. le clignotant
16. les feux avant
17. le kilométrique
18. l'indicateur de vitesse
19. le silencieux
20. le capot
21. le volant
22. le rétroviseur

23. le toit ouvrant
24. la ceinture de sécurité
25. la pédale
26. l'embrayage
27. le frein
28. le frein à main
29. le moteur
30. la batterie
31. l'indicateur de niveau d'huile (à moteur)
32. le radiator
33. la courroie de ventilateur

It won't start.	**Elle refuse de démarrer.**
	ehl ruh-fuez duh day-mah-ray
It's out of gas.	**Elle est en panne d'essence.**
	ehl ay-taw~ pahn day-saw~s
The check engine light is on.	**Le voyant de contrôle du moteur est allumé.**
	luh vwah-yaw~ duh koh~-trohl due moh-toehr ay-tah-lue-may
The oil light is on.	**Le voyant de niveau d'huile est allumé.**
	luh vwah-yaw~ duh nee-voh dweel ay-tah-lue-may
The brake light is on.	**Le voyant de contrôle des freins est allumé.**
	luh vwah-yaw~ duh koh~-trohl day frehn ay-tah-lue-may
It runs rough.	**La conduite est trop serrée.**
	lah koh~-dwee-tay troh suh-ray
The car is overheating.	**Le moteur chauffe.**
	luh moh-toehr shohf

Asking for Directions

Excuse me, please.	**Excusez-moi, s'il vous plaît.**
	ehks-kue-zay mwah seel voo play
How do I get to ____?	**Comment fais-je pour aller à ____?**
	koh-moh fay-zhuh pooh-rah-lay ah
Go straight.	**Allez tout droit.**
	ah-lay too dwah
Turn left.	**Tournez à gauche.**
	toohr-nay ah gohsh
Continue right.	**Continuez à droite.**
	koh~-teen-yue-ay ah dwaht
It's on the right.	**C'est à droite.**
	say-tah dwaht
Can you show me on the map?	**Pouvez-vous me montrer sur la carte?**
	poo-vay-voo muh moh~-tray suehr lah kahrt

Is it far from here?	**Est-ce loin d'ici?**
	ehs lweh dee-see
Is this the right way for ____?	**Est-ce que c'est la bonne route pour ____?**
	ehs kuh say lah buhn root pohr
I've lost my way.	**Je me suis perdu(e).**
	zhuh muh swee payhr-due
Could you repeat that, please?	**Est-ce que vous pouvez répéter, s'il vous plaît?**
	ehs kuh voo poo-vay ruh-puh-tay seel voo play
Thanks for your help.	**Merci pour votre aide.**
	mayhr-see pohr voh-trehd

For a full list of direction-related terms, see p5.

SORRY, OFFICER

What is the speed limit?	**Quelle est la limite de vitesse?**
	keh-lay lah lee-meet duh vee-tess
I wasn't going that fast.	**Je n'allais pas si vite.**
	zhuh nah-lay pah see veet
Where do I pay the fine?	**Où dois-je payer l'amende?**
	oo dwah-zhuh pay-ay lah-maw~d
How much is the fine?	**Combien est-ce que l'amende?**
	koh~-bee-yeh~ ehs kuh lah-maw~d
Do I have to go to court?	**Dois-je passer en justice?**
	dwah-zhuh pah-say aw~ zhues-tees
I had an accident.	**J'ai eu un accident.**
	zhay oo uh~-nahk-see-daw~
The other driver hit me.	**C'est l'autre conducteur qui m'est rentré dedans.**
	say loh-truh koh~-duek-toehr kee may raw~-tray duh-daw~
I'm at fault.	**C'est moi qui suis responsable.**
	say mwah kee swee ruh-spoh~-sah-bluh

BY TAXI

Where is the taxi stand?	**Où est la station de taxi?** *oo ay lah stah-see-yon duh tahk-see*
Is there a shuttle bus between the airport and my hotel?	**Y a-t-il une navette entre l'aéroport et mon hôtel?** *yah-tee-loon nah-veht aw~-truh lay-roh-pohr ay moh~-noh-tel*
I need to get to ____.	**Je désire aller à ____.** *zhuh day-seer ah-lay ah*
How much will that cost?	**Combien va coûter la course?** *koh~-bee-yeh~ vah koo-tay lah koohrs*
Can you take me / us to the train / bus station?	**Pouvez-vous m'emmener / nous emmener à la gare / à la gare routière?** *poo-vay-voo maw~m-nay / nooz-ah~-m-nay ah lah gahr / ah lah gahr roo-tee-yayhr*
I am in a hurry.	**Je me suis pressé(e).** *zhuh muh swee pruh-say*
Slow down.	**Veuillez ralentir.** *voeh-yay rah-law~-teehr*
Am I close enough to walk?	**Est-ce assez près pour y aller à pied?** *eh-sah-say pray poohr yah-lay ah pee-ay*

Listen Up: Taxi Lingo

Montez!	Get in!
Laissez vos bagages. Je m'en occupe.	Leave your luggage. I got it.
C'est ____ euros par baggage.	It's ____ for each bag.
Combien de passagers?	How many passengers?
Vous êtes pressés?	Are you in a hurry?

Please let me out here.	**Laissez-moi descendre ici, s'il vous plaît.** *leh-zay mwah duh-saw~-druh ee-see seel voo play*
That's not the correct change.	**Vous ne m'avez pas rendu la bonne monnaie.** *voo nuh mah-vay pah raw~-due lah buhn moh-nay*

For a full list of numbers, see p7.

BY TRAIN

How do I get to the train station?	**Comment puis-je me rendre à la gare?** *koh-maw~ pwee-zhuh muh raw~-drah lah gahr*
Would you take me to the train station?	**Pouvez-vous m'emmener à la gare?** *poo-vay-voo maw~-m-nay ah lah gahr*
How long is the trip to ____?	**Il y a combien de kilomètres jusqu'à ____?** *eel-yah koh~-bee-yeh~ duh kee-loh-meh-truh zhues-kah*
When is the next train?	**À quelle heure part le prochain train?** *ah keh-loehr pahr luh pro-shaw~-treh~*
Do you have a schedule?	**Avez-vous un horaire des départs?** *ah-vay-voo-zuh~-nohr-ayhr day day-pahr*

Do I have to change trains?	**Dois-je changer de train?** *dwah-zhuh shaw~-zhay duh treh~*
a one-way ticket	**un aller simple** *uh~-nah-lay seh~-pluh*
a round-trip ticket	**un aller-retour** *uh~-nah-lay ruh-toohr*
Which platform does it leave from?	**De quel quai le train part-il?** *duh kehl kay luh treh~ pahr-teel*
Is there a bar car?	**Y a-t-il un service de boissons?** *yah-teel uh~ sayhr-vees duh bwah-soh~s*
Is there a dining car?	**Y a-t-il un wagon-restaurant?** *yah-teel uh~ vah-goh~ reh-stoh-raw~*
Which car is my seat in?	**Dans quel wagon se trouve ma place?** *daw~ kehl vah-goh~ suh troov mah plahs*
Is this seat taken?	**Ce siège est-il pris?** *suh see-yehzh ey-teel pree*
Where is the next stop?	**Quel est le prochain arrêt?** *keh-lay luh proh-sheh~-nah-rey*
Would you please tell me how many stops to ____?	**Pouvez-vous me dire combien d'arrêts il y a avant ____?** *poo-vay-voo muh deer koh~-bee-yeh~ dah-rey eel-yah ah-vaw~*
What's the train number and destination?	**Quel est le numéro du train et sa destination?** *keh-lay luh nue-may-roh due treh~ ay sah deh-stee-nah-see-yoh~*

BY BUS

How do I get to the bus station?	**Comment puis-je me rendre à la gare routière?** *koh-maw~ pwee-zhuh muh raw~-druh ah lah gahr roo-tee-yayhr*
Would you take me to the bus station?	**Pouvez-vous m'emmener à la gare routière?** *poo-vay-voo maw~m-nay ah lah gahr roo-tee-yayhr*
May I please have a bus schedule?	**Puis-je avoir un horaire des cars?** *pwee-zhuh ah-vwahr uh~-noh-rayhr day kahr*
Which bus goes to ____?	**Quel car va à ____?** *kehl kahr vah ah*
Where does it leave from?	**D'où part-il?** *due pahr-teel*
How long does the bus take?	**Combien de temps prend le car pour aller à ____?** *koh~-bee-yeh~ duh taw~ praw~luh kahr poohr ah-lay ah*
How much is it?	**Combien ça coûte?** *koh~-bee-yeh~ sah koot*
Is there an express bus?	**Y a-t-il un service direct?** *yah-teel uh~ sayhr-vees dee-rekt*

Does it make local stops?	**Dessert-il toutes les villes?** *duh-zayhr-teel toot lay veel*
Does it run at night?	**Fonctionne-t-il pendant la nuit?** *foh~k-see-yoh~-teel paw~-daw~ lah nwee*
When is the next bus?	**À quelle heure part le prochain car?** *ah keh-loehr pahr luh proh-sheh~ kahr*
a one-way ticket	**un aller simple** *uh~-nah-lay seh~-pluh*
a round-trip ticket	**un aller-retour** *uh~-nah-lay ruh-toohr*
How long will the bus be stopped?	**Combien de temps dure l'arrêt?** *koh~-bee-yeh~ duh taaw~ duehr lah-rey*
Is there an air conditioned bus?	**Y a-t-il un car climatisé?** *yah-teel uh~ kahr klee-mah-tee-zay*
Is this seat taken?	**Ce siège est-il pris?** *suh see-yehzh ey-teel pree*
Where is the next stop?	**Quel est le prochain arrêt?** *keh-lay luh proh-sheh~-nah-rey*
Would you please tell me when we reach ____?	**Veuillez me dire quand nous atteignons ____?** *voeh-yay muh deer kaw~ noo-zah-teh-nyoh~*
Would you please tell me how to get to ____?	**Pouvez-vous me dire comment aller à ____, s'il vous plaît?** *poo-vay-voo muh deer koh-maw~ ah-lay ah ___ seel voo play*
I'd like to get off here.	**Je voudrais descendre ici.** *zhuh voo-dray duh-saw~-druh ee-see*

BY BOAT OR SHIP

Would you take me to the port?	**Pouvez-vous m'emmener au port?** *poo-vay-voo meh-men-ay oh pohr*
When does the boat sail?	**Quand le navire appareille-t-il?** *kaw~ luh nah-veer ah-pah-ray teel*
How long is the voyage?	**Combien de temps la traversée dure-t-elle?** *koh~-bee-yeh~-duh taw~ lah trah-vayhr-say duehr-tehl*
Where are the life preservers?	**Où sont les bouées de sauvetage?** *oo soh~ lay boo-ay duh sohv-tazh*
I would like a private cabin.	**Je voudrais une cabine individuelle.** *zhuh voo-dray oon kah-been eh~-dee-vee-due-ehl*
Is the trip rough?	**Le voyage, est-il difficile?** *luh vwah-yahzh ey-teel dee-fee-seel*
I feel seasick.	**J'ai le mal de mer.** *zhay luh mahl duh mayhr*
I need some Dramamine.	**Je voudrais de la Dramamine.** *zhuh voo-dray duh lah drah-mah-meen*
Where is the bathroom?	**Où puis-je trouver des WC?** *oo pwee-zhuh troo-vay day vay-say*
Does the ship have a casino?	**Y a-t-il un casino à bord?** *yah-teel uh~ kah-zee-noh ah bohr*
Will the ship stop at ports along the way?	**Le navire fera-t-il escale dans certains ports?** *luh nah-veer fuh-rah teel ehs-kahl daw~ sayhr-teh~ pohr*

BY SUBWAY

A very convenient, fast, safe and inexpensive way to cruise through a French city is to take its **Métro**. Note that subways close at night (the Paris Métro closes from 12:50 AM to 5:30 AM), so do allocate enough time for your trip back to your hotel!

Where is the subway station?	**Où se trouve la station du métro?** *oo suh troov lah stah-see-yoh~ due meh-troh*
Where can I buy a ticket?	**Où achete-t-on des billets?** *oo ah-sheh-toh~ day bee-yay*
Could I have a map of the subway, please?	**Pouvez-vous me donner un plan métro, s'il vous plaît?** *poo-vay voo muh duh-nay uh~ plaw~ meh-troh seel voo play*
Which line should I take for _____?	**Quelle ligne prend-t-on à _____?** *kehl leen praw~ toh~ ah*
Is this the right line for _____?	**Est-ce que c'est la bonne ligne à _____?** *ehs kuh say lah buhn lee-nah*
Which stop is it for _____?	**Quel arrêt pour _____?** *keh-lah-rey poohr*
How many stops is it to _____?	**Combien d' arrêts jusqu'à _____?** *koh~-bee-yeh~ dah-rey zhues-kah*
Is the next stop _____?	**L' arrêt prochain, c'est _____?** *lah-rey proh-sheh~ say*
Where are we?	**Où sommes-nous?** *oo suhm-noo*

Where do I change to _____?	**Où est-ce que je change à _____?** *oo ehs kuh zhuh shaw~zh ah*
What time is the last train to _____?	**Á quelle heure part le dernier train à _____?** *ah keh-loehr pahr luh dayhr-nyay treh~-nah*
Where?	**Où?** *oo*

SUBWAY TICKETS

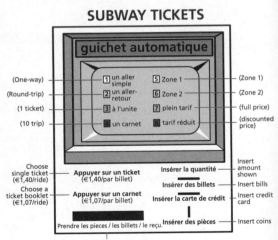

(One-way) — **1** un aller simple
(Round-trip) — **2** un aller-retour
(1 ticket) — **3** à l'unite
(10 trip) — **4** un carnet

5 Zone 1 — (Zone 1)
6 Zone 2 — (Zone 2)
7 plein tarif — (full price)
8 tarif réduit — (discounted price)

Choose single ticket (€1,40/ride) — **Appuyer sur un ticket** (€1,40/par billet)

Choose a ticket booklet (€1,07/ride) — **Appuyer sur un carnet** (€1,07/par billet)

Insérer la quantité — Insert amount shown

Insérer des billets — Insert bills

Insérer la carte de crédit — Insert credit card

Insérer des pièces — Insert coins

Prendre les pieces / les billets / le reçu. — Take change / tickets / receipt

TRAVELERS WITH SPECIAL NEEDS

Do you have wheelchair access?	**Ce navire est-il accessible aux personnes à mobilité réduite?** *suh nah-veer ey-teel ahk-seh-see-bluh oh payhr-suhn ah moh-bee-lee-tay ray-dweet*
Do you have elevators? Where?	**Y a-t-il des ascenseurs à bord? Où?** *yah-teel day-zah-saw~-soehrs ah bohr; oo*
Do you have ramps? Where?	**Y a-t-il des rampes à bord? Où?** *yah-teel day raw~-pah bohr; oo*
Are the restrooms handicapped accessible?	**Les toilettes sont-elles accessibles aux personnes à mobilité réduite?** *lay twah-leht soh~-tehl ahk-seh-see-bluh oh payhr-suhn ah moh-bee-lee-tay ray-dweet*
Do you have audio assistance for deaf persons?	**Offrez-vous des services audio aux malentendants?** *oh-fray-voo day sayhr-vees oh-dee-yoh oh mah-law~-taw~-daw~*
I am deaf / hearing impaired.	**Je suis sourd(e) / malentendant(e).** *zhuh swee soohr(d) / mah-law~-taw~-daw~(t)*
May I bring my service dog?	**Puis-je emmener mon chien aidant?** *pwee-zhuh aw~m-nay moh~ shee-yeh~-nay-daw~*
I am blind / visually impaired.	**Je suis aveugle / malvoyant(e).** *zhuh swee ah-voeh-gluh / mahl-vwah-yaw~(t)*
I need to charge my power chair.	**J'ai besoin d'assistance pour embarquer ma chaise roulante.** *zhay buh-zweh~ dah-see-staw~s poohr aw~-bahr-kay mah shehz roo-law~t*

CONVERSIONS

For exact conversions of all measurements, including currencies, go to **www.onlineconversion.com.** Here are some critical conversions for American travelers:

1 liter = .26 U.S. gallons

1 U.S. gallon = 3.8 liters

To convert U.S. gallons to liters, multiply by 3.8.

To covert liters to U.S. gallons, multiply by .26.

A liter is a little over a U.S. liquid quart, and thus a U.S. gallon is around 4 liters.

To convert inches to centimeters, multiply by 2.54.

To convert centimeters to inches, multiply by .39.

To convert feet to meters, multiply by .30.

To convert meters to feet, multiply by 3.28.

To convert yards to meters, multiply by .91.

To convert meters to yards, multiply by 1.09.

To convert miles to kilometers, multiply by 1.61.

To convert kilometers to miles, multiply by .62.

1 foot = .3m; 1 mile = 1.6km; 1m = 3.3 feet; 1 km = .6 miles

Train Travel   The best ground transportation for navigating France is the national train network, the **SNCF** (www.sncf.fr and www.voyages-sncf.com). Every major city and town in the country is served by rail, and the service is generally efficient and reasonably priced (other than during periods of labor strikes, which occur usually once a year). You can reserve and buy your train tickets online with a credit card and then collect them at the Automatic Tellers at the train station. Be aware, however, that the website takes Visa, MasterCard, and American Express, but the ATMs function only with Visa and MasterCard. Schedules and tickets are available before you leave home from **Rail Europe** at www.raileurope.com, ✆ **800/622-8600.**

Favorite Train Trips   The Eurostar between Paris's Gare du Nord and London's Waterloo Station takes only 2 hours and 40 minutes. You can even turn London into a day trip from Paris. Some travelers are attracted to the idea of traveling first-class on the EuroStar, but the extra comfort is minimal and, unless you have money to burn, usually isn't worth the higher cost. The Thalys train between Brussels and Paris takes only 80 minutes!

Air Travel   Flying time to Paris is 7 hours from New York, 9½ hours from Chicago, and 11 hours from Los Angeles. Flying time from the United Kingdom to Paris is under 1½ hours.

AIR TRAVEL

Major Airlines Serving France

- **Air Canada**   ✆ **888/247-2262** in the U.S. and Canada; **08-25-88-08-81** in France; www.aircanada.ca
- **Air France**   ✆ **800/237-2747** in the U.S.; **0826-460-950** in France; www.airfrance.com
- **American Airlines**   ✆ 800/433-7300 in the U.S.; **08-10-87-28-72** in France; www.aa.com
- **British Airways**   ✆ **800/247-9297** in the U.S.; **0844/493-0-787** in the U.K.; **08-25-82-54-00** in France; www.britishairways.com
- **Continental**   ✆ **800/231-0856** in the U.S.; **01-71-23-03-35** in France; www.continental.com
- **Delta**   ✆ **800/241-4141** in the U.S.; **0811-640-005** in France; www.delta.com
- **Qantas**   ✆ **800/227-4500** in the U.S.; **0811-980-002** in France; www.qantas.com

GETTING THERE

- **United**   © 800/538-2929 in the U.S.; 08-10-72-72-72 in France; www.unitedairlines.com

- **US Airways**   © 800/428-4322 in the U.S.; 08-10-63-22-22 in France; www.usairways.com

Top European Budget Airlines

- **www.easyjet.com**   Easyjet. Specializes in European cities.

- **www.flybmi.com**   Fly BMI. Specializes in the U.K.

- **www.germanwings.com**   German Wings. Specializes in German destinations.

- **www.ryanair.com**   Ryanair. Specializes in the U.K. and Ireland.

- **www.opodo.com**   Gives you a comparative look at all flights, airlines, and fares.

- **www.ebookers.com**   Compares all flights, fares, and airlines.

- **www.expedia.co.uk**   Compares all flights, fares, and airlines.

- **www.govoyages.com**   Online cut-rate fares with a Paris pick-up office.

- **www.flymycase.com**   Sends your luggage in advance of your journey.

- **www.moneysavingexpert.com**   Works out itineraries for you, and lets you know when the cheapest offers from each airline are available.

How to Get the Best Seats and Fares

Become a **frequent flyer;** even if you never get a free ticket, it will entitle you to a better choice of seats and other perks. Check **airline websites,** as they may offer even better deals than general online booking sites such as Travelocity. After you book online, call the airline to **confirm your seat** reservation. Check **consolidators,** known as bucket shops, in the Sunday travel sections of major newspapers such as *the New York Times,* but beware that they sometimes put you on charter flights, which may leave at inconvenient times. Tickets bought online may still be cheaper. If your flight is cancelled, don't wait on a long line to change it; **call the airline,** even if you're at the airport.

Avoid seats in the back of the plane, which can be noisy and cramped. Avoid seats near the toilets and pantries, which can be noisy as well. As a general rule, try for a seat as far forward as possible. Bulkhead seats have more legroom, but sometimes they are reserved for infants. If two of you are traveling together, reserve the aisle and window seats in a three-seat row. (Center seats go last, so you may have a free seat between you. If someone fills it, they will invariably be happy to switch with one of you.)

FUN FACTS

- France's tallest mountain is **Mount Blanc**, part of the range that runs across the border of France and Italy. Mount Blanc rises 15,771 ft. (4,731m) at its highest point in the French Alps.

- France's longest river is the **Loire**, which runs for 634 miles (1,021km). It begins 85 miles (137km) north of the Mediterranean Sea, and flows north.

- France's tallest building is the **Tour Montparnasse** in Paris. At a height of 689 ft. (210m), the Tour Montparnasse towers above Paris's 14th arrondissement. From its panoramic roof terrace above the 56th floor, you can see as far as 25 miles (40km) in clear weather. The view of the Montparnasse Cemetery, right below, is excellent; it's exciting to stand on a structure from which you actually look down at the Eiffel Tower.

CHAPTER THREE

LODGING

This chapter will help you find the right accomodations, at the right price—and the amenities you might need during your stay.

ROOM PREFERENCES

Would you please recommend _____	**Pourriez-vous me recommander _____**
	pooh-ree-yay-voo muh ruh-koh-maw~-day
a clean hostel?	**une auberge propre?**
	oo-noh-bayrzh proh-pruh
a moderately priced hotel?	**un hôtel au prix moyen?**
	uh~ noh-tehl oh pree mwah-yaw~
a moderately priced B&B?	**une chambre d'hôtes / un bed and breakfast au prix moyen?**
	oon shaw~-bruh doht / uh~ behd ahnd brehk-fahst oh pree mwah-yaw~
a good hotel / motel?	**un bon hôtel / motel?**
	uh~ buh-noh-tehl / moh-tehl
Does the hotel have _____	**Cet hôtel a-t-il _____**
	seh-toh-tel ah-teel
a pool?	**une piscine?**
	oon pee-seen
a casino?	**un casino?**
	uh~ kah-zee-noh
suites?	**des suites?**
	day sweet
terraces?	**des chambres donnant sur une terrace?**
	day shaw~-bruh duh-naw~ suehr oon tay-rahs

a fitness center?	**une salle de musculation?**
	oon sahl duh mues-kue-lah-see-yoh~
a spa?	**un spa?**
	uh~ spah
a private beach?	**une plage privée?**
	oon plazh pree-vay
a tennis court?	**un court de tennis?**
	uh~ koohr duh tay-nees
I would like a room for ____ people.	**Je voudrais une chambre pour ____ personnes.**
	zhuh voo-dray oon shaw~-bruh poohr ____ payhr-suhn

For a full list of numbers, see p7.

I would like ____	**Je voudrais ____**
	zhuh voo-dray
a king-sized bed.	**une chambre à très grand lit.**
	oon shaw~-bruh ah tray graw~ lee
a double bed.	**une chambre à lit à une place.**
	oon shaw~-bruh ah lee ah oon plahs
twin beds.	**des lits jumeaux.**
	day lee zhue-moh
adjoining rooms.	**des chambres communicantes.**
	day shaw~-bruh koh-mue-neek-aw~t

LODGING

Listen Up: Reservations Lingo

Nous sommes pleins.	We have no vacancies.
Combien de nuits désirez-vous rester?	How long will you be staying?
Fumeur ou non fumeur?	Smoking or nonsmoking?

a smoking room.	**une chambre fumeur** *oon shaw~-bruh fue-moehr*
nonsmoking room.	**une chambre non fumeur.** *oon shaw~-bruh noh~ fue-moehr*
a private bathroom.	**une salle de bain privée.** *oon sahl duh beh~ pree-vay*
a room with a shower.	**une chambre avec une douche.** *oon shaw~-bruh ah-vehk oon doosh*
a room with a bathtub.	**une chambre avec une baignoire.** *oon shaw~-bruh ah-vehk oon beh~-nwahr*
air conditioning.	**climatisation.** *klee-mah-tee-zah-see-yoh~*
television.	**un poste de télévision.** *pohst duh tay-lay-vee-zee-yoh~*
cable.	**le télévision par câble.** *luh tay-lay-vee-zee-yoh~ pahr kah-bluh*
satellite TV.	**le télévision par satellite.** *luh tay-lay-vee-zee-yoh~ pahr sah-teh-leet*
a telephone.	**un téléphone.** *un~ tay-lay-fohn*
Internet access.	**accès à l'Internet.** *ahk-say ah leh~-tayhr-neht*
high-speed Internet access.	**accès haute vitesse à l'Internet.** *ahk-say ot veet-ess ah leh~-tayhr-neht*
a refrigerator.	**un réfrigérateur.** *uh~ ray-free-zheh-rah-toehr*
a beach view.	**vue sur la mer.** *vue suehr lah mayhr*
a city view.	**vue sur la rue.** *vue suehr lah rue*

a kitchenette. **une kitchenette.**
oon kee-shee-neht

a balcony. **un balcon.**
uh~ bahl-koh~

a suite. **une suite.**
oon sweet

a penthouse. **une chambre terrasse.**
oon shaw~-bruh tay-rahs

I would like a room ____ **Je voudrais une chambre __**
zhuh voo-dray oon shaw~-bruh

on the ground floor. **au rez-de-chaussée.**
oh ray duh shoh-say

near the elevator. **à proximité d'un ascenceur.**
ah prok-see-mee-tay duh~ ah-saw~-soehr

near the stairs. **à proximité d'un escalier.**
ah prok-see-mee-tay duh~ ehs-kah-lee-yay

near the pool. **à proximité de la piscine.**
ah prok-see-mee-tay duh lah pee-zeen

away from the street. **à l'écart de la rue.**
ah lay-kahr duh lah rue

I would like a corner room. **Je voudrais une chambre d'angle.**
zhuh voo-dray oon shaw~-bruh daw~-gluh

Do you have ____ **Avez-vous ____**
ah-vay-voo

a crib? **un lit d'enfant?**
uh~ lee daw~-faw~

a foldout bed? **un lit dépliant?**
uh~ lee day-plee-yaw~

GUESTS WITH SPECIAL NEEDS

I need a room with ____
J'ai besoin d'une chambre ____
zhay buh-zweh~ doon shaw~-bruh

wheelchair access.
accessible en chaise roulante.
ahk-seh-see-bluh aw~ shehz roo-law~t

services for the visually impaired.
équipée pour malvoyant.
ay-kee-pay poohr mahl-vwahy-aw~

services for the hearing impaired.
équipée pour malentendant.
ay-kee-pay poohr mah-law~-taw~-daw~

I am traveling with a service dog.
Je voyage avec un chien aidant.
zhuh vwah-yahzh ah-vek uh~ shee-yeh~-nay-daw~

MONEY MATTERS

I would like to make a reservation.
Je désire faire une réservation.
zhuh day-zeer fayhr oon ray-zehr-vah-see-yoh~

How much per night?
Quel est le prix par nuit?
keh-lay luh pree pahr nwee

Do you have a ____
Avez-vous ____
ah-vay-voo

weekly rate?
un tarif hebdomadaire?
uh~ tah-reef ehb-doh-mah-dayhr

monthly rate?
un tarif mensuel?
uh~ tah-reef maw~-swehl

weekend rate?
le prix de fin de semaine?
luh pree duh feh~ duh smehn

We will be staying for ____ days / weeks / months.
Nous désirons rester ____ nuits / semaines / mois.
noo day-zeer-oh~ ruh-stay ____ nwee / smehn / mwah

For full coverage of numbers, see p7.

When is checkout time?	**À quelle heure la chambre doit-elle être libérée?** *ah keh-loehr lah shaw~-bruh dwah-tehl eh-truh lee-bay-ray*
Do you accept credit cards / travelers' checks?	**Acceptez-vous les cartes de crédit / les chèques de voyage?** *ahk-sehp-tay-voo lay kahrt duh kray-dee / lay shek duh vwah-yahzh*
May I see a room?	**Puis-je visiter l'une de vos chambres?** *pwee-zhuh vee-zee-tay loon duh voh shaw~-bruh*
How much extra are taxes?	**Combien ajoute-elle la taxe?** *koh~-bee-yeh~ ah-zhoo-tehl lah tahks*

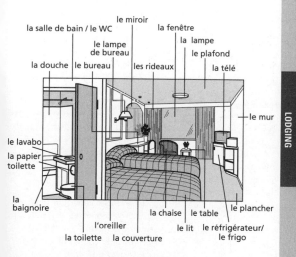

le miroir

la salle de bain / le WC

la fenêtre

le lampe de bureau

la lampe

le plafond

la douche   le bureau   les rideaux

la télé

le mur

le lavabo

la papier toilette

la baignoire

la chaise   le table

le plancher

l'oreiller

la toilette   la couverture

le lit   le réfrigérateur/ le frigo

LODGING

How much is the service charge, or is it included?	**Combien coûte le service, ou est-il compris?**
	koh~-bee-yeh~ koot luh suhr-vees oo ey-teel koh~-pree
I'd like to speak with the manager.	**Je voudrais m'entretenir avec le directeur.**
	zhuh voo-dray maw~-truh-tuh-neer ah-vek luh dee-rehk-toehr

IN-ROOM AMENITIES

I'd like _____	**Je voudrais _____**
	zhuh voo-dray
to place an international call.	**faire un appel à l'étranger.**
	fayhr uh~-nah-pel ah lay-traw~-zhay
to place a long-distance call.	**faire un appel longue distance.**
	fayhr uh~-nah-pel loh~g dee-staw~s
directory assistance in English.	**les renseignements en anglais.**
	lay raw~-seh~-nyuh-maw~-naw~-naw~-glay

Instructions for Dialing the Hotel Phone

Pour appeler une autre chambre, composez le numéro de chambre.	To call another room, dial the room number.
Pour faire un appel local, composez d'abord le neuf.	To make a local call, first dial 9
Pour appeler l'opératrice, composez le zéro.	To call the operator, dial 0.

room service.	**du service en chambre.**
	due sayhr-vee-saw~ shaw~-bruh
maid service.	**une femme de chambre.**
	oon fahm duh shaw~-bruh
the front desk.	**la réception.**
	lah ray-sehp-see-yoh~
Do you have room service?	**Offrez-vous du service en chambre?**
	oh-fray-voo due sayhr-vees aw~ shaw~-bruh
When is the kitchen open?	**Quand peut-on dîner?**
	kaw~ poeh-toh~ dee-nay
Do you serve breakfast?	**Servez-vous le petit-déjeuner?**
	sayhr-vay-voo luh ptee day-zhoeh-nay
When is breakfast served?	**À quelle heure est le petit déjeuner?**
	ah keh-loehr ey luh ptee day-zhuh-nay

For a full list of time-related terms, see p12.

Do you offer massages?	**Offrez-vous un service de massage?**
	oh-fray-voo uh~ sayhr-vees duh mah-sahzh
Do you have a lounge?	**Y a-t-il un bar-salon dans l'hôtel?**
	yah-teel uh~ bahr-sah-loh~ daw~ loh-tehl
Do you have a business center?	**Avez-vous un centre d'affaires?**
	ah-vay-voo uh~ saw~-truh dah-fayhr
Do you have Wi-Fi?	**Avez-vous l'accès Internet Wi-Fi?**
	ah-vay-voo lahk-seh eh~-tayhr-neht wee-fee

May I have a newspaper in the morning?	**Puis-je avoir un journal le matin?** *pwee-zhuh ah-vwahr uh~ zhoohr- ahl luh mah-teh~*
Do you offer a tailor service?	**Offrez-vous un service de raccommodage?** *oh-fray-voo uh~ sayhr-vees duh rah-koh-moh-dazh*
Do you offer a laundry service?	**Offrez-vous un service de lessive?** *oh-fray-voo uh~ sayhr-vees duh leh-seev*
Do you offer dry cleaning?	**Offrez-vous un service de nettoyage à sec?** *oh-fray-voo uh~ sayhr-vees duh nuh-twah-yahzh ah sek*
May we have _____	**Pourrions-nous avoir _____** *pooh-ree-yoh~-noo-zah-vwahr*
clean sheets today?	**des draps propres aujourd'hui?** *day drah proh-pruhz oh-zhoohr- dwee*
more towels?	**des serviettes supplémentaires?** *day sayhr-vee-yeht sue-play- maw~-tayhr*
more toilet paper?	**du papier toilette?** *due pah-pee-yay twah-leht*
extra pillows?	**des oreillers supplémentaires?** *day-zoh-ray-ay sue-play-maw~- tayhr*
Do you have an ice machine?	**Y a-t-il une machine à glace dans l'hôtel?** *yah-teel oon mah-sheen ah glahs daw~ loh-tehl*

Did I receive any ____	**Est-ce qu'il y a ____ pour moi?**
	ehs keel-yah ____ poohr mwah
messages?	**des messages**
	day meh-sahzh
mail?	**du courrier**
	due kooh-ree-yay
faxes?	**des télécopies**
	day tay-lay-koh-pee
May I have a spare key, please?	**Puis-je avoir une clé supplémentaire, s'il vous plaît?**
	pwee-zhuh ah-vwahr oon klay sue-play-maw~-tayhr seel voo play
May I have more hangers, please?	**Puis-je avoir des cintres supplémentaires, s'il vous plaît?**
	pwee-zhuh ah-vwahr day seh~-truh sue-play-maw~-tayhr seel voo play
I am allergic to down pillows.	**Je suis allergique aux oreillers à duvet d'oie.**
	zhuh swee-zah-layhr-zheek oh-zoh-ray-ay ah due-vay dwah
May I have a wake-up call?	**Puis-je demander un réveil téléphonique?**
	pwee-zhuh duh-maw~-day uh~ ray-vay tay-lay-foh-neek

For a full list of time-related terms, see p12.

Do you have alarm clocks?	**Avez-vous des réveils?**
	ah-vay-voo day ray-vay
Is there a safe in the room?	**Y a-t-il un coffre-fort dans la chambre?**
	yah-teel uh~ koh-fruh fohr daw~ lah shaw~-bruh
Does the room have a hair dryer?	**Y a-t-il un sèche-cheveux dans la chambre?**
	yah-teel uh~ sehsh-shuh-voeh daw~ lah shaw~-bruh

LODGING

HOTEL ROOM TROUBLE

May I speak with the manager?

Puis-je parler au responsable de l'hôtel?
pwee-zhuh pahr-lay oh ruh-spoh~sah-bluh duh loh-tehl

The _____ does not work.

_____ ne marche pas.
_____ nuh mahrsh pah

television

La telévision
lah tay-lay-vee-see-yoh~

telephone line

La ligne téléphonique
lah lee-nyuh tay-lay-foh-neek

air conditioning

La climatisation
lah klee-mah-tee-zah-see-yoh~

Internet access

L'accès à l'Internet
lahk-say ah leh~-tayhr-neht

cable TV

Les chaînes câblées
lay shehn kah-blay

There is no hot water.

Il n'y a pas d'eau chaude.
eel nyah pah doh shohd

The toilet is overflowing!

Les toilettes sont débordent!
lay twah-leht soh~ day-bohrd

This room is ____

> Cette chambre est ____
> *seht shaw~-bruh ay*

too loud.

> trop bruyante.
> *troh bwee-yaw~t*

too cold.

> pas assez chauffée.
> *pah-zah-say shoh-fay*

too warm.

> surchauffée.
> *suehr-shoh-fay*

too smoky.

> trop fumeuse.
> *troh fue-moehz*

This room has ____

> Il y a ____ dans cette chambre.
> *eel-yah ____ daw~ seht shaw~-bruh*

bugs.

> des insectes
> *day-zeh~-sehkt*

mice.

> des souris
> *day sooh-ree*

May I have a different room, please?

> Puis-je avoir une autre chambre, s'il vous plaît?
> *pwee-zhuh ah-vwahr oon oh-truh shaw~-bruh seel voo play*

Do you have a bigger room?

> Avez-vous une chambre plus spacieuse?
> *ah-vay-voo-zoon shaw~-bruh plue spah-see-yoehz*

I locked myself out of my room.

> J'ai oublié ma clé à l'intérieur de ma chambre.
> *zhay oo-blee-yay mah klay ah leh~-tay-ree-yoehr duh mah shaw~bruh*

Do you have any fans?

> Avez-vous des ventilateurs?
> *ah-vay-voo day vaw~-tee-lah-toehr*

The sheets are not clean.

> Les draps de mon lit sont sales.
> *lay drah duh moh~ lee soh~ sahl*

The towels are not clean.	**Les serviettes de ma salle de bains sont sales.**
	lay sayhr-vee-yeht duh mah sahl duh beh~ soh~ sahl
The room is not clean.	**Ma chambre n'a pas été nettoyée.**
	mah shaw~bruh nah pah-zay-tay neh-twah-yay
This room smells like smoke. I am allergic to smoke.	**Cette chambre sent de fumée. Je suis allergique à la fumée.**
	seht shaw~-bruh saw~ duh fue-may; zhuh swee-zah-layhr-zhee-kah lah fue-may
The guests ____ are being very loud.	**Les occupants de la chambre ____ de la mienne sont très bruyants.**
	lay-zoh-kue-paw~ duh lah shaw~-bruh ____ duh lah mee-yehn soh~ trey bwee-yaw~
next door	**à côté**
	ah koh-tay
above	**au-dessus**
	oh duh-sue
below	**en dessous**
	aw~ duh-soo

CHECKING OUT

I think this charge is a mistake.	**Je crois que ce montant-là est une erreur.**
	zhuh kwah kuh se moh~-taw~-lah ey-toon eh-roehr
Would you please explain this charge to me?	**Pourriez-vous m'expliquer ce montant-là?**
	poo-ree-yay-voo mehk-splee-kay suh moh~-taw~-lah
Thank you, we have enjoyed our stay.	**Merci, nous avons passé un bon séjour.**
	mayhr-see noo-zah-voh~ pah-say uh~ boh~ say-zhoohr

The service was excellent.	**Le service était excellent.**
	luh sayh-vee-zey-tay ehk-say-law~
Would you please call a cab for me?	**Pouvez-vous m'appeler un taxi, s'il vous plaît?**
	poo-vay-voo mah-play uh~ tahk-see seel voo play
Would someone please get my bags?	**Pouvez-vous faire amener mes bagages?**
	poo-vay-voo fayh-raw~-m-nay may bah-gazh

HAPPY CAMPING

I'd like a site for ____	**Je voudrais un emplacement pour ____**
	zhuh voo-dray uh~-naw~-plah-smaw~ poohr
a tent.	**une tente.**
	oon taw~t
a camper.	**un camping-car.**
	uh~ kaw~-peeng kahr
Are there ____	**Y a-t-il ____**
	yah-teel
bathrooms?	**des toilettes dans ce camping?**
	day twah-leht daw~ suh kaw~-peeng
showers?	**des douches?**
	day doosh
Is there running water?	**Y a-t-il l'eau courante?**
	yah-teel loh kooh-raw~t
Is the water drinkable?	**L'eau est-elle potable?**
	loh ey-tehl poh-tah-bluh
Where is the electrical hookup?	**Où est la borne de raccordement?**
	oo ay lah bohrn duh rah-kohrd-maw~

GOVERNMENT LODGING RATES

The French government examines and rates French hotels. There are five official categories based on facilities, location, and services provided. The categories are one-star, two-star, three-star, four-star, and, for hotels of great comfort, four-star L (luxury). The official criteria include: number of rooms, size of the reception area, number of elevators, heating and air-conditioning, round-the-clock hot water, soundproofing, and size of rooms (a room in a two-star hotel must be at least 9 sq. m/99 sq. ft. while in a four-star the minimum is 12 sq. m/132 sq. ft.). It's important to realize that these classifications do not include good taste or comfort, and that a three-star hotel could be preferable to a four-star property. That's why guidebook ratings are so important.

By North American standards, many French hotel rooms are small—sometimes painfully so. You may find yourself in an elegantly decorated room in the Latin Quarter where you can barely walk around the outside of your bed. The closet might be cramped, and the shower may demand a gymnast's flexibility. Remind yourself that, in France, bigger does not necessarily mean better. What you give up in space, you might gain in decor or view. The key to being satisfied is not to settle for less but to think differently. A small room can often feel especially cozy and secure.

THE BEST FRENCH HOTEL & MOTEL CHAINS

Accor This French megachain owns four major chains: Ibis ($), Mercure Hotels ($$), Novotel ($$$), and the more upscale Hotel Sofitel ($$$$)—which amounts to some 4,000 hotel worldwide. In the U.S., the same group owns Motel 6 © **800/515-5679**; www.accorhotels.com

Concorde Hotels Definitely the chain of prestige Concorde ($$$$$) has eight renowned hotels in Paris and many others around France. © **800/888-4747**; www.concorde-hotels.com

Relais & Châteaux These famed hotels and restaurants ($$$–$$$$$), some of the most exclusive properties in the world, have an elegant website, www.relaischateaux.com, where you can download their catalog free of charge. Or call © **800/735-2478**.

Timhôtel This chain ($$$), has brought a number of small, decent, independent hotels under its auspices, and given them the attention they deserve. They have some 15 hotels within Paris, all typically Parisian, and many others around the country. All are two- and three-star hotels with an average of 50 rooms. These represent a compromise between the big chains and the independents. Consult their catalog at **www.timhotel.com** or call each hotel directly (numbers are listed on the website); there is no central reservation number.

THE BEST AFFORDABLE HOTELS

Brittany

- **Hôtel d'Avaugour** (Dinan, Brittany; © **02-96-39-07-49**; www.avaugourhotel.com): Its exterior looks as antique as the fortifications ringing the medieval harbor, but a major restoration transformed the interior into a cozy getaway on the Norman coast. Amid Dinan's winding alleys, with views of the Channel, you've got the ingredients for an affordable escape.

Cote d'Azur

- **Hôtel Clair Logis** (St-Jean-Cap-Ferrat, Cûte d'Azur; © **04-68-81-03-27**; www.leclairlogis.com): The real estate surrounding this converted 19th-century villa is among the most expensive in Europe, but this hotel manages to keep its prices within reach. When you check into your room (named after a flower in the garden surrounding the place), you'll be in good company: Even General de Gaulle, who knew the value of a *centime*, stayed here.

LODGING

Languedoc

- **New Hôtel La Baume** (Nimes, Languedoc; ✆ **04-66-76-28-42**; www.new-hotel.com): The best features of this 17th-century mansion are the magnificent staircase that ornaments the interior courtyard and the overall sense of grandeur. In contrast to the stately exterior, the guest rooms are hypercontemporary and the bathrooms are in a post-modern style evocative of Philippe Starck's work.

Normandy

- **Les Maisons de Lèa** (Honfleur, Normandy; ✆ **02-31-14-49-49**; www.lesmaisonsdelea.com): It overlooks a Norman 18th-century port favored by Flaubert. The amenities aren't grand, but you'll sense that Madame Bovary could roll into view in her notorious carriage. The charming setting includes an appealing restaurant, and the price tag is reasonable.

Paris

- **Bel de Lutëce** (Paris; ✆ **01-43-26-23-52**; www.paris-hotel-lutece.com): It slumbers on Paris's "other island," the Ile St-Louis, which evades the crowds on the Ile de la Cité, across the bridge. You're still in the city, but you can imagine yourself in a country inn at this tasteful retreat on the Seine.

Rhone Valley

- **Ostellerie du Vieux-Pèrouges** (Pèrouges, Rhùne Valley; ✆ **04-74-61-00-88**; www.hostelleriedeperouges.com): This hotel, described as a museum of the 13th century, is one of the most significant in central France. Composed of a group of 13th-century buildings with low ceilings and thick walls, it evokes the France of another day and doesn't overcharge.

HOW TO GET THE BEST ROOMS AND RATES

Contact both the main reservation number and the individual hotel; the latter may have better rates. Even if you book online, call the hotel to discuss special needs, such as a quiet room, a corner room (often larger and brighter, but for the same price), a nonsmoking room, a room on an upper floor, a room that has been recently redecorated, and so on. Traveling with kids? Ask if they can stay for free, or if a suite is cheaper than two rooms. If it's a business hotel, try to stay on a weekend, when rates are lower. If it's a tourist hotel, try to stay midweek, when rates are lower. Check online rates for the hotel's own website; they may be cheaper. Look into air/land packages, available through travel agencies or airlines. You still travel independently, but get group rates. Find out about room taxes, hidden service charges, airport transfers, and parking costs. Ask if breakfast is included. Simply ask for a better rate; many hotels won't mention it unless you ask.

French Hotel Sites To rent a room click www.france.com (one of the most comprehensive sites), www.france-hotel-guide.com, www.frenchexperience.com, www.hotelnetdiscount. com, www.hotels.com, www.hotelsparis.fr, www.hotel supermarket.com, www.paris-anglo.com, www.travel-in-france.com, www.travnet.com, www.viamichelin.com, www.virtuallythere.com.

French Apartment Sites To rent an apartment for an extended stay in France, consult: www.untours.com, www.localflat.com, www. guestapartment.fr, www.paris-anglo.com, www.homerental.fr.

Alternate Lodging One of France's most delightful housing options is to rent a farmhouse or rooms in a country house, called a *gîte*. Rentals are usually for a week, but this varies. Consult the website www.untours.com or www.gites-de-france.fr/eng for properties in all French regions. For shorter stays, try a *chambre d'hôte*, the French equivalent to the bed-and-breakfast. You'll stay in the private homes of individuals who welcome overnight visitors in old farmhouses or mills. Many serve meals from local recipes, with local wines. Guests often eat with the family or with other boarders.

LODGING

CHAPTER FOUR

This chapter includes a menu reader and the language you need to communicate in a range of dining establishments and food markets.

FINDING A RESTAURANT

Would you please recommend a good ____ restaurant?	**Pouvez-vous nous recommander un bon restaurant ____** *poo-vay-voo noo ruh-koh-maw~-day uh~ boh~ruh-stoh-raw~*
local	**à spécialités locales?** *ah spay-see-yah-lee-tay loh-kahl*
Italian	**italien?** *ee-tah-lee-yeh~*
French	**français?** *fraw~-say*
German	**à spécialités allemandes?** *ah spay-see-yah-lee-tay ahl-maw~d*
Spanish	**espagnoles?** *eh-spah~-nyohl*
Chinese	**chinoises?** *shee-nwahz*
Japanese	**japonaises?** *zhah-poh~-nehz*
Asian	**à spécialités asiatiques?** *ah spay-see-yah-lee-tay ah-zee-yah-teek*
steakhouse	**spécialisé dans les steaks?** *spay-see-yah-lee-zay daw~ lay stayk*

family	**familial?**
	fah-mee-lee-yahl
seafood	**de fruits de mer?**
	day fhwee duh mayhr
vegetarian	**végétarien?**
	vay-zhay-tah-ree-yeh~
buffet-style	**de style buffet?**
	duh steel bue-fay
Greek	**grec?**
	grehk
budget	**pas cher?**
	pah shayhr

Which is the best restaurant in town?
Quel est le meilleur restaurant de la ville?
keh-lay luh may-yoehr ruh-stoh-raw~ duh lah veel?

Is there an all-night restaurant nearby?
Y a-t-il un restaurant ouvert toute la nuit pas loin d'ici?
yah-teel uh~ ruh-stoh-raw~ oo-vayhr toot lah nwee pah lweh~ dee-see

Is there a restaurant that serves breakfast nearby?
Y a-t-il un restaurant qui sert des petits déjeuners pas loin d'ici?
yah-teel uh~ ruh-stoh-raw~ kee sayhr day ptee day-zhoeh-nay pah lweh~ dee-see

Is it very expensive?
Est-il très cher?
ey-teel tray shayhr

Will I need a reservation?
Aurai-je besoin d'une réservation?
oh-ray-zhuh buh-zweh~ doon ray-suhr-vah-see-yoh~

Do they have a dress code?
Y a-t-il une tenue de rigueur?
yah-teel oon tuh-nue duh ree-goehr

Do they also serve lunch?	**Servent-ils aussi le déjeuner?** *sayhrv-teel oh-see luh day-zheuh-nay*
What time do they serve dinner? For lunch?	**À quelle heure serve-t-on le dîner?** **Le déjeuner?** *ah keh-loehr sayhrv-ton luh dee-nay; luh day-zhoeh-nay*
What time do they close?	**À quelle heure ferment-ils?** *ah keh-loehr fayhrm-teel*
Do you have a take-out menu?	**Avez-vous un menu de plats à emporter?** *ah-vay-voo uh~ muh-nue duh plah ah aw~-pohr-tay*
Do you have a bar?	**Avez-vous un bar?** *ah-vay-voo-zuh~ bahr*
Is there a café nearby?	**Y a-t-il un café pas loin d'ici?** *yah-teel uh~ kah-fay pah lweh~ dee-see*

GETTING SEATED

Are you still serving?	**Est-ce qu'il est encore possible de manger?** *ehs keel ay-taw~-kohr poh-see-bluh duh maw~-zhay*
How long is the wait?	**De combien est l'attente?** *duh koh~-bee-yeh~ ay lah-taw~t*
Do you have a non-smoking section?	**Avez-vous une section non fumeur?** *ah-vay-voo-zoon sehk-see-yoh~ noh~ fue-moehr*
I'd like a table for ____, please.	**Je voudrais une table pour ____ personnes, s'il vous plaît.** *zhuh voo-dray oon tah-bluh poohr ____ payhr-suhn seel voo play*

For a full list of numbers, see p7.

Do you have a quiet table?	**Avez-vous une table calme?** *ah-vay-voo-zoon tah-bluh kahlm*

Listen Up: Restaurant Lingo

Fumeur ou non fumeur?	Smoking or
fue-moehr oo noh~fue-moehr	nonsmoking?
Vous devez porter une	You'll need a tie and
cravate et une veste.	a jacket.
voo duh-vay pohr-tay	
oon krah-vaht ay oon vehst	
Les shorts sont interdits.	No shorts are allowed.
lay shohrt soh~-teh~-tayhr-dee	
Vous désirez quelque chose	May I bring you
à boire?	something to drink?
voo day-zee-ray kehl-kuh	
shohz ah bwahr	
Vous désirez voir la carte	Would you like to see
des vins?	a wine list?
voo day-zee-ray vwahr	
lah kahrt day veh~	
Vous désirez savoir quels	Would you like to hear
sont nos plats du jour?	our specials?
voo day-zee-ray sah-vwahr	
kehl soh~ noh plah due zhoohr	
Vous êtes prêt à / prête(s)	Are you ready to order?
à commander?	
voo-zeht preh ah /	
preh-tah koh~-maw~-day	
Je suis désolé, votre carte	I'm sorry, your credit
de crédit a été rejetée.	card was declined.
zhuh swee day-zoh-lay	
voh-truh kahrt duh kray-	
dee ah ay-tay ruh-zhuh-tay	

May we sit outside /	**Pouvons-nous nous asseoir à**
inside, please?	**l'extérieur / à l'intérieur?**
	poo-voh~-noo noo-zah-swahr ah
	lehk-stay-ree-yoehr / ah leh~-tay-
	ree-yoehr

May we sit at the counter?	**Pouvons-nous nous asseoir au comptoir?**
	poo-voh~-noo noo-zah-swahr oh koh~p-twahr
May I have a menu, please?	**Puis-je avoir un menu, s'il vous plaît?**
	pwee-zhuh ah-vwahr uh~ muh-nue seel voo play

ORDERING

Do you have a special tonight?	**Avez-vous un plat spécial, ce soir?**
	ah-vay-voo-zuh~ plah spay-see-yahl suh swahr
What do you recommend?	**Qu'est-ce que vous recommandez?**
	keh-skuh voo ruh-koh-maw~-day
May I see a wine list?	**Puis-je avoir la carte des vins?**
	pwee-zhuh ah-vwahr lah kahrt day veh~
Do you serve wine by the glass?	**Servez-vous du vin au verre?**
	sayhr-vay-voo due veh~-noh vayhr
May I see a drink list?	**Puis-je voir une liste des boissons?**
	pwee-zhuh vwahr oon leest day bwah-soh~
I would like it cooked ____	**Je le voudrais ____**
	zhuh luh voo-dray
rare.	**bleu.**
	bloeh
medium rare.	**à point.**
	ah pweh~
medium.	**rouge.**
	roozh
medium well.	**cuit.**
	kwee

well.	**bien cuit.**
	bee-yeh~ kwee
charred.	**cuit à fond.**
	kwee-tah foh~
Do you have a ____ menu?	**Avez-vous un menu ____**
	ah-vay-voo-zuh~ muh-nue
diabetic	**pour diabétiques?**
	poohr dee-yah-bay-teek
kosher	**kasher?**
	kah-shayhr
vegetarian	**végétarien?**
	vay-zhay-tah-ree-yeh~
children's	**pour enfants?**
	poohr aw~-faw~
Can you tell me what is in this dish?	**Pouvez-vous me dire ce qu'il y a dans ce plat?**
	poo-vay-voo muh deer suh keel-yah ah daw~ suh plah
How is it prepared?	**Comment est-il cuit?**
	koh-maw~ ey-teel kwee
What kind of oil is that cooked in?	**Avec quelle sorte d'huile est-il preparé?**
	ah-vek kehl sohrt dweel ey-teel pruh-pah-ray
I'd like some oil, please.	**Je voudrais de l'huile, s'il vous plaît.**
	zhuh voo-dray de lweel seel voo play
Do you have any low-salt dishes?	**Avez-vous des plats à faible teneur en sel?**
	ah-vay-voo day plah ah feh-bluh tuh-noehr aw~ sehl
No salt, please.	**Pas de sel, s'il vous plaît.**
	pah duh sehl seel voo play

May I have that on the side, please?	**Puis-je avoir cela sur une assiette séparée, s'il vous plaît?**
	pwee-zhuh ah-vwahr suh-lah suehr oo-nah-see-yeht say-pah-ray seel voo play
Dressing on the side, please.	**La sauce à part, s'il vous plaît.**
	lah soh-sah pahr seel voo play
May I make a substitution?	**Puis-je remplacer cela par autre chose?**
	Pwee-zhuh raw~-plah-say suh-lah pahr oh-truh shohz
I'd like to try that.	**Je voudrais essayer cela.**
	zhuh voo-dray eh-say-ay suh-lah
Is that fresh?	**C'est frais?**
	say fray
Waiter!	**Monsieur / Madame, s'il vous plaît!**
	moh~-syoehr / mah-dahm seel voo play
May I have extra butter, please?	**Puis-je avoir un peu plus de beurre, s'il vous plaît?**
	pwee-zhuh ah-vwahr uh~ poeh plue duh beur, seel voo play
More bread, please.	**Plus de pain, s'il vous plaît.**
	plue duh peh~ seel voo play
No butter, please.	**Pas de beurre, s'il vous plaît.**
	pas duh boehr seel voo play
I am lactose intolerant.	**Je suis allergique aux produits laitiers.**
	zhuh swee-zah-layhr-zheek oh proh-dwee lay-tee-yay
Would you recommend something without milk?	**Pouvez-vous me recommander quelque chose qui ne contienne pas de lait?**
	poo-vay-voo muh ruh-koh~-maw~day kehl-kuh shohz kee nuh koh~-tee-yeh~ pah duh lay

I am allergic to ____	**Je suis allergique ____** *zhuh swee-zah-layhr-zheek*
seafood.	**aux poissons et aux fruits de mer.** *oh pwah-soh~-nay oh fhwee duh mayhr*
shellfish.	**aux fruits de mer.** *oh fhwee duh mayhr*
nuts.	**aux noix.** *oh nwah*
peanuts.	**aux cacahuettes.** *oh kah-kah-oo-eht*
Water ____, please.	**De l'eau ____, s'il vous plaît.** *duh loh seel voo play*
with ice	**avec des glaçons** *ah-vehk day glah-soh~*
without ice	**sans glaçons** *saw~ glah-soh~*
I'm sorry, I don't think this is what I ordered.	**Je suis désolée(e), mais je ne pense pas que c'est ce que j'ai commandé.** *zhuh swee day-zoh-lay may zhuh nuh paw~s pah kuh say skuh zhay koh~-maw~-day*
My meat is over / under cooked.	**Ma viande est trop cuite / pas assez cuite.** *mah vee-yahnd ay troh kweet / pahz ah-say kweet*
My vegetables are a little over / under cooked.	**Mes légumes sont un peu trop cuits / pas assez cuits.** *may lay-guem soh~-tuh~ poeh troh kwee / pah-zah-say kwee*
There's a bug in my food!	**Il y a un insecte dans ma nourriture!** *eel-yah uh~-neh~-sekt daw~ mah nooh-ree-teuhr*

DINING

May I have a refill?	**Puis-je avoir la même boisson?**
	pwee-zhuh ah-vwahr lah mehm
	bwah-soh~
A dessert menu, please?	**La carte des desserts, s'il vous plaît?**
	lah kahrt day day-zayhr seel
	voo play

DRINKS

alcoholic	**de l'alcool / une boisson alcoolisée**
	duh lahl-kool / oon bwah-soh~-
	nahl-koo-lee-zay
neat / straight	**sec**
	sehk
on the rocks	**avec des glaçons**
	ah-vehk day glah-soh~
with (seltzer or soda)	**avec du soda**
water	*ah-vehk due soh-dah*
beer	**la bière**
	lah bee-yayhr
brandy	**le cognac**
	luh koh~-nyak
coffee	**un café**
	uh~ kah-fay
iced coffee	**un café glacé**
	uh~ kah-fay glah-say
latté	**un café au lait**
	uh~ kah-fay oh lay
cognac	**le cognac**
	luh koh~-nyak
fruit juice	**le jus de fruits**
	luh zhue duh fhwee

For a full list of fruit, see p125.

gin	**le gin**
	luh zheen
hot chocolate	**un chocolat chaud**
	uh~ shoh-koh-lah shoh

lemonade	**un citron pressé**
	uh~ see-troh~ pruh-say
liqueur	**une liqueur**
	oon lee-koehr
milk	**un lait**
	uh~ lay
milkshake	**un milk-shake**
	uh~ meehlk-shayk
non-alcoholic	**non alcoolisée / une boisson non alcoolisée**
	noh~-nahl-koo-lee-zay / oon bwah-soh~ noh~-nahl-koo-lee-zay
rum	**le rhum**
	luh ruhm
tea	**un thé**
	uh~ tay
vodka	**le vodka**
	luh vohd-kah
wine	**le vin**
	luh veh~
dry white wine	**le vin blanc**
	luh veh~ blaw~
a full-bodied wine	**le vin corsé**
	luh veh~ kohr-say
house wine	**le vin maison**
	luh veh~ may-zoh~
a light-bodied wine	**le vin léger**
	luh veh~ lay-zhay
red wine	**le vin rouge**
	luh veh~ roozh
rosé	**le vin rosé**
	luh~ veh~ roh-zay
sparkling sweet wine	**le vin mousseux et doux**
	luh beh~ moo-soeh ay doo
sweet wine	**le vin doux**
	luh veh~ doo

SETTLING UP

Check, please.	**L'addition, s'il vous plaît!** *lah-dee-see-yoh~ seel voo play*
I'm stuffed!	**Je n'en peux plus!** *zhuh naw~ poeh plue*
The meal was excellent.	**Ce repas était excellent.** *suh ruh-pah ay-tay ehk-suh-law~*
There's a problem with my bill.	**Il y a un problème avec l'addition.** *eel-yah uh~ proh-blehm ah-vek lah-dee-see-yoh~*
Is the tip included?	**Le service est-il compris?** *luh sayhr-vees ey-teel koh~-pree*
My compliments to the chef!	**Tous mes compliments au chef!** *too may koh~-plee-maw~ oh shehf*

MENU READER

French cuisine varies broadly from region to region, but we've tried to make our list of classic dishes as encompassing as possible.

SOUPS (LES POTAGES)

crème d'asperges / de bolets / d'huîtres: cream of asparagus / mushroom / oyster soup

crème vichyssoise: cold potato-leek soup

la gratinée à l'oignon: French onion soup

potage bilibi: cream of mussel soup

potage Crécy: carrot soup

potage cressonnière: watercress soup

potage parmentier: potato soup

potage printanier: mixed vegetable soup

potage Saint-Germain: puréed split pea with ham soup

soupe au pistou: pesto soup with vegetables, white beans, and pasta

soupe aux moules: mussel soup

velouté de tomates / d'asperges / de volaille / d'huîtres: rich tomato / asparagus / chicken / oyster soup

TERRINES, PÂTÉS, CONFITS, & MEAT IN ASPIC

confit de canard / d'oie / de porc: preserved duck / goose / pork
foie gras: fattened goose / duck liver
galantine: boned meat or poultry, rolled or stuffed, served cold
gelée: aspic
pâté de campagne: country-style pâté, generally with a more rustic texture
pâté de canard: duck pâté
pâté en croûte: pâté baked in puff pastry
rillettes: pot of spreadable minced meat (pork, poultry) or fish
terrine / pâté de foie de volaille: poultry liver terrine / pâté
terrine de lapin: rabbit terrine

CLASSIC BISTRO / SIDE DISHES (LES ENTRÉES)

le croque-monsieur: grilled ham and cheese sandwich on sliced bread
l'omelette aux fines herbes: omelet with minced herbs
le pizza margarita: pizza topped with cheese and herbs, without vegetables or meat
les pommes frites: French fries
le sandwich mixte: gruyère and ham on French bread
la tarte à l'oignon: onion tart

FISH / SEAFOOD (LES POISSONS / LES FRUITS DE MER)

bouillabaisse: provençal fish stew
coquilles Saint-Jacques: lightly breaded scallops sautéed or baked with lemon juice, cayenne pepper, garlic, butter, and parsley
darne de saumon: salmon filet
homard cardinal: lobster cooked with mushrooms and truffles in béchamel sauce
homard Thermidor: Lobster baked in spicy mustard sauce and gratinéed
moules à la poulette: mussels in creamy white wine sauce
moules marinière: mussels in white wine with shallots, onions, and herbs

plateau de fruits de mer: assorted seafood platter
raie au beurre noir: skate in brown butter sauce
saumon à l'oseille: salmon with sorrel sauce
sole bonne femme: sole with potatoes, shallots, parsley, and
  mushrooms
truite au bleu: trout cooked in hot water and vinegar very
  soon after gutting, causing its skin to turn blue
truite aux amandes: sautéed trout in a crème fraîche and
  almond sauce
truite meunière: seasoned trout rolled in flour, fried in butter,
  and served with butter and lemon
For a full list of fish, see p123.
For a full list of various meats, see p121.

BEEF (LE BŒUF)
l'assiette anglaise: potted meat
bœuf bourguignon: beef stewed in red wine with onions,
  mushrooms, and bacon
carbonnade: beef stew
entrecôte maître d'hôtel: steak with butter and parsley
filet de bœuf Rossini: beef filet with foie gras
fondue bourguignonne: Burgundy-style fondue (small pieces of
  meat cooked in boiling oil and then dipped in various sauces)
la moelle: beef marrow
steak tartare: steak tartare

LAMB (L'AGNEAU)
carré d'agneau: rack of lamb
côtelettes d'agneau: lamb chops
epaule d'agneau farcie: stuffed lamb shoulder
navarin: lamb stew
navarin de mouton: mutton stew with spring vegetables

VEAL (LE VEAU)
l'agneau de lait: milk-fed lamb
l'agneau de pré-salé: salted lamb
blanquette de veau: veal stew
escalope de veau normande: thin slices of veal in cream sauce
escalope de veau milanaise: thin slices of veal in tomato sauce

PORK (LE PORC)

cassoulet: casserole with white beans and combinations of sausages, pork, lamb, goose, or duck

choucroute: sauerkraut with ham and sausages

le cochon de lait: suckling pig

côtelettes de porc: pork chops

croque-monsieur: toasted ham and cheese sandwich

RABBIT (LE LAPIN)

gibelotte de lapin: fricasseed rabbit in red or white wine

le lapereau: young rabbit

lapin à la Lorraine: rabbit in mushroom and cream sauce

lapin à la moutarde: rabbit in mustard sauce

le lapin de garenne: wild rabbit

râble de lièvre: saddle of hare

POULTRY (LE VOLAILLE)

aspic de volaille: poultry in aspic

le blanc de canard: duck breast

canard à l'orange: duck in orange sauce

canard aux cerises: duck in cherry sauce

le canard sauvage: wild duck

le caneton: duckling

filet de canard au poivre vert: duck filet in green peppercorn sauce

coq au vin: chicken in red wine sauce

poulet à l'estragon: chicken in tarragon-cream sauce

poulet chasseur: chicken with white wine and mushrooms

le poulet fermier: free-range chicken

suprême de volaille: boneless chicken breast

VEGETABLE DISHES (LES LEGUMES, LES CRUDITÉS, ET LES SALADES)

l'assiette de crudités: raw vegetables

chou-fleur au gratin: cauliflower baked in cream, topped with gruyere

epinards à la crème: creamed spinach

gratin dauphinois: thin-sliced potatoes baked with cheese

poivron farci: stuffed green pepper
salade composée: main-course salad (with meat, cheese, and raw vegetables)
salade mixte: mixed salad
salade verte: green salad
salade de tomates: tomato salad
salade russe: diced vegetables in mayonnaise
For a full list of vegetables, see p126.

DESSERTS / PASTRIES (LES DESSERTS / LES PÂTISSERIES)

baba au rhum: small rum-soaked cake
bavaroise: custard dessert with gelatin and cream
chausson aux pommes: apple turnover
chocolat amer: dark, bitter chocolate
clafoutis: custard and fruit tart
financier: small almond cake
fondant au chocolat: chocolate dessert akin to a brownie
gâteau au fromage: cheesecake
génoise: sponge cake
les flottantes / œufs à la neige: thin custard topped with soft meringue
madeleine: lemon tea cake
mille-feuille: napoleon
mont-blanc: pastry with whipped cream, chestnut purée, and baked meringue
pain au chocolat: croissant (chocolate-filled)
pâte feuilletée: puff pastry
pêche melba: vanilla ice cream with a poached peach and raspberry sauce
petits fours: bite-sized, beautifully-decorated pastries
poire belle-Hélène: pear with chocolate sauce
profiteroles: cream puffs
religieuse: cream puffs with chocolate icing
sabayon: thin custard made with Marsala

sable: shortbread cookie

saint-Honoré: cake made with two types of pastry and cream filling

savarin: ring-shaped yeast cake in sweet syrup

soufflé au chocolat: chocolate soufflé

tarte au citron / aux fraises / aux pommes / aux abricots / aux framboises: lemon / strawberry / apple / apricot / raspberry tart

tarte tatin: upside-down apple tart

vacherin glacé: baked-Alaska-type dessert

SAUCES / METHODS OF PRESENTATION

basquaise: with ham, tomatoes, and peppers

béchamel: white sauce

bonne femme: with mushrooms and white wine

en brochette: on a skewer

aux câpres: in caper sauce

chasseur: with white wine and herbs

à la crème / à la normande: in cream sauce

au gratin: topped with cheese

jardinière: with mixed vegetables

maître d'hôtel: with butter and parsley

milanaise: in Italian-style tomato sauce

à la moutarde: in mustard sauce

à la nage: in wine and vegetable sauce

en papillote: baked in foil or parchment paper

piperade: with peppers and tomatoes

à la provençale: in olive oil (with herbs, garlic, and tomato)

sauce aurora: white sauce with tomato purée

sauce Béarnaise: hollandaise sauce (with capers)

sauce au beurre noir: dark browned butter sauce

sauce cresson: watercress sauce

sauce Mornay: white sauce with cheese

sauce noisette: light browned butter sauce

sauce à l'oseille: sorrel sauce

au vin rouge: in red wine sauce

HERBS / SPICES / CONDIMENTS

l'ail / la gousse d'ail: garlic / garlic clove

l'aneth: dill

l'anis: anise

le basilique: basil

la feuille de laurier: bay leaf

le carvi: caraway

le chervil: chervil

les ciboulettes: chives

le clou de girofle: clove

la confiture: jam

le coriandre: cilantro / coriander

l'estragon: tarragon

l'huile: oil

le laurier: bay leaf

la marjolaine: marjoram

la marjolaine sauvage: oregano

la mayonnaise: mayonnaise

le mélange d'épices: allspice

le miel: honey

la moutarde: mustard

l'origan: oregano

le persil: parsley

le poivre rose / vert: pink / green peppercorns

le romarin: rosemary

le safran: saffron

la sauge: sage

le sel / le sel marin: salt / sea salt

le sucre en poudre: sugar (granular)

le sucre en morceaux: sugar cubes

le thym: thyme

la verveine: verbena

le vinaigre: vinegar

NUTS / LEGUMES / FANCY FUNGI

les amandes: almonds

l'arachide: peanut

les haricots blancs: white beans

les haricots d'Espagne: kidney beans

les lentilles: lentils

les marrons: chestnuts

les morilles: morels

la noisette: hazelnut

la noix: walnut

la pâte d'amandes: almond paste

les pignons: pine nuts

les pistaches: pistachio nuts

les truffes: truffles

BUYING GROCERIES

In France, like most other countries, locals shop for food either at outdoor markets, specialty stores or, less commonly than in the United States, large supermarkets.

GROCERY VENUES

bakery	**la boulangerie**
	lah boo-law~-zhree
butcher	**la boucherie**
	lah boo-shree
cheese shop	**la fromagerie**
	lah froh-mahzh-ree
delicatessen	**le traiteur**
	luh treh-toehr
open-air market	**le marché en plein air**
	luh mahr-shay ehn pleh~-nayhr
pastry shop	**la pâtisserie**
	lah pah-tee-sree
pork butcher	**la charcuterie**
	la shahr-kue-tree
supermarket	**le supermarché**
	luh sue-payhr-mahr-shay

AT THE SUPERMARKET

checkout counter	**le comptoir**
	luh koh~-p-twahr
cash register	**la caisse**
	lah kehs
section / aisle	**le rayon**
	luh ray-oh~
produce	**les primeurs**
	lay pree-moehr
frozen food	**les plats congelés / surgelés**
	lay plah koh~zhlay / suehr-zhlay

Which aisle has ____	**Dans quel rayon se trouvent / trouve ____**
	aw~ kehl ray-oh~ suh troov
spices?	**les épices?**
	lay-zay-pees
toiletries?	**les produits de toilette?**
	lay proh-dwee duh twah-leht
paper plates and napkins?	**les assiettes et les serviettes en papier?**
	lay-zah-see-yeht ay lay sayhr-vee-yeh-taw~ pah-pee-yay
canned goods?	**les conserves?**
	lay koh~-sayhrv
snack food?	**les amuse-gueule?**
	lay-zah-muez goehl
baby food?	**la nourriture pour bébé?**
	lah nooh-ree-teuhr poohr bay-bay
water?	**l'eau?**
	loh
juice?	**le jus de fruits?**
	luh zhues duh fhwee
bread?	**le pain?**
	luh peh~
cheese?	**le fromage?**
	luh froh-mahzh
fruit?	**le fruit?**
	luh fhwee
cookies?	**les biscuits?**
	lay bees-kwee

Bread and Rice

brown rice	**le riz brun**
	luh ree bruh~
country-style loaf	**le pain de campagne**
	luh peh~ duh kaw~-pah-nyuh

French bread: large / small	**la baguette / la flûte**
	lah bah-geht / lah fluet
rye bread	**le pain de seigle**
	luh peh~ duh seh-gluh
sourdough bread	**le pain au levain**
	luh peh~ oh luh-veh~
white rice	**le riz blanc**
	luh ree blahn
whole-grain bread	**le pain complet**
	luh peh~ koh--play
wild rice	**le riz sauvage**
	luh ree sohvahzh

Dairy

butter	**le beurre**
	luh boehr
cream	**la crème**
	lah krehm
milk, whole / skim	**le lait entier / écremé**
	luh lay aw~-tee-yay / ay-kray-may
yogurt	**le yaourt**
	luh yah-oohr

Cheese

bleu cheese	**le fromage bleu**
	luh froh-mahzh bloeh
cream cheese	**le fromage frais**
	luh froh-mahzh fray
firm	**un crottin**
	uh~ kroh-teh~
goat cheese	**le (fromage de) chèvre**
	luh (froh-mahzh duh) sheh-vruh
semisoft cheeses	**les fromages à croûte fleurie**
	lay fro-mahzh ah kroot fleuh-ree

Eggs

free-range	**les œufs de la ferme** *lay-zoeh duh lah fayhrm*
large / extra large	**les œufs grands / très grands** *lay-zoeh graw~ / tray graw~*
small	**les œufs petits** *lay-zoeh puhtee*

AT THE BUTCHER SHOP

Is the meat fresh?	**Cette viande est-elle fraîche?** *seht vee-yand ey-tehl frehsh*
Is the fish fresh?	**Le poisson est-il frais?** *luh pwah-soh~ ey-teel fray*
Is the seafood fresh?	**Les fruits de mer sont-ils frais?** *lay fhwee duh mayhr soh~-teel fray*
Do you sell ____	**Vendez-vous de la viande de ____** *vaw~-day-voo duh lah vee-yand duh*
I would like a cut of ____	**Je voudrais un morceau ____** *zhuh voo-dray uh~ mohr-soh*
tenderloin.	**de filet.** *duh fee-lay*
T-bone.	**d'aloyau.** *dahl-wah-yoh*
brisket.	**de poitrine.** *duh pwah-treen*
rump roast.	**de rôti de croupe.** *duh roh-tee duh kroop*
pork chops.	**de côtelette de porc.** *duh koht-leht duh pohr*
filet.	**tournedos.** *toohr-nuh-doh*

I would like _____	**Je voudrais_____**
	zhuh voo-dray
the breast.	**le blanc.**
	luh blahn
chops.	**la côte.**
	lah koht
free-range.	**fermier.**
	fayhr-mee-yay
liver.	**le foie.**
	luh fwah
milk-fed.	**de lait.**
	duh lay
sweetbreads.	**le ris.**
	luh ree
Would you trim the fat?	**Pouvez-vous enlever le gras?**
	poo-vay-voo aw~-luh-vay luh grah
May I smell it?	**Puis-je le / la / les sentir?**
	pwee-zhuh luh / lah / lay saw~-teer
Would you _____	**Pouvez-vous _____**
	poo-vay-voo
filet it?	**le couper en filets?**
	luh koo-pay aw~ fee-lay
debone it?	**le désosser?**
	luh day-zoh-say
remove the head and tail?	**enlever la tête et la queue?**
	aw~-luh-vay lah teht ay lah koeh

Beef (Le Bœuf)

ground beef	**le bœuf haché**
	luh boehf ah-shay
sirloin steak	**le faux-filet**
	luh foh-fee-lay
tripe	**les tripes**
	lay treep
veal	**le veau**
	luh voh

Other Meats

bacon	**le lard**
	luh lahr
frog legs	**les cuisses de grenouille**
	lay kwees duh gruh-nwee
ham	**le jambon**
	luh zhahm-boh~
hare	**la lièvre**
	luh lee-yeh-vruh
headcheese	**le fromage de tête**
	luh froh-mazh duh teht
horsemeat	**la viande de cheval**
	lah vee-yand duh shuh-vahl
lamb	**l'agneau / le mouton**
	lah-nyoh / luh moo-toh~
leg of lamb	**le gigot**
	luh zhee-goh
rack of lamb	**le carré d'agneau**
	luh kah-ray dah-nyoh
pork	**le porc**
	luh pohr
rack of pork ribs	**le carré de porc**
	luh kah-ray duh pohr
rabbit	**le lapin**
	luh lah-peh~
sausage	**le saucisson**
	luh soh-see-soh~
dried sausage	**le saucisson sec**
	luh soh-see-soh~ sehk
fresh sausage	**la saucisse / le boudin**
	lah soh-sees / luh boo-deh~
snails	**les escargots**
	lay-zehs-kahr-goh

Poultry

chicken	**le poulet**
	luh poo-lay
duck	**le canard**
	luh kah-nahr
duck breast	**le blanc de canard**
	luh blaw~ duh kah-nahr
goose	**l'oie**
	lwah
pigeon / squab	**le pigeon**
	luh pee-zhyoh~
pheasant	**le faisan**
	luh fay-zaw~
turkey	**la dinde**
	lah deh~d

Fish

catfish	**la barbotte**
	lah bahr-boht
flounder	**le flet**
	luh flay
halibut	**le flétan**
	luh flay-taw~
herring	**le hareng**
	luh ah-raw~g
mackerel	**le maquereau**
	luh mah-kroh
salmon	**le saumon**
	luh soh-moh~
sardine	**la sardine**
	lah sahr-deen
sea bass	**le bar**
	luh bahr
shark	**le requin**
	luh ruh-keh~

skate	**la raie**
	lah ray
sole	**le sole**
	luh sohl
swordfish	**l'espadon**
	leh-spah-doh~
trout	**la truite**
	lah tweet
turbot	**le turbot**
	luh tuehr-boh

Seafood

clams	**les palourdes**
	lay pah-loohrd
crab	**le crabe**
	luh krahb
crayfish	**l'écrevisse**
	lay-kray-vees
eel	**la lamproie**
	lah law~-pwah
lobster	**le homard**
	luh oh-mahr
mussels	**les moules**
	lay mool
octopus	**le poulpe**
	luh poolp
oyster	**l'huître**
	lwee-truh
scallop	**la coquille**
	lah koh-kee
shrimp	**la crevette**
	lah kruh-veht
squid	**le calmar**
	luh kahl-mahr

AT THE PRODUCE STAND / MARKET
Fruits

apple	**la pomme**
	lah puhm
apricot	**l'abricot**
	lah-bree-koh
banana	**la banane**
	lah bah-nahn
blackberries	**la mûre**
	lah muehr
blueberry	**la myrtille**
	lah meer-tee
cantaloupe	**le cantaloup**
	luh kaw~-tah-loo
cherry	**la cerise**
	lah suh-reez
coconut	**la noix de coco**
	lah nwah duh koh-koh
cranberry	**la canneberge**
	lah kah-nuh-bayhrzh
fig	**la figue**
	lah feeg
grapefruit	**le pamplemousse**
	luh paw~-pluh-moos
grapes (green, red)	**le raisin (vert, noir)**
	luh ray-zeh~ vayhr nwahr
gooseberry	**la groseille à maquereau**
	lah groh-zay ah mah-kroh
honeydew	**le melon miel**
	luh muh-loh~ mee-yehl
kiwi	**le kiwi**
	luh kee-wee
lemon	**le citron**
	luh see-troh~

lime	**le citron vert**
	luh see-troh~ vayhr
mango	**la mangue**
	lah maw~g
melon	**le melon**
	luh muh-loh~
orange	**l'orange**
	loh-raw~zh
blood orange	**la sanguine**
	lah saw~-gween
papaya	**la papaye**
	lah pah-pay
peach	**la pêche**
	lah pehsh
pear	**la poire**
	lah pwahr
pineapple	**l'ananas**
	law~-naw~-nahs
plum	**la prune**
	lah pruen
prune	**le pruneau**
	luh prue-noh
raspberry	**la framboise**
	lah fraw~-bwahz
strawberry	**la fraise**
	lah frehz
tangerine	**la mandarine**
	lah maw~-dah-reen
watermelon	**la pastèque**
	lah pah-stek

Vegetables

artichoke	**l'artichaut**
	lahr-tee-shoh
arugula	**la roquette**
	lah roh-keht

asparagus	**les asperges**
	lay-zah-spayrzh
avocado	**l'avocat**
	lah-voh-kah
beans	**les haricots**
	lay-zah-ree-koh
green beans	**les haricots verts**
	lay-zah-ree-koh vayhr
broccoli	**le brocoli**
	luh broh-koh-lee
cabbage	**le chou**
	luh shoo
carrot	**la carotte**
	lah kah-roht
cauliflower	**le chou-fleur**
	luh shoo-floehr
celery	**le céleri**
	luh say-lay-ree
corn	**le maïs**
	luh may-ees
cucumber	**le concombre**
	luh koh~-koh~-bruh
eggplant	**l'aubergine**
	loh-bayhr-zheen
endive	**la chicorée**
	lah shee-koh-ray
curly	**frisée**
	free-zay
Belgian	**l'endive**
	law~-deev
garlic	**l'ail**
	lie
leek	**le poireau**
	luh pwah-roh

lettuce	**la salade verte**
	lah sah-lahd vayhrt
romaine	**la laitue (romaine)**
	lah lay-tue
mushroom	**le champignon**
	luh shaw~-pee-nyoh~
black olives	**les olives noires**
	lay-zoh-leev nwahr
green olives	**les olives vertes**
	lay-zoh-leev vayhrt
onion	**l'oignon**
	loh-nyoh~
red pepper	**le poivron rouge**
	luh pwah-vroh roozh
green pepper	**le poivron vert**
	luh pwah-vroh vayhr
pepper (chili)	**le piment**
	luh pee-maw~
habañero pepper	**le piment habanero**
	luh pee-maw~ ah-bah-nyuh-roh
chipotle pepper	**le piment chipotle**
	luh pee-maw~ shee-poht-lay
jalapeno pepper	**le piment jalapeno**
	luh pee-maw~ yah-lah-peh-nyoh
cayenne (fresh) pepper	**le piment de cayenne**
	luh pee-maw~ duh kah-yehn
potato	**la pomme de terre**
	lah puhm duh tayhr
shallot	**l'échalote**
	lay-shah-loht
sorrel	**l'oseille**
	loh-zay
spinach	**les épinards**
	lay-zay-pee-nahr
squash	**la courge**
	lah koorzh

tomato	**la tomate** *lah toh-maht*
yam	**la patate douce** *lah pah-taht doos*
zucchini	**la courgette** *lah koohr-zheht*

AT THE DELI

What kind of salad is that?	**Quelle sorte de salade est-ce?** *kehl sohrt duh sah-lahd ehs*
What kind of cheese is that?	**Quelle sorte de fromage est-ce?** *kehl sohrt duh froh-mahzh ehs*
What kind of bread is that?	**Quelle sorte de pain est-ce?** *kehl sohrt duh peh~-nehs*
I'd like some of this, please.	**J'en voudrais celui-ci, s'il vous plaît.** *zhaw~ voo-dray seh-lwee-see seel voo play*
I'd like _____, please.	**Je voudrais _____, s'il vous plait.** *zheh voo-dray seel voo-play*
a sandwich	**un sandwich** *uh~ saw~-d-weesh*
a salad	**une salade** *oon sah-lahd*
tuna salad	**au thon** *oh toh~*
chicken salad	**au poulet** *oh poo-lay*
ham	**au jambon** *oh jaw~-boh~*
roast beef	**au rosbif** *oh rohz-beef*
some cole slaw	**du céleri rémoulade** *due say-lay-ree ray-moo-lahd*
mustard	**de la moutarde** *duh lah moo-tahrd*

mayonnaise	**du mayonnaise**
	duh lah may-oh-nehz
a pickle	**un cornichon**
	uh~ kohr-nee-shoh~
about a pound	**cinq cent grammes**
	seh~k saw~ grahm
about a half-pound	**deux cent cinquante grammes**
	doeh saw~ grahm
about a quarter-pound	**cent vingt-cinq grammes**
	saw~ veh~-seh~k grahm
Is the salad fresh?	**La salade est-elle fraîche?**
	lah sah-lahd ey-tehl fresh
Is that smoked?	**C'est fumé?**
	say fue-may
May I have a package of tofu?	**Puis-je avoir du tofou?**
	pwee-zhuh ah-vwahr due toh-foo

FRENCH DINING

Plan on spending a good amount of time *au table*—dining. In France, "everything" happens here, from lively conversation to business transactions. The French love *la bonne bouffe* (slang for "good eats"). This cuts across socio-economic barriers. From the business executive to the factory worker, eating is a serious undertaking. A sandwich and a cold drink are not a meal. In Paris, as in other urban centers, people are taking less and less time for lunch, but on the whole, the way one eats here remains of paramount importance.

French meals have a natural structure and an inherent balance. The appetizer or *entrée* (the main dish is not an entree, as in the U.S.) is followed by the *plat principal* or main dish, and then cheese, salad, dessert, and coffee or *tisane* (herb tea). One drinks wine or water when dining in France. Soft drinks here are tolerated at *aperitif* time or in cafes, but not with food.

Time is part of the dining experience. If you want to do as the French, don't be tempted to sit down to a meal for less than an hour. In France, one learns to love to linger, to order a second coffee and a cognac or *calvados*, to talk. The French love to debate around the table. Shouldn't you, too? Some of your best moments in France will be the indulgence of doing nothing but nursing a tiny glass of Poire William or Armagnac.

Dining Times   The French eat at prescribed hours. Don't complain; it's this rigidity that helps preserve French culture. The French live to eat, not the other way around. Of course, you have more leeway in the big cities—primarily Paris, where global habits have infiltrated urban lifestyles. But in the smaller towns and in the countryside, if you plan to have a proper midday meal, you must be at the table between noon and 1:30pm. After 2pm don't expect a restaurant to serve you; in most cases don't even expect to be treated with sympathy. *C'est trop tard* (it's too late). In the provinces, dinner is usually between 7:30 and 9:00pm. Earlier or later may be problematic. You can always get something to eat in local bars or cafes, a *croque monsieur* or a sandwich jambon, but to the French that is not eating.

Another Tip   If you want to do as the French do, avoid sharing dishes or asking for substitutions in fixed menus, or any other variation in the form, style, and rhythm of the local culinary culture. Innovation at the table is appreciated if it's coming from the chef-artist, not from the customer.

A word on portions: The French meal is based on balance. Portions are not intended to impress the customer. In fact, big in France does not mean better. You should therefore not judge your meal by the amount of food on your plate. Flavor and presentation are the key criteria. The "doggy bag" is practically unknown; attempts to take uneaten portions of your dinner with you are usually not understood. Remember to explain that this is an American custom and that leftovers are not really for the dog; otherwise you may end up with 3 kilos of food scraps from the kitchen, because the French love their canines.

Tipping   The French don't consider service charges and tips to be the same thing. All restaurants in France include service, usually 15% to 17%, in the price. You should not, and are not expected to, leave an additional 15% or 20%. The French tip, or *pour boire,* is simply the few coins you leave in the dish to show your appreciation after you've paid the bill. A few euros is usually all that's needed. Note too that credit card forms in France do not have a place for you to write in a tip, so you must leave it in cash. If you do try to write it in, the waiter is unlikely to get it. Non-French credit cards, without an embedded chip, have a tendency not to work in some establishments, so make sure you have a backup means of paying your bill.

OUR FAVORITE DISHES

You'll want to try as many regional dishes as you can during your French stay. Here are a few of our favorites.

Bouillabaisse is a Mediterranean-style fish stew with tomatoes, saffron, mussels, shellfish, and the catch of the day. Each version is different, depending on the whim of the creator. Good ones are becoming hard to find. Two other regional variations of seafood soup are **bourride** and **chaudrée**.

Cassoulet is a casserole of white navy beans, shallots, and a variety of meats such as pork, lamb, sausage, and goose or duck, originating in the Languedoc region of France. It's perfect for the winter.

Choucroute is a dish of Alsatian origin that's often served in *brasseries* because it's such a good accompaniment to a strong draft beer. It consists of sauerkraut topped with a variety of sausages, cuts of pork, ham, and boiled potatoes.

Couscous is a specialty of North Africa originally brought to France by colonialists. It consists of a hearty blend of mutton, chicken, and a spicy beef sausage (*merguez*) in a light stock with boiled zucchini, carrots, onions, turnips, and chickpeas. It's spooned over a fine semolina-like base, called couscous, from which the dish gets its name. A hot red paste called *harissa* can be stirred into the broth.

Farce consists of spiced ground meat, usually pork, used for stuffing cabbage (*chou farci*), green pepper (*poivron vert farci*), or tomatoes (*tomates farcies*).

Fondue is a Swiss Alps specialty, popular in France, especially in the ski regions. There are two types: bourguignon beef (small chunks of beef cooked on long forks in pots of hot oil and accompanied by a variety of sauces); and Savoyard cheese melted and flavored with kirsch or white wine, lapped up with chunks of stale French bread on long forks.

Hachis Parmentier consists of mashed potatoes and ground meat topped with a *béchamel* sauce and served in a casserole.

Paella is a Portuguese and Spanish dish with a rice base, saffron, pimiento, chicken, pork, and shellfish, cooked in a special two-handled metal pan. It's served mostly in the south and southwest.

Pot-au-feu is made from boiled meat and marrow bone with vegetables in a broth.

Raclette is a dish consisting of melted cheese scraped onto potatoes, pickles, and ham. The cheese is melted at the table and served on tiny plates.

FAVORITE FRENCH DESSERTS

Baba au Rhum is a dense white cake soaked with a sugary rum sauce.

Charlotte consists of light pastry fingers assembled with a sweet cream mounted with fresh fruit.

Fondant au Chocolat is a moist chocolate cake with melted chocolate in the center.

Fraise or **Frambroise Nature** is a seasonal dessert made from fresh strawberries or raspberries with powdered sugar, *crème fraîche*, or sorbet.

Profiteroles are puff pastry balls with vanilla ice cream in the middle, served with a hot bittersweet chocolate sauce.

Tarte Tatin is a caramelized upside-down apple pie served warm with *crème fraîche*.

CHAPTER FIVE

SOCIALIZING

Whether you're meeting people in a bar or a park, you'll find the language you need, in this chapter, to make new friends.

GREETINGS

Hello!	**Bonjour!**
	boh~-zhoohr
How are you?	**Comment allez-vous?** *formal /*
	Ça va? *informal*
	koh-maw~-tah-lay-voo / sah vah
Fine, thanks.	**Bien, merci.**
	bee-yeh~ mayhr-see
And you?	**Et vous?** *formal /* **Et toi?** *informal*
	ay voo / ay twah
I'm exhausted.	**Je suis épuisé(e).**
	zhuh swee-zay-pwee-zay
I have a headache.	**J'ai mal à la tête.**
	zhay mah-lah lah teht
I'm terrible.	**Je vais très mal.**
	zhuh vay treh mahl
I have a cold.	**J'ai un rhume.**
	zhay uh~ ruem
Good morning.	**Bonjour!**
	boh~-zhoohr
Good evening.	**Bonsoir!**
	boh~-swahr
Good afternoon.	**Bon après-midi!**
	boh~-nah-pray mee-dee
Good night.	**Bonne nuit!**
	buhn nwee

135

Listen Up: Common Greetings

Bonjour! *boh~-zhoohr*	Hello!
Ravi(e) de faire votre connaissance. *rah-vee duh fayhr voh-truh koh~-nay-saw~s*	It's a pleasure.
Enchanté(e). *aw~-shaw~-tay*	Charmed.
Ravi(e). *rah-vee*	Delighted.
Ça va? *sah vah*	How's it going?
Au revoir! *oh r'vwahr*	Goodbye!
À la prochaine! *ah lah proh-shen*	See you around!
À bientot! *ah bee-yeh~-toh*	See you later!

THE LANGUAGE BARRIER

I'm sorry, I don't understand very well.	**Désolé(e), je ne comprends pas bien.** *day-zoh-lay zhuh nuh koh~-praw~ pah bee-yeh~*
Would you speak slower, please?	**Pouvez-vous parler plus lentement, s'il vous plaît?** *poo-vay-voo pahr-lay plue law~-t-maw~ seel voo play*
Would you speak louder, please?	**Pouvez-vous parler plus fort, s'il vous plaît?** *poo-vay-voo pahr-lay plue fohr seel voo play*
Do you speak English?	**Parlez-vous anglais?** *pahr-lay-voo-zaw~-glay*

I speak ____ better than French.	**Je parle le ____ mieux que le français.**
	zhuh pahrl luh ____ mee-yoeh kuh luh fraw~-say

For languages, see English / French dictionary.

I'm sorry, would you spell that, please?	**Je suis désolé(e), pouvez-vous épeler, s'il vous plaît?**
	zhuh swee day-zoh-lay poo-vay-voo-zeh-play seel voo play
Would you please repeat that?	**Pouvez-vous répéter, s'il vous plaît?**
	poo-vay-voo ray-pay-tay seel voo play
How do you say ____?	**Comment dit-on ____?**
	koh-maw~ dee-toh~
Would you show me that in this dictionary?	**Pouvez-vous me montrer cela dans ce dictionnaire?**
	poo-vay-voo muh moh~-tray suh-lah daw~ suh deek-see-yoh-nayhr

Common Curses

Merde alors!	Oh shit!
mayhr-dah-lohr	
Fils de pute!	Son of a bitch! (Son of a whore!)
fees duh puet	
Merde!	Damn!
mayhrd	
Trou du cul!	Asshole!
troo due kue	
Nous sommes foutus!	We're screwed! (We're fucked!)
noo suhm foo-tue	
Enfoiré! / Salaud!	Bastard!
aw~-fwah-ray / sah-loh	
Putain!	Fuck! / Fucker!
pue-teh~	
C'est foutu!	That's fucked up!
say foo-tue	

GETTING PERSONAL

Europeans are typically more formal than Americans. Remember to use the formal forms of speech until given permission to employ more familiar speech.

INTRODUCTIONS

What is your name?	**Comment vous appelez-vous?** *koh-maw~ voo-zah-play-voo*
My name is ____.	**Je m'appelle ____.** *zhuh mah-pehl*
I'm very pleased to meet you.	**Ravi(e) de vous rencontrer.** *rah-vee duh voo raw~-koh~-tray*
May I introduce my ____	**Laissez-moi vous présenter ____** *leh-zay-mwah voo pray-zaw~-tay*
How is your ____	**Comment va votre ____** *koh-maw~ vah voh-truh*
aunt / uncle?	**mon oncle / ma tante?** *moh~-noh~kluh / mah taw~t*
boss?	**mon patron / ma patronne?** *moh~ pah-troh~ / mah pah-truhn*
boyfriend / girlfriend?	**mon petit ami / ma petite amie?** *moh~ puh-tee-tah-mee / mah puh-tee-tah-mee*
brother / sister?	**mon frère / ma sœur?** *moh~ frayhr / mah seuhr*
cousin?	**mon cousine / ma cousine?** *moh~ koo-zeh~ / mah koo-zeen*
family?	**ma famille?** *mah fah-mee*
father?	**mon père?** *moh~ payhr*
fiancé / fiancée?	**mon fiancé / ma fiancée?** *moh~ fee-yaw~-say / mah fee-yaw~-say*
friend?	**mon ami(e)?** *moh~-nah-mee*

grandparents?	**mes grand-parents?**
	may graw~-pah-raw~
husband?	**mon mari?**
	moh~ mah-ree
mother?	**ma mère?**
	mah mayhr
neighbor?	**mon voisin / ma voisine?**
	moh~ vwah-zeh~ / mah vwah-zeen
nephew / niece?	**mon neveu / ma niece?**
	moh~-neh-voeh / mah nee-yehs
parents?	**mes parents?**
	may pah-raw~
partner?	**mon partenaire?**
	moh~ pahrt-nayhr
son / daughter?	**mon fils / ma fille?**
	moh~ fees / mah fee-yuh
wife?	**ma femme?**
	mah fahm
Are you married / single?	**Vous êtes marié(e) / célibataire?**
	voo-zeht mah-ree-yay / say-lee-bah-tayhr
I'm married.	**Je suis marié(e).**
	zhuh swee mah-ree-yay
I'm single.	**Je suis célibataire.**
	zhuh swee say-lee-bah-tayhr
I'm divorced.	**Je suis divorcé(e).**
	zhuh swee dee-vohr-say
I'm a widow / widower.	**Je suis veuf / veuve.**
	zhuh swee voehf / voehv
We're separated.	**Nous sommes séparés.**
	noo suhm say-pah-ray

I live with my boyfriend / girlfriend.	**Je vis avec mon petit ami / ma petite amie.**
	zhuh vee ah-vek moh~ puh-tee-tah-mee / mah puh-tee-tah-mee
How old are you / your children?	**Quel âge avez vous / ont vos enfants?**
	keh-lahzh ah-vay-voo / oh~ voh-zaw~-faw~
Wow, that's very young.	**Oh là, c'est très jeune.**
	oh lah say tray zhoehn
What grade are they in?	**En quelle classe sont-ils?**
	aw~ kehl klahs soh~-teel
Your wife / daughter is beautiful.	**Ta femme / fille est belle.**
	tah fahm / fee-yuh ay behl
Your husband / son is handsome.	**Ton mari / fils est beau.**
	toh~ mah-ree / fees ay boh
What a beautiful baby!	**Quel beau bébé!**
	kehl boh bay-bay
Are you here on business?	**Vous êtes ici en voyage d'affaires?**
	voo-zeht ee-see aw~ vwah-yahz dah-fayhr
I am vacationing.	**Je suis en vacances.**
	zhuh swee-zaw~ vah-kaw~s
I'm attending a conference.	**Je participe à une conférence.**
	zhuh pahr-tee-see-pah oon koh~-fay-hraw~s
How long are you staying?	**Combien de temps restez-vous ici?**
	koh~-bee-yeh~ duh taw~ ruh-stay-voo-zee-see
What are you studying?	**Vous vous spécialisez en quoi?**
	voo voo spay-see-ah-lee-zay aw~ kwah
I'm a student.	**Je suis étudiant(e).**
	zhuh swee-zay-tue-dee-yaw~(t)
Where are you from?	**D'où êtes-vous?**
	doo eht-voo

NATIONALITIES

I am ____	**Je suis ____**
	zhuh swee(z)
American.	**américain** *m* / **américaine** *f.*
	ah-may-ree-keh~ / ah-may-ree-kehn
Canadian.	**canadien** *m* /**canadienne** *f.*
	kah-nah-dee-yeh~ / kah-nah-dee-yehn
Chinese.	**chinois** *m* / **chinoise** *f.*
	shee-nwah / shee-nwahz
English.	**anglais** *m* / **anglaise** *f.*
	aw~-glay / aw~-glehz
French.	**français** *m* / **française** *f.*
	fraw~-say / fraw~-sehz
German.	**allemand** *m* /**allemande** *f.*
	ahl-maw~ / ahl-maw~-d
Irish.	**irlandais** *m* / **irlandaise** *f.*
	eer-law~-day / eer-law~-dehz
Italian.	**italien** *m* / **italienne** *f.*
	ee-tahl-yeh~ / ee-tahl-yehn
Russian.	**russe** *m* / *f.*
	ruehs
Spanish.	**espagnol** *m* / **espagnole** *f.*
	ehs-pah-nyohl

See English / French dictionary for more nationalities.

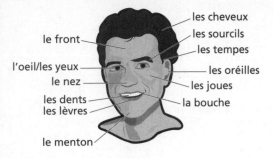

les cheveux
les sourcils
les tempes
le front
les oréilles
l'oeil/les yeux
les joues
le nez
les dents
la bouche
les lèvres
le menton

PERSONAL DESCRIPTIONS

African-American	**Il / Elle est afro-américain(e).**
	eel / ehl ay ah-froh-ah-may-ree-keh~(n)
Asian	**Il / Elle est asiatique.**
	eel / ehl ay ah-see-ah-teek
biracial	**Il / Elle est métis / métisse.**
	eel / ehl ay may-tee / may-tees
black	**Il / Elle est noir(e).**
	eel / ehl ay nwahr
blond(e)	**le blond / la blonde**
	luh bloh~ / lah blohd
blue eyes	**Il / Elle a les yeux bleus.**
	eel / ehl ah lay-zyoeh bloeh
brown eyes	**Il / Elle a les yeux bruns.**
	eel / ehl ah lay-zyoeh bruh~
brunette	**le brun / la brune**
	luh bruh~ / lah bruen
curly hair	**Il / Elle a les cheveux frisés.**
	eel / ehl ah lay shuh-voeh free-zay

eyebrows	**les sourcils**
	lay soohr-see
eyelashes	**les cils**
	lay see
face	**le visage**
	luh vee-zahzh
fat	**Il / Elle est gros / grosse.**
	eel / ehl ay groh(s)
freckles	**les taches de rousseur**
	lay tash duh roo-soehr
green eyes	**Il / Elle a les yeux verts.**
	eel / ehl ah lay-zyoeh veyhr
hazel eyes	**Il / Elle a les yeux noisette.**
	eel / ehl ah lay-zyoeh nwah-zeht
kinky hair	**Il / Elle a les cheveux crépus.**
	eel / ehl ah lay shuh-voeh kray-pue
long hair	**Il / Elle a les cheveux longs.**
	eel / ehl ah lay shuh-voeh loh~
mocha-skinned	**Il / Elle a le teint foncé.**
	eel / ehl ay luh teh~ foh~-say
moles	**les grains de beauté**
	lay greh~ duh boh-tay
pale	**Il / Elle a le teint clair.**
	eel / ehl ay luh teh~ klayhr
redhead	**le roux / la rousse**
	luh roo / lah roos
short	**Il / Elle est petit(e).**
	eel / ehl ay puh-tee(t)
short hair	**Il / Elle a les cheveux courts.**
	eel / ehl ah lay shuh-voeh koohr
straight hair	**Il / Elle a les cheveux raides.**
	eel / ehl ah lay shuh-voeh rayd
tall	**Il / Elle est grand(e).**
	eel / ehl ay graw~-(d)

tanned	**Il / Elle est basané(e).**
	eel / ehl ay bah-zah-nay
thin	**Il / Elle est mince.**
	eel / ehl ay meh~s
white	**Il / Elle est blanc / blanche.**
	eel / ehl ay blaw~ / blaw~sh

See diagram, p142, for facial features.
See diagram, p236, for body parts.

DISPOSITIONS AND MOODS

angry	**fâché(e)**
	fah-shay
anxious	**anxieux** *m* **/anxieuse** *f*
	aw~k-see-yoeh / aw~k-see-yoehz
confused	**confus(e)**
	koh~-fueh / koh~-fuehz
depressed	**deprimé(e)**
	day-pree-may
enthusiastic	**enthousiaste**
	aw~-too-zee-ahst
happy	**heureux** *m* **/ heureuse** *f*
	oeh-roeh / oeh-roehz
sad	**triste**
	treest
stressed	**stressé(e)**
	struh-say
tired	**fatigué(e)**
	fah-tee-gay

PROFESSIONS

What do you do for a living?	**Quelle est votre profession?**
	keh-lay voh-truh proh-feh-see-yoh~
Here is my business card.	**Voici ma carte de visite.**
	vwah-see mah kahrt duh vee-zeet

I am ____	**Je suis ____**
	zhuh swee
an accountant.	**comptable.**
	koh~p-tah-bluh
an artist.	**artiste.**
	ahr-teest
a craftsperson.	**artisan(e).**
	ahr-tee-saw~(n)
a designer.	**styliste.**
	stee-leest
a doctor.	**médecin.**
	may-duh-seh~
an editor.	**rédacteur** *m* **/ rédactrice** *f.*
	ruh-dahk-toehr / ruh-dahk-treese
an educator.	**dans l'enseignement.**
	daw~ law~-seh~-nyuh-maw~
an engineer.	**ingénieur.**
	eh~zhay-nyoehr
a government employee.	**fonctionnaire.**
	foh~k-see-yoh~-nayhr
a homemaker.	**femme au foyer.**
	fah-moh fwah-yay
a lawyer.	**avocat(e).**
	ah-voh-kah(t)
a military professional.	**dans l'armée.**
	daw~ lahr-may
a musician.	**musicien** *m* **/ musicienne** *f.*
	mue-zee-see-yeh~(n)
a nurse.	**infirmier** *m* **/ infirmière** *f.*
	eh~-feer-mee-yayh(r)
a salesperson.	**représentant(e) commercial(e).**
	ruh-pray-saw~-taw~(t) koh-mayhr-see-yahl
a writer.	**écrivain.**
	ay-kree-veh~

DOING BUSINESS

I'd like to make an appointment.	**Je voudrais prendre rendez-vous.** *zhuh voo-dray praw~-druh raw~-day-voo*
I'm here to see ____.	**J'ai rendez-vous avec ____.** *zhay raw~-day-voo ah-vek*
I need to photocopy this.	**J'ai besoin de photocopier ceci.** *zhay buh-zweh~ duh foh-toh-koh-pee-yay suh-see*
May I use a computer here?	**Puis-je utiliser un ordinateur ici?** *pwee-zhuh oo-tee-lee-zay uh~-nohr-dee-nah-toehr ee-see*
What's the password?	**Quel est le mot de passe?** *keh-lay luh moh duh pahs*
May I access the Internet here?	**Puis-je accéder à l'Internet d'ici?** *pwee-zhuh ahk-say-day ah leh~-tayhr-neht dee-see*
May I send a fax?	**Puis-je envoyer une télécopie?** *pwee-zhuh aw~-vwah-yay oon tay-lay-koh-pee*
May I use the phone?	**Puis-je faire un appel?** *pwee-zhuh fayhr uh~-nah-pehl*

PARTING WAYS

Keep in touch.	**Restons en contact.** *ruh-stoh~-naw~ koh~-tahkt*
Please write or e-mail.	**Correspondons par poste ou par courriel.** *koh-ruh-spoh~-doh~ pahr pohst oo pahr kooh-ree-yehl*
Here's my phone number. Call me!	**Voici mon numéro de téléphone. Appelez-moi!** *vwah-see moh~-nue-may-roh duh tay-lay-fohn; ah-play mwah*

May I have your phone number / e-mail, please?	**Puis-je avoir votre numéro de téléphone / adresse courriel?** *pwee-zhuh ah-vwahr voh-truh nue-may-roh duh tay-lay-fohn / ah-drehs kooh-ree-yehl*
May I have your card?	**Puis-je avoir votre carte de visite?** *pwee-zhuh ah-vwahr voh-truh kahrt duh vee-zeet*
Give me your address and I'll write.	**Donnez-moi votre adresse pour que je vous écrive.** *duh-nay mwah voh-truh ah-drehs poohr kuh zhuh voo-zay-kreev*

TOPICS OF CONVERSATION

As in the United States or anywhere in the world, the weather and current affairs are common conversation topics.

THE WEATHER

It's _____. / Is it always so _____?

sunny	**Il fait beau. / Fait-il toujours si beau?** *eel fay boh / fay-teel too-zhoor see boh*
raining / rainy	**Il pleut. / Fait-il toujours si plu-vieux?** *eel ploeh / fay-teel too-zhoor see plue-vee-yoeh*
cloudy	**Le temps est nuageux. / Est-il toujours si nuageux?** *luh taw~ ay nue-wah-zhoeh / ey-teel too-zhoor see nue-wah-zhoeh*

humid	**Le temps est humide. / Est-il toujours si humide?**
	luh taw~ ay-tue-meed / ey-teel too-zhoor see oo-meed
warm	**Il fait chaud. / Fait-il toujours si chaud?**
	eel fay shoh / fay-teel too-zhoor see shoh
cool	**Il fait frais. / Fait-il toujours si frais?**
	eel fay fray / fay-teel too-zhoor see fray
windy	**Il fait du vent. / Fait-il toujours si venteux?**
	eel fay due vaw~ / fay-teel too-zhoor see vaw~-toeh
What's the forecast for tomorrow?	**Quel temps est prévu pour demain?**
	kehl taw~ ay pray-vue poohr duh-meh~

THE ISSUES

What do you think about _____	**Quelle est votre position à propos _____**
	keh-lay voh-truh poh-zee-see-yoh~ ah proh-poh
democracy?	**de la démocracie en général?**
	duh lah day-moh-krah-see aw~-zhay-nay-rahl
socialism?	**du socialisme?**
	due soh-see-yah-lee-smuh
the environment?	**de l'environnement?**
	duh leh~-vee-roh~-maw~
women's rights?	**des droits de la femme?**
	day dhwah duh lah fahm
gay rights?	**des droits des homosexuels?**
	day dhwah day-zoh-moh-sehk-sue-ehl

the French economy?	**de l'économie française?** *duh lay-koh-noh-mee fraw~-sehz*
the French / American election?	**de l'election française / americaine?** *duh lehl-ehk-see-yoh~ fraw~-sehz / ah-may-ree-kehn*
the war in _____?	**de la guerre en _____?** *duh lah guehr aw~*
What party do you belong to?	**Vous êtes membre de quel parti politique?** *voo-zeht maw~-bruh duh kehl pahr-tee poh-lee-teek*

RELIGION

Do you go to church / temple / mosque?	**Allez-vous à la messe / synagoge / mosquée?** *ah-lay-voo-zah lah mehs / see-nah-guhg / muh-skay*
Are you religious?	**Êtes-vous pratiquant(e)?** *eht-voo prah-tee-kaw~(t)*
I'm _____ / I was raised _____	**Je suis _____ / J'ai reçu une éducation _____** *zhuh swee / zhay ruh-sue oon ay-due-kah-see-yoh~*
agnostic.	**agnostique.** *ahg-noh-steek*
atheist.	**athée.** *ah-tay*
Buddhist.	**bouddhiste.** *boo-deest*
Catholic.	**catholique.** *kah-toh-leek*
Hindu.	**hindouiste.** *eh~-doo-eest*
Jewish.	**juif *m* / juive *f*.** *zhweef / zhweev*

Muslim.	**musulman(e).**
	mue-suel-maw~(n)
Orthodox Christian.	**chrétien orthodoxe.**
	khreh-tee-yeh~-nohr-toh-doks
Protestant.	**protestant(e).**
	proh-teh-staw~(t)

I'm spiritual but I don't go to church.
Je suis spirituel m / spirituelle f mais je ne vais pas à la messe.
zhuh swee spee-ree-twehl may zhuh nuh vay pah-zah lah mehs

I don't believe in that.
Je ne crois pas en cela.
zhuh nuh khwah pah-zaw~ suh-lah

That's against my beliefs.
Cela va à l'encontre de mes croyances.
suh-lah vah ah law~-koh~truh duh may khwah-yaw~s

I'd rather not talk about it.
Je préfère ne pas en parler.
zhuh pray-fayhr nuh pah-zaw~ pahr-lay

GETTING TO KNOW SOMEONE

Following are some fun topics for you to explore with friends you meet.

MUSICAL TASTES

What kind of music do you like?
Quel type de musique aimez-vous?
kehl teep duh mue-zeek ay-may-voo

I like ____	**J'aime ____**
	zhehm
calypso.	**le calypso.**
	luh kah-leep-soh
classical.	**la musique classique.**
	lah mue-zeek klah-seek

country and western.	**le country.** *luh kuhn-tree*
disco.	**le disco.** *luh dees-koh*
jazz.	**le jazz.** *luh zhahz*
New Age.	**la musique New Age.** *lah mue-zeek nyue ahzh*
opera.	**l'opéra.** *loh-pay-rah*
pop.	**la musique pop.** *lah mue-zeek pohp*
reggae.	**le reggae.** *luh reh-gay*
rock'n'roll.	**le rock.** *luh rohk*
show-tunes / musicals.	**les comedies musicales.** *lay koh-may-dee mue-zee-kahl*
techno.	**la techno.** *lah tehk-noh*

HOBBIES

What do you like to do in your spare time?	**Qu'est-ce que vous aimez faire pendant votre temps libre?** *kehs kuh voo-zay-may fayhr paw~-daw~ voh-truh taw~ lee-bruh*
I like ____	**J'aime ____** *zhehm ____*
camping.	**aller camper.** *ah-lay kaw~-pay*
cooking.	**cuisiner.** *kwee-zee-nay*
dancing.	**danser.** *daw~-say*
drawing.	**dessiner.** *deh-see-nay*

eating out.	**manger au restaurant.**
	maw~-zhay oh ruh-stoh-raw~
going to the movies.	**aller au cinéma.**
	ah-lay oh see-nay-mah
hanging out.	**passer du temps avec mes amis.**
	pah-say due taw~ ah-vek may-zah-mee
hiking.	**faire de la marche.**
	fayhr duh lah mahrsh
painting.	**peindre.**
	peh~-druh
playing the guitar.	**jouer de la guitare.**
	zhoo-ay duh lah gee-tahr
playing the piano.	**jouer du piano.**
	zhoo-ay due pee-yah-noh

For other instruments, see English / French dictionary.

reading.	**lire.**
	leer
sewing.	**faire de la couture.**
	fayhr duh lah koo-tuehr
shopping.	**faire les magasins.**
	fayhr lay mah-gah-zeh~
sports.	**faire du sport.**
	fayhr due spohr
traveling.	**voyager.**
	vwah-yah-zhay
watching TV.	**regarder la télé.**
	ruh-gahr-day lah tay-lay
Do you like to dance?	**Aimez-vous danser?**
	ay-may-voo daw~-say
Would you like to go out?	**Voulez-vous sortir avec moi?**
	voo-lay-voo sohr-teer ah-vek mwah
May I buy you dinner sometime?	**Puis-je vous inviter à dîner un de ces soirs?**
	pwee-zhuh voo-zeh~-vee-tay ah dee-nay uh~ duh say swahr

What kind of food do you like?	**Quel type de nourriture aimez-vous?**
	kehl-teep duh nooh-ree-tuehr ay-may-voo

For a full list of cuisines, see p100.

Would you like to go ____	**Voulez-vous aller ____ avec moi?**
	voo-lay-voo-zah-lay ____ ah-vek mwah
to a movie?	**au cinéma**
	oh see-nay-mah
to a concert?	**à un concert**
	ah uh~ koh~-sayhr
to the zoo?	**au zoo**
	oh zoh
to the beach?	**à la plage**
	ah lah plahzh
to a museum?	**au musée**
	oh mue-zay
for a walk in the park?	**faire une promenade au parc**
	fayhr oon proh-meh-nahd oh pahr
dancing?	**danser**
	daw~say
Would you like to get ____	**Voulez-vous ____ avec moi?**
	voo-lay-voo ____ ah-vek mwah
lunch?	**déjeuner**
	day-zhoeh-nay
coffee?	**prendre un café**
	preh~-druh uh~ kah-fay
dinner?	**dîner**
	dee-nay

What kind of books do you like to read?	**Quel type de livres aimez-vous lire?**
	kehl teep duh lee-vruh ay-may-voo leer
I like ____	**J'aime ____**
	zhehm
autobiographies.	**les autobiographies.**
	lay-zoh-toh-bee-yoh-grah-fee
biographies.	**les biographies.**
	lay bee-yoh-grah-fee
dramas.	**les romans dramatiques.**
	lay roh-maw~ drah-mah-teek
history.	**les livres d'histoire.**
	lay lee-vruh dees-twahr
mysteries.	**les romans policiers.**
	lay roh-maw~ poh-lee-see-yay
novels.	**les romans.**
	lay roh-maw~
romance.	**les romans d'amour.**
	lay roh-maw~ dah-moohr
Westerns.	**les romans-western.**
	lay roh-maw~-vehs-tayhrn

For dating terms, see Nightlife in Chapter 10.

THE FRENCH CHARACTER & POLITICS

It's hard to make generalizations about a people; however, most visitors note a significant difference between Parisians and people from the provinces. First, the pace in Paris is far more hectic and Parisians have less time to chatter and are often *ennervé* (irritable) due to the stress of work, traffic, and less-than-pure air quality. Even folk from the provincial cities have a hard time tolerating the way of life in Paris.

It's harder and harder to identify regional characteristics these days, but it is accurate to note that there is strong regional pride among people from diverse French regions such as Brittany, the Pyrenees, the Ardèche, and Alsace. Although young people no longer speak the regional languages, lots of elderly people still do. There has been a movement not to lose Provençal, Basque, Breton, and of course Corsican, where the cultural identity is fierce.

Despite France's overwhelmingly Catholic population, the vast majority of French people defend the strict division of church and state and do not practice any religion. Additionally, the French tend to be socially open, sexually free, and very pro-choice. There is no stigma at all about cohabitation, and a great many couples, even those with children, are legally unmarried. France even passed a law called the PACS recognizing the legal and fiscal rights of unwed, single-sex couples.

After the September 11, 2001, terrorist attacks and the beginning of the war in Iraq, a propaganda war in the U.S. directed at France created a period of tension and some large misconceptions about U.S.-Franco relations.

It's true that Washington's decision to invade Iraq in 2003 drove a wedge between the United States and its ally, and George W. Bush became one of the most unpopular American presidents ever in the eyes of the French. When Bush visited

France to observe the 60th anniversary of the June 1944 D-Day invasion of Normandy, relations remained somewhat icy between Bush and French President Jacques Chirac, who had criticized the way the American president was handling the postwar situation in Iraq. When Bush arrived in Paris in June 2004, thousands of antiwar and anti-Bush protesters marched in the streets of Paris. Bush declared, "We have great relations with France," but the opinion poll released the same week showed 78 percent of the French people no longer trusted the politics of the United States.

It's important to remember, though, that the French as a people are not anti-American, and that you will not have negative experiences in France because you are American. The French do have a strong sense of national pride and enjoy talking about politics. You may encounter individuals who do not agree with Washington, D.C., or with your views, either. But you'll rarely find anyone who takes out his or her political or cultural biases on you as an individual. In fact, you'll find that in large measure the French have a limitless admiration for American popular culture and affection for the American people.

The France-bashing that Americans witnessed on U.S. television only served to reinforce unfounded myths. A majority of the French oppose the war in Iraq without UN and international consensus, but France is one of the most active players in the collaborative war against terror, and remains a close ally to the U.S.

LIVELY CONVERSATION STARTERS

- **Smoking Habits and Anti-Smoking Laws in The U.S. and France**   The French love to cite the intolerance of Americans who ban smoking everywhere. In France there are still some 20 million or so smokers, and more than 20% of French doctors continue to smoke. To be fair, the smoking scene is getting better; more people are quitting, more public places are attempting to maintain the law that requires restaurants and bars to provide no-smoking areas, and the airports are pretty much smoke-free.

- **Franco-American Relations** Why the French do/don't hate Americans, why Americans/the French think Americans/the French hate them, and so on. This is a subject filled with lively differences of opinion.

- **Opinions of I.M. Pei's Modern Glass Pyramid at The Louvre** No one is too worked up about Pei and the Louvre anymore, nor about the Pompidou Center or even the newer Mitterrand National Library. But it's true that the French do like to criticize the government's initiatives. That doesn't mean they'd prefer something else, they just enjoy complaining. It's an art form.

- **The War in Iraq, The Urban Unrest in France** These subjects are worth debating with French friends, but be prepared to hear points of view that differ from your own. France has a large Muslim population and a significant Jewish community, and discussions of Iraq or oil or the immigrant groups in France often end up as debates on the Palestine question and American hegemony.

Remember that heated talk in France is not a reason to break up with a friend or refuse to wolf down a dozen oysters and a bottle of Sancerre with your partner in conversation.

DINING AT HOME

If you're invited to a French friend's for dinner, always bring something, usually a nicely wrapped bouquet of flowers. Tell the florist that they're a gift—*pour offrir*—and they'll be dolled up for the same price. A decent bottle of wine or champagne is standard. Don't bring a bottle of table wine (*vin de table*) or any bottle with a plastic cork or with blue metal wrapping over the cork. Trust us. Even simple, unpretentious, and modest Parisians know a thing or two about wine. Small gifts from home are highly appreciated. If you happen to think of it in advance, a bottle of Californian wine will be greeted with pleasant curiosity.

After dinner, you may offer to help with the dishes, but there is a good chance that you will not be encouraged to enter the kitchen or be invited to help out. Although you'll want to be polite, don't be overly insistent on helping.

Be prepared to spend a lot more time sitting around the table at the end of the meal, drinking coffee, eating clementines, sipping cognac or Calvados, and talking. This is one of the great pleasures of being in France.

THE BEST FRENCH LANGUAGE SCHOOLS

The Alliance Française has offices throughout the United States and around the world (including Paris), where you can take French language courses and attend lectures, films, and cultural activities. For details, go to **www.fiaf.org**. In New York City, try the French Institute Alliance Francaise (© **212/355-6100**). In Washington, D.C., call © **202/234-7911**.

Another great source of cultural and linguistic information for Paris-bound travelers is **www.info-france-usa.org**. For language study, you can try **Berlitz** at **www.berlitz.com**.

In France, there are many language schools providing short- and long-term French classes for English-speakers. The www.paris-anglo.com website lists all the Paris area programs. Here are three:

- **The Alliance Française**   © **01-42-84-90-00**; www.alliancefr. org.
- **Institut de Langue et de Culture Françaises, Institut Catholique de Paris**   © **01-44-39-52-00**; www.icp.fr/ilcf.
- **Berlitz France**   © **01-53-30-18-18**; www.berlitz.com.

CHAPTER SIX

MONEY & COMMUNICATIONS

This chapter covers money, the mail, phone and Internet service, and other tools you need to connect with the outside world.

MONEY

Do you accept _____	**Acceptez-vous** _____ *ahk sehp-tay-voo*
Visa / MasterCard / Discover / American Express / Diners' Club?	**la carte Visa / MasterCard / Discover / American Express / Diners' Club?** *lah kahrt vee-zah / mahs-tayhr-kahrd / dees-koh-vayhr / ah-may-ree-keh-nek-spres / day-nayhrz kloohb*
credit cards?	**les cartes de crédit?** *lay kahrt duh kray-dee*
bills?	**les coupures / billets?** *lay koo-puehr / bee-yay*
coins?	**les pièces?** *lay pee-yes*
checks?	**les chèques?** *lay shek*
travelers' checks?	**les chèques de voyage?** *lay shek duh vwah-yazh*
money transfers?	**les virements?** *lay veer-maw~*
May I wire transfer funds here?	**Puis-je virer des fonds d'ici?** *pwee-zhuh vee-ray day foh~-dee-see*

COMMUNICATIONS

Would you please tell me where to find ____	**Pouvez-vous m'indiquer ____** *poo-vay-voo meh~-dee-kay*
a bank?	**un bureau de banque?** *uh~ bue-roh duh baw~k*
a credit bureau?	**une institution de crédit?** *oo-neh~-stee-tue-see-yoh~ duh kray-dee*
an ATM?	**une billeterie automatique?** *uh~ bee-yeh-tree oh-toh-mah-teek*
a currency exchange?	**un bureau de change?** *uh~ bueh-roh duh shaw~zh*
May I have a receipt, please?	**Puis-je avoir un reçu, s'il vous plaît?** *pwee-zhuh ah-vwahr uh~ reh-sue seel voo play*
Would you please tell me ____	**Pouvez-vous me dire ____** *poo-vay-voo muh deer*
today's interest rate?	**quel est le taux de change aujourd'hui?** *keh-lay luh toh duh shaw~zh oh-zhoohr-dwee*
the exchange rate for dollars to ____?	**quel est le taux de change du dollar en ____?** *keh-lay luh toh duh shaw~zh due doh-lahr en*
Is there a service charge?	**Y a-t-il des frais bancaires?** *yah-teel day frey baw~-kayhr*

En panne

Before you stick your coins or bills in a vending machine, watch out for the little sign that says *En panne* or *Hors service* (Out of Service).

Listen Up: Bank Lingo

Signez ici, s'il vous plaît. *seen-yay-zee-see seel voo play*	Please sign here.
Voici votre reçu. *vwah-see voh-truh ruh-sue*	Here is your receipt.
Puis-je voir une pièce d'identité, s'il vous plaît? *pwee-zhuh vwahr oon pee-yes dee-deh~-tee-tay seel voo play*	May I see your ID, please?
Nous acceptons les chèques de voyage. *noo-zahk-sehp-toh~ lay shek duh vwah-yahzh*	We accept travelers' checks.
Nous n'acceptons que les espèces. *noo nahk-sehp-toh~ kuh lay-zehs-pehs*	Cash only.

COMMUNICATIONS

May I have a cash advance on my credit card?	**Puis-je retirer de l'argent sur ma carte de crédit?** *pwee-zhuh ruh-tee-ray duh lahr-zhaw~ suehr mah kahrt duh kray-dee*
Will you accept a credit card?	**Acceptez-vous les cartes de crédit?** *ahk-sehp-tay-voo lay kahrt duh kray-dee*
May I have smaller bills, please?	**Puis-je avoir des billets plus petits, s'il vous plaît?** *pwee-zhuh ah-vwahr day bee-yay plue puh-tee seel voo play*
Can you make change?	**Pouvez-vous faire de la monnaie?** *poo-vay-voo fayhr duh lah moh~-nay*

ATM Machine

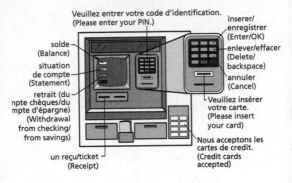

Veuillez entrer votre code d'identification.
(Please enter your PIN.)

solde
(Balance)

situation
de compte
(Statement)

retrait (du
 npte chèques/du
mpte d'épargne)
(Withdrawal
from checking/
from savings)

inserer/
enregistrer
(Enter/OK)

enlever/effacer
(Delete/
backspace)

annuler
(Cancel)

Veuillez insérer
votre carte.
(Please insert
your card)

Nous acceptons les
cartes de credit.
(Credit cards
accepted)

un reçu/ticket
(Receipt)

I only have bills.	**Je n'ai que des billets.** *zhuh nay kuh day bee-yay*
May I have some coins, please?	**Puis-je avoir quelques pièces, s'il vous plaît?** *pwee-zhuh ah-vwahr kehl-kuh pee-yehs seel voo play*

PHONE SERVICE

Where can I buy or rent a cell phone?	**Où puis-je acheter ou louer un téléphone portable?** *oo pwee-zhuh ahsh-tay oo loo-way uh~ tay-lay-fohn pohr-tah-bluh*
What rate plans do you have?	**Quels tarifs proposez-vous?** *kehl tah-reef proh-poh-zay-voo*
Is this good in the whole country?	**Est-ce que c'est valable pour tout le pays?** *ehs-kuh say vah-lah-bluh poohr too luh pay-ee*

May I have a prepaid phone card?	**Puis-je avoir une carte téléphonique prépayée?** *pwee-zhuh ah-vwahr oon kahrt tay-lay-foh-neek pray-pay-ay*
Where can I buy a phone card?	**Où puis-je acheter une carte téléphonique?** *oo pwee-zhuh ahsh-tay oon kahrt tay-lay-foh-neek*
May I add more minutes to my phone card?	**Puis-je ajouter des minutes sur ma carte téléphonique?** *pwee-zhuh ah-zhoo-tay day mee-nuet suehr mah kahrt tay-lay-foh-neek*

MAKING A CALL

May I dial direct?	**Puis-je composer le numéro directement?** *pwee-zhuh koh~-poh-zay luh nue-may-roh dee-rehkt-maw~*
Operator, please.	**Je voudrais l'opératrice, s'il vous plaît.** *zhuh voo-dray loh-pay-rah-trees seel voo play*
I'd like to make an international call.	**Je voudrais faire un appel à l'étranger.** *zhuh voo-dray fayhr uh~-nah-peh-lah lay-traw~-zhay*
I'd like to make a collect call.	**Je voudrais faire un appel en PCV.** *zhuh voo-dray fayhr uh~-nah-peh-law~ pay-say-vay*
I'd like to use a calling card.	**Je voudrais faire un appel à l'aide d'une carte téléphonique.** *zhuh voo-dray fayhr uh~-nah-peh-lah lehd doon kahrt tay-lay-foh-neek*

COMMUNICATIONS

Listen Up: Phone Lingo

Bonjour. *boh~-zhoohr*	Hello.
Quel numéro? *kehl nue-may-roh*	What number?
Désolé(e), la ligne est occupée. *day-zoh-lay lah lee-ney-toh-kue-pay*	I'm sorry, the line is busy.
Veuillez raccrocher puis composer de nouveau le numéro. *voeh-yay rah-kroh-shay pwee koh~-poh-zay duh noo-voh luh nue-may-roh*	Please hang up the phone and redial.
Désolé(e), ça ne répond pas. *day-zoh-lay sah nuh ray-poh~ pah*	I'm sorry, nobody answers.
Il reste dix minutes sur votre carte. *eel rehst dee mee-nuet suehr voh-truh kahrt*	Your card has ten minutes left.

I'd like to bill the call to my credit card.	**Je voudrais facturer cet appel sur ma carte de crédit.** *zhuh voo-dray fahk-tueh-ray seh-tah-pehl suehr mah kahrt duh kray-dee*
May I bill the charges to my room?	**Puis-je ajouter cet appel à ma note d'hôtel?** *pwee-zhuh ah-zhoo-tay seh-tah-pehl ah mah noht doh-tehl*

May I bill the charges to my home phone?	**Puis-je facturer cet appel sur la note de téléphone de mon domicile?** *pwee-zhuh fahk-tueh-ray seh-tah-pehl suehr lah noht duh tay-lay-fohn duh moh~ doh-mee-seel*
Information, please.	**Je voudrais les renseignements, s'il vous plaît.** *zhuh voo-dray lay raw~-seh~-nyuh-maw~ seel voo play*
Would you please give me the number for ____?	**Je voudrais le numéro de ____, s'il vous plaît.** *zhuh voo-dray luh nue-may-roh duh ____ seel voo play*
I just got disconnected.	**J'étais coupé(e).** *zheh-tay koo-pay*
The line is busy.	**La ligne est occupée.** *lah lee-ney-toh-kue-pay*

INTERNET ACCESS

Would you tell me where to find an Internet café?	**Pouvez-vous m'indiquer un cybercafé?** *poo-vay-voo meh~-dee-kay uh~-see-behr-kah-fay*
Is there a wireless hub / Wi-Fi access nearby?	**Y a-t-il un hub Ethernet sans fil / Wi-Fi près d'ici?** *yah-teel uh~-nuhb ay-tayhr-neht saw~ feel / wee-fee pray dee-see*

COMMUNICATIONS

How much do you charge per minute / hour?	**Combien prenez-vous par minute / heure?**
	koh~-bee-yeh~ pruh-nay-voo pahr mee-nuet / oehr
Can I print here?	**Puis-je imprimer des documents ici?**
	pwee-zhuh eh~-pree-may day doh-kue-maw~-zee-see
Can I burn a CD?	**Puis-je graver un CD ici?**
	pwee-zhuh grah-vay uh~ say-day ee-see
Would you please help me change the preference to English?	**Pouvez-vous m'aider à configurer l'anglais comme langue préférée?**
	poo-vay-voo may-day ah koh~-fee-gueh-ray law~-glay kohm law~g pray-fay-ray
May I scan something in here?	**Puis-je scanner quelque chose ici?**
	pwee-zhuh skah-nay kehl-kuh shoh-zee-see
Can I upload photos from my digital camera?	**Puis-je télécharger vers l'amont des photos de mon appareil photo numérique?**
	pwee-zhuh tay-lay-shahr-zhay vayhr law~-moh~ day foh-toh duh moh~-nah-pah-ray foh-toh nue-may-reek
Do you have a USB port so I can load some music on my MP3 player?	**Avez-vous un port USB pour que je puisse importer de la musique sur mon lecteur MP3?**
	ah-vay-voo-zuh~ pohr oo-ehs-bay poohr kuh zhuh pwees eh~-pohr-tay duh lah mue-zeek suehr moh~ lehk-toehr ehm-pay-twhah
Do you have a machine compatible with iTunes?	**Avez-vous un système compatible avec iTunes?**
	ah-vay-voo-zuh~ see-stehm koh~-pah-tee-bluh ah-vek ee-tuehn

Do you have a Mac?	**Avez-vous un Mac?** *ah-vay-voo-zuh~ mahk*
Do you have a PC?	**Avec-vous un compatible PC?** *ah-vay-voo-zuh~ koh~-pah-tee-bluh pay-say*
Do you have a newer version of this software?	**Avez-vous une version plus récente de ce logiciel?** *ah-vay-voo-zoon vayhr-see-yoh~ plue ray-saw~t duh suh loh-zhee-see-yehl*
How fast is your connection speed here?	**La vitesse d'accès est de combien de bauds ici?** *lah vee-tess dahk-say ay duh koh~-bee-yeh~ duh boh-dee-see*
Do you have broadband?	**Avez-vous l'accès à l'Internet à large bande?** *ah-vay-voo lahk-say ah leh~-tayhr-neht ah lahrzh bahnd*

GETTING MAIL

Excuse me, can you tell me where to find the post office?	**Excusez-moi, pouvez-vous me dire où se trouve la poste?** *ek-skue-zay mwah poo-vay-voo muh deer oo suh troov lah pohst*
May I send an international package?	**Puis-je envoyer un colis à l'étranger d'ici?** *pwee-zhuh aw~-vwah-yay uh~ koh-lee ah lay-traw~-zhay dee-see*
Do I need a customs form?	**Ai-je besoin de remplir un formulaire de douane?** *ay-zhuh buh-zweh~ duh raw~-pleer uh~ fohr-mue-layhr duh doo-wahn*

Do you sell insurance?	**Offrez-vous une formule assurance?** *oh-fray-voo-zoon fohr-muel ah-sueh-raw~s*
Please, mark it fragile.	**Apposez un tampon "Fragile", s'il vous plaît.** *ah-poh-zay uh~ taw~-poh~ frah-zheel seel voo play*
Please, handle with care.	**Manipulez-le doucement, s'il vous plaît.** *mah-nee-pue-lay-luh doos-maw~ seel voo play*
Do you have more twine?	**Avez-vous de la ficelle, s'il vous plaît?** *ah-vay-voo duh lah fee-sehl seel voo play*
Would you please tell me where to find a DHL office?	**Pouvez-vous me dire où se trouve l'agence DHL la plus proche?** *poo-vay-voo muh deer oo suh troov lah-zhaw~s day-ahsh-ehl lah plue prohsh*
Do you sell stamps?	**Est-ce que vous vendez des timbres?** *ehs kuh voo vaw~day day taw~-bruh*
Do you sell postcards?	**Est-ce que vous vendez des cartes postales?** *ehs kuh voo vaw~-day day kahrt poh-stahl*

Listen Up: Postal Lingo

Au suivant!	Next!
oh swee-vaw~	
Veuillez le poser ici.	Set it here.
voeh-yay luh poh-zay	
ee-see	
Quelle classe?	Which class?
kehl klahs	
Vous désirez?	What kind of service would you
voo day-zee-ray	like?
En quoi puis-je vous	How can I help you?
être utile?	
aw~ kwah pwee-zhuh	
voo-zeh-truh oo-teel	
le guichet de dépôt	dropoff window
luh gee-shay duh day-poh	
le guichet de récupération	pickup window
luh gee-shay duh ray-kue-	
pay-rah-see-yoh~	

I'd like to send this first class / priority mail.

Je voudrais le service rapide / prioritaire.
zhuh voo-dray luh sayhr-vees rah-peed / pree-oh-ree-tayhr

How much to send that express / air mail?

Combien coûte l'envoi accéléré / par avion?
koh~-bee-yeh~ koot law~-vwah ahk-say-lay-ray / pahr ah-vee-yoh~

Do you offer overnight delivery?

Offrez-vous un service de livraison sous 24 heures?
oh-fray-voo-zuh~ sayhr-vees duh lee-vray-zoh~ soo vaw~-kah-truh oehr

How long will that take?	**Combien de jours est-ce que l'envoi prendra?** *koh~-bee-yeh~ duh zhoohr ehs kuh law~-vwah praw~-drah*
I'd like to buy an envelope, please.	**Je voudrais acheter une enveloppe, s'il vous plaît.** *zhuh voo-dray ahsh-tay oo-naw~-vuh-lohp seel voo play*
May I send it airmail?	**Puis-je l'envoyer par avion?** *pwee-zhuh law~-vwah-yay pahr ah-vee-yoh~*
I'd like to send it certified / registered mail.	**Je voudrais l'envoyer en recommandé.** *zhuh voo-dray law~-vwah-yay aw~ ruh-koh-maw~-day*

MONEY MATTERS

Cash   France uses the euro, which is currently about 20% higher than the U.S. dollar. If you want today's rates, or to buy foreign currency, call **BHD Worldwide** at © 888/465-6150, or log on to www.nyforeignexchange.com. You can also try **www.xe.com** or contact **American Express** at © 800/528-4800 or www.americanexpress.com.

U.S. cash is readily changed in many French banks and change offices, but it's not usually accepted in stores, restaurants, or hotels. To be safe, store your cash in two different places, so you don't risk losing everything at once. Men should keep wallets in front pockets. When you change money, ask for a certain amount in small bills; they come in handy for tips and other small charges.

Western Union (© 800/325-6000; www.westernunion. com) has offices all over Paris and in most French cities, so you can have money wired to you easily if need be.

Traveler's Checks   These have gone the way of the dinosaur, because ATMs are everywhere. You can get **American Express** checks by calling © 800/221-7282 or logging on to www.americanexpress.com. **Visa** offers traveler's checks through Citibank locations nationwide (© 800/732-1322; www.international. visa.com). **MasterCard** (© 800/223-9920; www.mastercard. com) also sells them.

ATMs   It's best to bring a small amount of euros with you to avoid ATM lines at the airport when you arrive. There are ATMs in virtually every town in France, so you needn't bring too much cash with you. Keep in mind that you're likely to be charged a hefty withdrawal fee both by the French bank that operates the ATM and by your bank at home. Make sure you have a PIN for international use; it may be shorter than the number you use at home. Find out your daily withdrawal limit.

If you need to change a large amount of cash in Paris, the *rue Vivienne* near the French Bourse hosts a row of professional currency exchange shops which usually offer the best rates in the city and take no commission.

Credit Cards   It's generally a good idea to bring two credit cards in case one gets lost or your bank at home refuses to honor one. **Visa** and **MasterCard** are accepted virtually everywhere in France, with **American Express** a distant third. Get an **international PIN** before you leave home, which could be different from the one you use at home. Find out your daily withdrawal limit. Keep in mind that you're charged interest from the day of your withdrawal, even if you pay your monthly bill on time. You'll also be charged a fee for exchanging dollars into euros. Keep your card numbers in a separate place to facilitate their replacement if they're lost or stolen. You should also have a record of the numbers to call should you need to report a lost or stolen card. Card companies go berserk when they see a bill from an unfamiliar destination, so it's always good to call and let them know where you're going and how long you'll be away. You don't want charges to be declined thousands of miles from home.

STAYING IN TOUCH

You'll find cybercafes in all French cities and Internet connections in most hotels. Remember to take with you your log-in and password if you are unaccustomed to checking your e-mail from a distance. As a backup, use **www.mail2web.com** to get your e-mail from any server. For a global list of cybercafes, contact **www.cybercaptive.com** or **www.cybercafes.com.** For a list in Paris, try www.parispubs.com/cyber.php.

Regular Mail   You can receive mail at central post offices in most towns. It should be addressed "*Poste Restante, Poste Central*," followed by the name of the town and its postal code.

To collect your mail you will usually need a passport, and there may be a charge of a euro or less. French post offices are usually open 9am to 7pm, Monday to Friday, and 9am to noon on Saturday. In smaller towns, offices may close for lunch. In Paris, the main office is open 24 hours, though lines at lunchtime are formidable. The central office of the Louvre is at 52 rue du Louvre. The nearest metro is Louvre.

Remember that you can buy stamps (*timbres*), with less queuing, from *tabacs* (tobacco shops). Standard letters (20 grams or less) and postcards within France and to E.U. countries (including the U.K. and Ireland), cost 0.50€. To the U.S. the cost is 0.90€.

Using a Cellphone   The three letters that define much of the world's wireless capabilities are **GSM** (Global System for Mobiles), a big, seamless network that makes for easy cross-border cellphone use throughout the world. In the U.S., T-Mobile and Cingular use this system. All Europeans use it, too.

If your phone is on a multi-band GSM system, you can make and receive calls in France. Just call your wireless operator and ask for "international roaming." Unfortunately, per-minute charges can be high—usually $1 to $1.50 per minute. Another option is to rent a phone before you leave from **InTouchUSA.com** (✆ **703/222-7161**) or **CellularAbroad.com** (✆ **800/287-5072**). You can also buy an "unlocked" world phone before your trip. This allows you to install a cheap, pre-paid SIM card (found at local retailers).

Phone Calls   To call the U.S. from France, using your **AT&T** calling card, dial ✆ 0800 99 00 11. An English-language voice will ask you for the number you are calling. The number for **Sprint** is ✆ **0-800/99-0087**. **Bell Canada** is ✆ **0-800/99-0016** or **0-800/99-0216**.

COMMUNICATIONS

To call France from the U.S. or Canada, dial the international access code (011), plus the country code (33), then the local number minus the 0.

To make a **direct international call** from France to the U.S. or Canada, dial the international code (00), then the country code (1), the area code, and the local number.

To make a **local or long distance call in France**, dial the 10-digit number, including the area code.

For **directory assistance** in French, dial ☎ **12**. For English, dial ☎ **0-800/364-775**. For an international operator in English, dial ☎ **0 33** plus the country code (☎ **0011** for the U.S. and Canada).

Useful Phone Numbers in France

- **Medical Emergencies** ☎ 15
- **Police** ☎ 17
- **Fire** ☎ 18
- **Poison Control Center** ☎ 01-40-05-48-48
- **SOS Help** (English-language crisis line) ☎ 01 46 21 46 46
- **Directory Assistance** (French) ☎ 12
- **Directory Assistance** (English) ☎ 0-800/364-775
- **Collect Calls to the U.S.** ☎ 00 1

World Time Zones   France is 6 hours later than the East Coast of the U.S., 9 hours later than Los Angeles, and 1 hour behind the U.K. Thus when it's noon in Paris, it's 6am in New York, 3am in L.A., and 11am in London.

Note that the French use the 24-hour clock; 10am is 10h, while 10pm is 22h.

CHAPTER SEVEN

CULTURE

CINEMA

Is there a movie theater nearby?	**Y a-t-il un cinéma près d'ici?** *yah-teel uh~ see-nay-mah pray dee-see*
Would you please tell me what's playing tonight?	**Pouvez-vous me dire quels films passent ce soir?** *poo-vay-voo muh deer kehl feelm pahs suh swahr*
Is that in English or French?	**Est-ce un film en français ou en anglais?** *ehs uh~ feelm aw~ fraw~-say oo aw~-naw~-glay*
Are there English subtitles?	**Y a-t-il des soustitres en anglais?** *yah-teel day soo-tee-truh aw~-naw~-glay*
Is the theater air conditioned?	**La salle est-elle climatisée?** *lah sahl ey-tehl klee-mah-tee-zay*
How much is a ticket?	**Combien coûte un billet?** *koh~-bee-yeh~ koo-tuh~ bee-yay*
Do you have a discount for ____	**Offrez-vous une réduction aux ____** *oh-fray-voo-zoon ray-duek-see-yoh~-noh*
seniors?	**personnes âgées?** *payhr-suh-nah-zhay*
students?	**étudiants?** *zay-tue-dee-yaw~*
children?	**enfants?** *zaw~-faw~*

CULTURE

175

What time is the next showing?	**À quelle heure commence la prochaine séance?** *ah keh-loehr koh~-maw~s lah proh-shen say-aw~s*
How long is the movie?	**Combien de temps dure ce film?** *koh~-bee-yeh~ duh taw~ duehr suh feelm*
May I buy tickets in advance?	**Puis-je acheter des billets à l'avance?** *pwee-zhuh ahsh-tay day bee-yay ah lah-vaw~s*
Is it sold out?	**C'est complet?** *say koh~-play*
When does it begin?	**Quand commence-t-il?** *kaw~ koh-maw~-steel*

PERFORMANCES

Do you have ballroom dancing?	**Y a-t-il de la danse de salon ici?** *yah-teel duh lah daw~s duh sah-loh~-nee-see*
Are there any plays showing right now?	**Quelle pièce avez-vous en ce moment?** *kehl pee-yehs ah-vay-voo-zaw~ suh moh~-maw~*
Is there a dinner theater?	**Y a-t-il une salle de dîner théâtre?** *yah-teel oon sahl duh dee-nay tay-ah-truh*
Where can I buy tickets?	**Où achete-t-on des billets?** *oo ah-sheh-toh~ day bee-yay*
Do you offer a student discount?	**Offrez-vous un tarif réduit aux étudiants?** *oh-fray-voo-zuh~ tah-reef ray-dwee oh-zay-tue-dee-yaw~*

Listen Up: Box Office Lingo

Quel film désirez-vous voir?
kehl feelm day-zee-ray-voo vwahr
What would you like to see?

Combien de personnes?
koh~-bee-yeh~ duh payhr-suhn
How many?

Deux adultes?
doeh-zah-duelt
For two adults?

Avec du beurre? Du sel?
ah-vek due boehr; due sehl
With butter? Salt?

Désirez-vous autre chose?
day-zee-ray-voo-zoh-truh shohz
Would you like anything else?

I need ____ seats.	**J'ai besoin de places ____** *zhay buh-zweh~ duh plahs*
aisle	**côté couloir.** *koh-tay kool-wahr*
orchestra	**parterre.** *pahr-tayhr*
What time does the play start?	**À quelle heure la pièce commence-t-elle?** *ah keh-loehr lah pee-yes koh~-maw~-s-tehl*
Is there an intermission?	**Y a-t-il un entracte?** *yah-teel uh~-naw~-trahkt*
Is there an opera house?	**Y a-t-il une salle d'opéra?** *yah-teel oon sahl doh-pay-rah*

Is there a local symphony?	**Y a-t-il un orchestre philharmonique local?**
	yah-teel uh~-nohr-keh-struh fee-lahr-moh~-neek loh-kahl
May I purchase tickets over the phone?	**Puis-je acheter des billets par téléphone?**
	pwee-zhuh ahsh-tay day bee-yay pahr tay-lay-fohn
What time is the box office open?	**À quelle heure le bureau de location ouvre-t-il?**
	ah keh-loehr luh bueh-roh duh loh-kah-see-yoh~ oo-vruh-teel
I need space for a wheelchair.	**J'ai besoin de suffisamment d'espace pour une chaise roulante.**
	zhay buh-zweh~ duh sue-fee-zah-maw~ day-spahs poohr oon shez roo-law~t
Do you have private boxes available?	**Avez-vous des loges privés de libres?**
	ah-vay-voo day lohzh pree-vay duh lee-bruh
I'd like a program, please.	**Je voudrais un programme, s'il vous plaît.**
	zhuh voo-dray uh~ proh-grahm seel voo play
Could you please show us our seats?	**Pouvez-vous nous montrer où sont nos places?**
	poo-vay-voo noo moh~-tray oo soh~ noh plahs

MUSEUMS, GALLERIES & SIGHTS

Do you have a museum guide?	**Avez-vous un guide des musées de la ville?** *ah-vay-voo-zuh~ geed day mue-zay duh lah veel*
Do you have guided tours?	**Offrez-vous des excursions?** *oh-fray-voo day-zhek-skuehr-see-yoh~*
What are the museum hours?	**Quelles sont les heures d'ouverture de ce musée?** *kehl soh~ lay-zoehr doo-vayhr-tuehr duh suh mue-zay*
Do I need to make an appointment?	**Ai-je besoin de m'inscrire à l'avance?** *ay-zhuh buh-zweh~ duh meh~-skreer ah lah-vaw~s*
Is there an admission fee?	**L'entrée est-elle payante?** *law~-tray ey-tehl pay-aw~t*
Do you offer _____	**Offrez-vous _____** *oh-fray-voo*
student discounts?	**des tarifs réduit aux étudiants?** *day tah-reef ray-dwee oh-zay-tue-dee-yaw~*
senior discounts?	**des tarifs réduits aux personnes âgées?** *day tah-reef ray-dwee oh payhr-suh-nah-zhay*
services for the hearing impaired?	**des services pour malentendants?** *day sayhr-vees poohr mah-law~-taw~-daw~*
audio tours in English?	**une visite audioguidée en anglais?** *oon vee-zeet oh-toh-gee-day aw~-naw~-glay*

FROMMER'S FAVORITE FRENCH MOMENTS

- Enjoying a picnic on the **Pont des Artes,** in Paris, at sunset. Position yourself over the Seine and watch the world stroll by. It's a religious experience.

- Spending an hour beneath the stained glass windows of **Chartres Cathedral** (1194–1260), less than an hour by train from Paris's Gare Montparnasse station, and experiencing medieval architecture at its height. This was the first cathedral to use flying buttresses, which support the walls, making it possible to create soaring spaces, with more glass and light.

- Basking in the soft, magical light of **Provence** and the **Riviera** as you drive through lavender fields, stopping for lunch in medieval villages overlooking the vineyards, and visiting some of France's greatest modern art museums. Highlights are *Aix-en-Provence* (Cezanne's studio), *Biot* (the Léger Museum), *Cagnes-sur-Mer* (the Museum of Modern Mediterranean Art), *Cap d'Antibes* (the Picasso Museum), *La Napoule* (the Henry Clews Museum), and *Menton* (the Cocteau Museum).

- Offering your oiled body to the sun on the beaches of **St. Tropez.** The real miracle is that the charm of this place manages to survive the hype and the hordes of visitors—particularly in the early morning light.

- Sampling local wines at a family-run restaurant in **Burgundy.** Castles rise from the vineyards and medieval churches mark the land of the good life for those who savor fine cuisine and wine in historic settings. Our favorite towns: the ancient capital of Dijon, Alsi Auxerre, Vézelay, Autun, and Beaune.

- Scouring the **Musée du Louvre** for your favorite master pieces. The Mona Lisa and the Venus de Milo are the museum's greatest draws, but the Louvre holds other works equally worthy of your attention.

- Savoring the art of **French cuisine.** The food here is as sensual as it is cerebral.

- Skiing in the **French Alps** and stopping for lunch at a mountain chalet on your way down the slopes. Our favorite ski resorts are Chamonix, Courcheval, and Megève.

- Exploring the **Loire Valley** and its *châteaux*, particularly by bike. Getting a feel for the ancien regime through the stunning Renaissance homes and palaces throughout the region. Not to miss: Chambord, Chenonceau, and Azay-le-Rideau.

- Visiting the *château de* **Versailles,** a 40-minute train ride from Paris, and wandering through the 233-foot Hall of Mirrors, the Grans Appartements, and the gardens. The most spectacular palace in the world was built by an army of laborers (as many as 45,000) and flaunts the spoils of a vanished era. Louis XIV sought to build a palace that would be the envy of Europe and created a symbol of opulence copied but never duplicated.

- Shopping—or window shopping—on Paris's right bank on **rue du Faubourg St-Honoré** and its extension, **rue St-Honoré.** The most glamorous shops are along these streets, stretching between the Palais Royal to the east and the Palais de l'Elysée to the west.

- Pay tribute to the fallen heroes on **Normandy**'s D-Day beaches. On June 6, 1944, the largest armada ever assembled departed on rough seas and in a dense fog from England. For about a week, the future of the western world hung in a bloody and brutal balance between the Nazi and Allied armies. Today you'll find only the sands and wind-torn, green-gray seas of a rather chilly beach. But you can

CULTURE

picture the struggles of determined soldiers who paid a terrible price to establish a beachhead on the continent.

- Biking through the **Dordogne** region. The rivers meander through countryside that's among the most verdant and historic in France. This is where wealthy, sophisticated Parisians buy and restore their second homes, made from ancient stone. The area is underpopulated but dotted with monuments, *châteaux*, medieval villages, and venerable churches.

The SNCF makes it easy to transport bikes on the nation's railways, but you can rent bikes in almost every sizeable town. You'll never go wrong if your route parallels the riverbanks of the Lot, the Vézere, the Dordogne, or any of their tributaries. Canoe trips on the Dordogne are equally memorable. Try to get to Salat on market day, and to reserve tickets far in advance for the prehistoric caves of Les Eyzies-de-Tayac. Falling asleep at the small deluxe hotel Le Vieux Logis (www.vieux-logis.com) in the village of Trémolet is as close to heaven as it gets.

For bike trips, try www.backroads.com, www.butterfield.com, and www.abercrombiekent.com.

THE MOST CHARMING VILLAGES

France actually has an Association of the Most Beautiful Villages in France. The 146 villages on the list share features such as location in the countryside, relative isolation from the mainstream tourist scene, and preservation of a traditional way of life. We've picked some of our favorites. For a complete list, log on to www.cometofrance.com/PBVF.html.

Gordes in Provence This is a candidate for *le plus beau village de France*. The perfect harmony of facades and terraced gardens has seduced artists and Parisians for decades. Houses covered in golden stone rise to a massive Renaissance château perched on top of this stunning village.

Riquewihr in Alsace   A perfect blend of quality wines and traditional architecture make Riquewihr the jewel of the Alsatian vineyard trail. Behind walls enveloped in vines is a world of architectural beauty, with lovingly maintained Gothic and Renaissance houses adorned with carved balconies and doors. A visit will transport you back in time.

Vézelay in Burgundy   Once believed to contain the tomb of Mary Magdalene, this small medieval town was one of the greatest pilgrimage sites of the Christian world. Nowadays, Vézelay's ancient charm is well-known throughout Europe, so avoid the summer crowds. The ramparts and gates have been preserved. The main street, bordered by historic homes, leads to the Basilica of Saint Magdalen, a masterpiece of Romanesque art.

Montrésor in Centre   Often overshadowed by its lofty neighbor Château de Chenonceau, Montrésor is a pleasant stop on any car or bike tour of the Loire Valley. In the 11th century, the count of Anjou built a fortress to block entrance to the Tours plateau. The fortress is now a private residence with breathtaking works of art on public view, including paintings by Raphael and Caravaggio. The doors of the château open on summer evenings for a village-wide medieval fete.

La Roque-Gageac in Perigord   Wedged between the Dordogne River and high cliffs, La Roque's ancient manors and fairy-tale castle never cease to charm. Many of the Renaissance homes are built directly into the cliff that looms above.

Coaraze on the French Riviera   Coaraze is one of the prettiest medieval mountaintop villages in France, only a half-hour from the sea. You'll want to explore the narrow, winding cobblestone streets, shaded by olive trees, sit in sunny squares bursting with color, and enjoy stunning views of the valley far below. The 13th-century church is an extra treat.

CULTURE

CHAPTER EIGHT

SHOPPING

This chapter covers the phrases you'll need for shopping in a variety of settings: from the mall to the town square artisan market. We also throw in the terminology you'll need to visit the barber or hairdresser.

For coverage of food and grocery shopping, see Chapter 4, Dining.

GENERAL SHOPPING TERMS

Would you please tell me _____	**S'il vous plaît, pouvez-vous m'indiquer _____** *seel voo play poo-vay-voo meh~-dee-kay*
how to get to a mall?	**comment aller au centre commercial le plus près?** *koh~-maw~-tah-lay oh saw~-truh koh~-mayhr-see-yahl luh plue pray*
the best place for shopping?	**le meilleur endroit pour faire des courses?** *luh may-yoehr aw~-dhwah poohr fayhr day koohrs*
how to get downtown?	**comment aller au centre-ville?** *koh~-maw~-tah-lay oh saw~-truh veel*
Where can I find a _____	**Où puis-je trouver _____** *oo pwee-zhuh troo-vay*
shoe store?	**un magasin qui vende des chaussures?** *uh~ mah-gah-zeh~ kee vaw~-d day shoh-suehr*
clothing store?	**un magasin qui vende des vêtements?** *uh~ mah-gah-zeh~ kee vaw~-d day veht-maw~*

184

designer fashion boutique?	**une boutique haute couture?** *oon boo-teek oht koo-tuehr*
vintage clothing store?	**une friperie?** *oon fhree-pay-ree*
jewelry store?	**une bijouxterie?** *oon bee-zhoo-tree*
bookstore?	**une librairie?** *oon lee-bray-ree*
toy store?	**un magasin des jouets?** *uh~ mah-gah-zeh~ day zhoo-ay*
stationery store?	**une papeterie?** *oon pah-pay-tree*
cigar store / tobacco shop?	**un magasin qui vende des cigares / un tabac?** *uh~ mah-gah-zeh~ kee vaw~d day day see-gahr / uh~ tah-bahk*
antique shop?	**un antiquaire?** *uh~-naw~-tee-kwayhr*
souvenir shop?	**un magasin qui vende des souvenirs?** *uh~ mah-gah-zeh~ kee vaw~d day soov-neer*
flca market?	**un marché à puces?** *uh~ mahr-shay ah pues*

CLOTHES SHOPPING

'd like to buy _____	**Je voudrais acheter _____** *zhuh voo-dray ahsh-tay*
some men's shirts.	**des chemises pour homme.** *day shmeez pooh-ruhm*
some women's shoes.	**des chaussures pour femme.** *day shoh-suehr poohr fahm*
some children's clothes.	**des vêtements pour enfant.** *day veht-maw~ pooh-raw~-faw~*
some toys for my kids.	**des jouets pour mes enfants.** *day zhoo-ay poohr may-zaw~-faw~*

les boucles d'oreille
le collier
la robe
la montre

la chemise
la cravate
le veston
la ceinture
le pantalon
les chaussures

| I'm looking for a size ____ | **Je cherche une taille ____** |
| | *zhuh shayhrsh oon tie* |

For a full list of numbers, see p7.

small.	**petit.**
	puh-tee
medium.	**moyen.**
	mwah-yeh~
large.	**large.**
	lahrzh
extra-large.	**extra-large.**
	ehk-strah-lahrzh
I'm looking for ____	**Je suis à la recherche ____**
	zhuh sweez ah lah ruh-shayhrsh
a silk blouse.	**d'un chemisier en soie.**
	duh~ shmee-zee-yay aw~ swah
cotton pants.	**d'une paire de pantalons en coton.**
	doon payhr duh paw~-tah-loh~- naw~ koh-toh~

les lunettes

le tee-shirt

le jean

les chaussures de tennis

a hat.	**d'un chapeau.**
	duh~ shah-poh
sunglasses.	**de lunettes de soleil.**
	duh lue-neht duh soh-lay
some underwear.	**de sous-vêtements.**
	duh soo veht-maw~
socks.	**de chausettes.**
	duh shoh-seht
a sweater.	**d'un pull.**
	duh~ puehl
a swimsuit.	**d'un maillot de bain.**
	duh~ mie-yoh duh beh~
a coat.	**d'un manteau.**
	duh~ maw~-toh
May I try it on?	**Puis-je l'essayer?**
	pwee-zhuh leh-say-yay
Do you have fitting rooms?	**Avez-vous des cabines d'essayage?**
	ah-vay-voo day kah-been deh-say-yazh

This is ____	**C'est ____**
	say
too tight.	**trop étroit.**
	troh ay-twah
too loose.	**trop flou.**
	troh floo
too long.	**trop long.**
	troh loh~g
too short.	**trop court.**
	troh koohr
This fits great!	**C'est parfait comme taille!**
	say pahr-fay kohm tie
Thanks, I'll take it.	**Merci, je le *m* / la *f* prends.**
	mayhrsee zhuh luh / lah praw~
Do you have that ____	**Est-ce que vous avez cet article**
	____
	ehs kuh voo-zah-vay seh-tahr-tee-kluh
in a smaller / larger size?	**dans une taille plus petite / grande?**
	daw~-zoon tie plue puh-teet / graw~d
in a different color?	**dans une autre couleur?**
	daw~-zoo-noh-truh koo-loehr
How much is it?	**Ça coûte combien?**
	sah koot koh~-bee-yeh~

ARTISAN MARKET SHOPPING

Is there a craft / artisans market?	**Y a-t-il un marché d'artisans?**
	yah-teel uh~ mahr-shay dahr-tee-zaw~
That's beautiful. May I take a look at it?	**C'est très beau. Puis-je le regarder de plus près?**
	say tray boh; pwee-zhuh luh ruh-gahr-day duh plue pray

When is the farmers' market open?	**Quelles sont les heures d'ouverture du marché de producteurs?** *kehl soh~ lay-zoehr doo-vayhr-tuehr due mahr-shay duh proh-duek-toehr*
Is that open every day of the week?	**Est-il ouvert tous les jours de la semaine?** *ey-teel oo-vayhr too lay zhoohr duh lah smehn*
How much does that cost?	**Combien est-ce que cela coûte?** *koh~-bee-yeh~ ehs kuh suh-lah koot*
Oh, that's too expensive!	**Oh là, c'est trop cher m / chère f!** *oh lah say troh shayhr*
How much for both?	**Combien coûte tous les deux?** *koh~-bee-yeh~ koot too lay doeh*
Is there a cash discount?	**Y a-t-il un escompte de caisse?** *yah-teel uh~-nuh-skoh~t duh kehs*
No thanks. Maybe I'll come back.	**Non, merci. Peut-être je reviens.** *noh~ mayhr-see; poeh-teh-truh zhuh ruh-vee-yeh~*
Would you take €_____?	**Accepteriez-vous _____ euros?** *ahk-sehp-tay-ree-yay-voo _____ oeh-roh*

For a full list of numbers, see p7.

Okay, it's a deal. I'll take it / them!	**D'accord. Je le m / la f / les pl prends!** *dah-kohr; zhuh luh / lah / lay praw~*
Do you have a less expensive one?	**Est-ce que vous en avez moins cher m / chère f?** *ehs kuh voo-zaw~-nah-vay mweh~ shayhr*
Is tax included?	**La taxe est-elle comprise?** *lah tahks ey-tehl koh~-preez*
May I have a VAT form?	**Puis-je avoir un formulaire TVA?** *pwee-zhuh ah-vwahr uh~ fohr-mue-layhr tay-vay-ah*

BOOKSTORE / NEWSSTAND SHOPPING

Is there a bookstore / newsstand nearby?	**Y a-t-il un libraire / kiosque à journaux près d'ici?** *yah-teel uh~ lee-brayhr / kee-ohsk ah zhoohr-noh pray dee-see*
Do you have _____	**Avez-vous _____** *ah-vay-voo*
books in English?	**des livres en anglais?** *day lee-vruh-zaw~-naw~-glay*
current newspapers?	**des journaux récents?** *day zhoohr-noh ray-saw~*
international newspapers?	**des journaux internationaux?** *day zhoohr-noh eh~-tayhr-nah-see-yoh~-noh*
magazines?	**des magazines?** *day mah-gah-zeen*
books about local history?	**des livres sur l'histoire de cette région?** *day lee-vruh suehr lees-twahr duh seht ray-zhee-yoh~*
picture books?	**des livres d'image?** *day lee-vruh dee-mahzh*

SHOPPING FOR ELECTRONICS

With some exceptions, shopping for electronic goods in France is generally not recommended. Many DVDs, CDs, and other products contain different signal coding than what is used in the United States and Canada to help deter piracy. Radios are probably the biggest exception, though, and lots of U.S. market goods are available.

Can I play this in the United States?	**Est-ce que cela va marcher aux États-Unis?** *ehs kuh suh-lah vah mahr-shay oh zay-tah-zue-nee*

Will this game work on my game console in the United States?

Est-ce que ce jeu va marcher sur ma console de jeu aux États-Unis?
ehs kuh suh zhoeh vah mahr-shay suehr mah koh~-sohl duh zhoeh oh-zay-tah-zue-nee

Do you have this in a U.S. market format?

Avez-vous cela en format américain?
ah-vay-voo suh-lah aw~ fohr-mah ah-may-ree-keh~

Can you convert this to a U.S. market format?

Pouvez-vous convertir cela au format américain?
poo-vay-voo koh~-vayhr-teer suh-lah oh fohr-mah ah-may-ree-keh~

Will this work with a 110 VAC adapter?

Est-ce que cela va marcher avec un adaptateur 110 VCA?
ehs kuh suh-lah vah mahr-shay ah-vek uh~-nah-dahp-toehr saw~-dees vay-say-ah

Do you have an adapter plug for 110 to 220?

Est-ce que vous avez un adaptateur 110 à 220?
ehs kuh voo-zah-vay-zuh~-nah-dahp-toehr saw~-dee-zah saw~-veh~

Do you sell electronics adapters here?

Est-ce que vous vendez des adaptateurs pour appareils électroniques?
ehs kuh voo vaw~-day day-zah-dahp-toehr poohr ah-pah-ray ay-lehk-troh-neek

Is it safe to use my laptop with this adapter?

Est-ce sans risque d'utiliser mon ordinateur portable avec cet adaptateur?
ehs saw~ reesk due-tee-lee-zay moh~-nohr-dee-nah-toehr pohr-tah-bluh ah-vek seh-tah-dahp-toehr

If it doesn't work, may I return it?	**Si cela ne marche pas, puis-je le ramener?**
	see suh-lah nuh mahrsh pah pwee-zhuh luh rah-mnay
May I try it here in the store?	**Puis-je l'essayer ici, dans le magasin?**
	pwee-zhuh leh-say-ay ee-see daw~ luh mah-gah-zeh~

AT THE BARBER / HAIRDRESSER

Do you have a style guide?	**Avez-vous des photos avec les différents styles?**
	ah-vay-voo day foh-toh ah-vek lay dee-fay-raw~ steel
I'd like a trim.	**Je voudrais une coupe.**
	zhuh voo-dray-zoon koop
I'd like it bleached.	**Je voudrais une couleur.**
	zhuh voo-dray-zoon koo-loehr
Would you change the color?	**Pouvez-vous changer ma couleur?**
	poo-vay-voo shaw~-zhay mah koo-loehr
I'd like it darker.	**Je la voudrais plus foncée.**
	zhuh lah voo-dray plue foh~-say
I'd like it lighter.	**Je la voudrais plus claire.**
	zhuh lah voo-dray plue klayhr
Would you just touch it up a little?	**Pouvez-vous faire une simple retouche?**
	poo-vay-voo fayhr oon seh~-pluh ruh-toosh
I'd like it curled.	**Je voudrais une mise en plis.**
	zhuh voo-dray-zoon mee-zaw~ plee
Do I need an appointment?	**Ai-je besoin d'un rendez-vous?**
	ay-zhuh buh-zweh~ duh~ raw~-day-voo

Wash, dry, and set.	**Je voudrais un shampooing et un brushing, s'il vous plaît.**
	zhuh voo-dray uh~ shaw~-poo-een ay uh~ bruh-sheen seel voo play
Do you do perms?	**Faites-vous des permanentes?**
	feht-voo day payhr-maw~-naw~t
Please use low heat.	**Vérifiez que le séchoir ne soit pas trop chaud, s'il vous plaît.**
	vay-ree-fee-yay kuh luh say-shwahr nuh swah pah troh shoh seel voo play
Please don't blow dry it.	**Pas de brushing, s'il vous plaît.**
	pah duh bruh-sheen seel voo play
Please dry it curly.	**Faites-les boucler, s'il vous plaît.**
	feht-lay boo-klay seel voo play
Please dry it straight.	**Lissez-les, s'il vous plaît.**
	lee-say lay seel voo play
Would you fix my braids?	**Pouvez-vous me refaire mes nattes?**
	poo-vay-voo muh ruh-fayhr may naht
Would you fix my highlights?	**Pouvez-vous me refaire mes mèches?**
	poo-vay-voo muh ruh-fayhr may mehsh
Do you wax?	**Est-ce que vous faites des épilations à la cire?**
	ehs kuh voo feht day-zay-pee-lah-see-yoh~ ah lah seer
Please wax my _____	**Épilez-moi _____ à la cire, s'il vous plaît.**
	ay-pee-lay mwah _____ ah lah seer seel voo play
legs.	**les jambes**
	lay zhahmb
bikini line.	**le maillot**
	luh mah-yoh

eyebrows.	**les sourcils** *lay soohr-seel*
under my nose.	**sous le nez** *soo luh nay*
Please trim my beard.	**Raccourcissez-moi un peu la barbe, s'il vous plaît.** *rah-koohr-see-say mwah uh~ poeh lah bahrb seel voo play*
May I have a shave, please?	**Puis-je me faire raser, s'il vous plaît?** *pwee-zhuh muh fayhr rah-zay seel voo play*
Use a fresh blade, please.	**Utilisez une lame neuve, s'il vous plaît.** *oo-tee-lee-zay oon lahm noehv seel voo play*
Sure, cut it all off.	**D'accord, coupez-la f / coupez-les pl complètement.** *dah-kohr koo-pay lah / les koh~ pleht-maw~*

UNDERSTANDING THE VAT

France has a VAT (value added tax) of 19.6%! When you purchase, in the same store on the same day, a minimum of 175€ worth of goods that you plan to export with you, you are eligible for a VAT rebate of 13%. Ask in the store for the VAT Détaxe form. You'll need to show your passport.

You can get your rebate either by applying for a refund on your credit card (a process that takes time), or by claiming a cash refund when you leave the country (a service that costs you a commission). When leaving France by plane, present your purchased items, the détaxe form, your passport, and boarding pass to the Customs official at the Détaxe Window. (Don't make the mistake of packing your items in checked luggage before détaxing your purchases.) You will then be directed to a window where you can get your refund in cash, minus the commission. When leaving France for another European Union country—if you go by train to the U.K. or Germany, for example—you cannot apply for the refund in France.

Foodstuffs   Don't try to bring unprocessed foods (fruits, vegetables, meats, and so on) back to the U.S. The Department of Agriculture has laws restricting their importation, and well-trained beagles are on hand to sniff out your favorite cheeses and *pâtés*.

Shipping   Shipping fees can double the cost of goods; you'll also pay U.S. duty on items that are valued for more than $50. The good news is that détaxe is automatically applied to any item shipped to a U.S. destination—no need to worry about the 175€ minimum on purchases bought in France and carried with you. Some stores, however, have a $100 minimum for shipping. You can also mail small packages home yourself from any post office (PT&T).

BEST BUYS

Beauty Products   Designer makeup at retail is likely to cost the same as it does in the U.S.—or even more. But if you spend at least 175€ at a **duty-free shop** (non-airport type), you can qualify for a VAT détaxe (you need to spend at least 175€) and see at least 15% melt off your bill. Paris offers the most duty-free stores, but any town with tourist business should have at least one. Ask your concierge for a perfumerie that participates in the détaxe program. Don't buy American brands, even at a duty-free shop—they're more expensive. Ask for free samples!

Crafts   Moustier Ste-Marie in Provence is known for a type of *faience* (earthenware) decorated with animals. You'll find tiles in the south; check out Salernes. L'Occitane, a Provençal brand, runs boutiques in Provence and Paris. You'll find **copper cooking pots** in northern France, especially in the Normandy village of Villedieu-les-Poêles, not far from Mont-St-Michel. Northeastern France, near Strasbourg, is the home of **Baccarat crystal**.

Fashion   You can find knockoffs everywhere in France in the two major dime-store chains **Monoprix** (owned by Galeries Lafayette) and Prisunic (owned by Au Printemps). Hérmes scarves tend to be cheaper outside of France.

Food   You can bring **cheeses** into the U.S. that have aged more than 90 days—that means hard, moldy cheeses, not soft, runny ones. Dijon mustard makes a great gift. You can buy **chocolates** at any market, but the best chocolatiers are in Paris or Lyon. You should consume handmade fresh chocolate within 3 days. The big outlets in Paris are La Maison du Chocolate and Christian Constant.

Kitchenware   Copper-lined casseroles and thick-walled roasters should last a lifetime once you recover from the shock of their prices. You can buy used copperware at almost any flea market.

In Paris, hit rue Montmartre in the second *arrondissement* (not in Montmartre) for a choice of kitchen and restaurant supplies.

Porcelain For delicate porcelains, head to Limoges, where factory shops sell local wares and a few seconds. Shops are closed from noon to 2pm. In Limoges, head for Bernardaud and Reynaud. In Paris, head for rue de Paradis, where you'll find suppliers from all the big French factories. If you can carry a piece with you, rather than shipping it, you may save 20% to 25%.

CLOTHING SIZES

The website **www.onlineconversion.com** will help you make conversions for shoes, clothing, rings, etc. Keep in mind that in France, half sizes are rarely used.

Children's Shoes

US	French
3½	18
4½	19
5½	20
6½	21
7	22
7½–8	23
8½	24
9	25
9½–10	26
10½–11	27
11½	28
12–12½	29
13	30
13½-1	31
1½	32
2–2½	33
3–3½	34

Women's Shoes

US	French
3½	35
4½	36
5–5½	37
6–6½	38
7–7½	39
8	40
8½	41
9–9½	42
12½–13	47

Men's Pants (waist)

US (in)	France (cm)
30	76
32	81
34	86
36	91
38	97
40	102

Men's Shoes

US	French
7	39
7½	40
8	41
8½–9	42
9½–10	43
10½	44
11–11½	45
12	46

Men's Socks

US	France
9½	39
10	40
10½	41
11	42
11½	43
12	44
12½	45

Women's Blouses & Sweaters

US	France
32	40
34	42
36	44
38	46
40	48
42	50
44	52

Womens' Dresses & Suits

US	France
6	34
8	36
10	38
12	40
14	42
16	44
18	46

Men's Shirts (collar)

US	France
14	36
14½	37
15	38
15½	39
16	40
16½	41
17	42

Men's Jackets

US	France
34	44
36	46
38	48
40	50
42	52
44	54
46	56

CHAPTER NINE
SPORTS & FITNESS

STAYING FIT

Is there a gymnasium nearby?
Y a-t-il un gymnase près d'ici?
yah-teel uh~ zheem-nahz prey dee-see

Do you have free weights?
Avez-vous des altères?
ah-vay-voo day-zahl-tayhr

I'd like to go for a swim.
Je voudrais aller nager.
zhuh voo-dray-zah-lay nah-zhay

Do I have to be a member?
L'entrée est-elle réservée aux membres?
law~-tray ey-tehl ray-zehr-vay oh maw~-bruh

May I come here for one day?
Puis-je entrer pour un séance à l'unité?
pwee-zhuh aw~-tray poohr uh~ say-aw~s ah lue-nee-tay

How much does a membership cost?
Combien coûte l'abonnement?
koh~-bee-yeh~ koot lah-buhn-maw~

I need to get a locker, please.	**Je voudrais un casier, s'il vous plaît.**
	zhuh voo-dray uh~ kahz-yay seel voo play
Do you have locks for those?	**Avez-vous des cadenas pour les casiers?**
	ah-vay-voo day kahd-nah poohr lay kahz-yay
Do you have a treadmill?	**Y a-t-il un tapis roulant ici?**
	yah-teel uh~ tah-pee roo-law~ ee-see
Do you have a stationary bike?	**Y a-t-il un vélo d'exercice?**
	yah-teel uh~ vaylo dehk-sayhr-sees
Do you have a handball / squash court?	**Avez-vous un terrain de jeu de hand-ball / squash?**
	ah-vay-voo-zuh~ tuh-reh~ duh zhoeh duh ahnd bahl / skwahsh
Are they indoors?	**Sont-ils couverts?**
	soh~-teel koo-vayhr
I'd like to play tennis.	**J'aime jouer au tennis.**
	zhehm zhoo-ay oh teh-nees
Would you like to play?	**Voulez-vous jouer avec moi?**
	voo-lay-voo zhoo-ay ah-vek mwah
I'd like to rent a racquet.	**Je voudrais louer une raquette.**
	zhuh voo-dray loo-ay oon rah-keht
I need to buy some new balls.	**Je voudrais acheter des balles neuves.**
	zhuh voo-dray ahsh-tay day bahl noehv
I lost my safety glasses.	**J'ai perdu mes lunettes protectrices.**
	zhay payhr-due may lue-neht proh-tehk-trees
May I rent a court for tomorrow?	**Puis-je louer un court pour demain?**
	pwee-zhuh loo-ay uh~ koohr poohr duh-meh~

Do you have clean towels? **Avez-vous des serviettes propres?**
ah-vay-voo day sayhr-vee-yeht proh-pruh

Where are the showers /
locker rooms? **Où sont les douches / vestiaires, s'il vous plaît?**
oo soh~ lay doosh / vehs-tee-yayhr seel voo play

Do you have a workout
room for women only? **Avez-vous une salle d'entraîne-ment réservée aux femmes?**
ah-vay-voo-zoon sahl daw~-treh~-maw~ ray-zehr-vay oh fahm

Do you have aerobics
classes? **Avez-vous des cours d'aérobic?**
ah-vay-voo day koohr dah-eyh-roh-beek

Do you have a women's
pool? **Avez-vous une piscine réservée aux femmes?**
ah-vay-voo-zoon pee-seen ray-sehr-vay oh fahm

Let's go for a jog. **Allons faire un jogging.**
ah-loh~ fayhr uh~ zhoh-gheeng

That was a great workout. **Je me suis bien entraîné(e).**
zhuh muh swee bee-yeh~ aw~-treh~-nay

CATCHING A GAME

Where is the stadium? **Où se trouve le stade?**
oo suh troov luh stahd

Who is the best goalie? **Qui est le meilleur gardien de but?**
kee ay luh may-yoehr gahr-dee-yeh~ duh bue

Is there a women's team? **Y a-t-il une équipe féminine?**
yah-teel oon ay-keep fay-mee-neen

Do you have any amateur / professional teams?	**Avez-vous des équipes amateurs / professionnelles?** *ah-vay-voo day-zay-keep ah-mah-toehr / proh-feh-see-yoh-nehl*
Is there a game I could play in?	**Y a-t-il un événement sportif auquel je pourrais participer?** *yah-teel uh~-nay-vay-nuh-maw~ spohr-teef oh-kehl zhuh pooh-ray pahr-tee-see-pay*
Which is the best team?	**Quelle est la meilleure équipe?** *keh-lay lah may-yoehr ay-keep*
Will the game be on television?	**Le match va-t-il passer à la télévision?** *luh mahtch vah-teel pah-say ah lah tay-lay-veez-yoh~*
Where can I buy tickets?	**Où puis-je acheter des places?** *oo pwee-zhuh ahsh-tay day plahs*
The best seats, please.	**Les meilleures places, s'il vous plaît.** *lay may-yoehrs plahs seel voo play*
The cheapest seats, please.	**Les places les moins chères, s'il vous plaît.** *lay plahs lay mweh~ shayhr seel voo play*

How close are these seats?	**Ces places sont-elles près du terrain?**
	say plahs soh~-tehl pray due tuh-reh~
May I have a private box?	**Puis-je avoir un box privé?**
	pwee-zhuh ah-vwahr uh~ bohks pree-vay
Wow! What a game!	**Quel match!**
	kehl mahtch
Go! Go! Go!	**On va gagner!** *repeat several times*
	oh~ vah gah-nyay
Oh no!	**Oh non!**
	oh noh~
Give it to them!	**Montrez leur!**
	moh~-tray loehr
Go for it!	**Vas-y!**
	vah-zee
Score!	**Marque un but!**
	mahrk uh~ bue
What's the score?	**Quel est le score?**
	keh-lay luh skohr
Who's winning?	**Qui est en train de gagner?**
	kee eh-taw~ treh~ duh gah-nyay

HIKING

Where can I find a guide to hiking trails?	**Où puis-je trouver un guide des randonnées régionales?**
	oo pwee-zhuh troo-vay uh~ gheed day raw~-doh~-nay ray-zhee-oh~-nahl
Do we need to hire a guide?	**Est-il nécessaire d'embaucher un guide?**
	ey-teel nay-suh-sayhr daw~-boh-shay uh~ gheed

Where can I rent equipment?	**Où puis-je louer du matériel d'escalade?** *oo pwee-zhuh loo-ay due mah-tayh-ree-yehl dehs-kah-lahd*
Do they have rock climbing there?	**Y a-t-il des endroits où on peut faire de la varappe?** *yah-teel day-zaw~-dhwah oo oh~ poeh fayhr duh lah vah-rahp*
We need to get more ropes and carabiners.	**Nous avons besoin de cordes et de mousquetons supplémentaires.** *noo-zah-voh~ buh-zweh~ duh kohrd ay duh moos-kuh-toh~ sue-play-maw~-tayhr*
Where can we go mountain climbing?	**Où est-il possible de faire de l'escalade?** *oo ey-teel poh-see-bluh duh fayhr duh lehs-kah-lahd*
Are the routes well marked?	**Les routes sont-elles bien signalisées?** *lay root soh~-tehl bee-yeh~ see-nyah-lee-zay*

Are the routes in good condition?	**Les chemins sont-ils en bon état?** _lay shuh-meh~ soh~-teel aw~ boh~-nay-tah_
What is the altitude there?	**Quelle est l'altitude là-bas?** _keh-lay lahl-tee-tued lah bah_
How long will it take?	**Combien de temps cela prendra-t-il?** _koh~-bee-yeh~ duh taw~ suh-lah praw~-drah-teel_
Is it very difficult?	**Est-ce très difficile?** _ehs tray dee-fee-seel_
I'd like a challenging climb, but I don't want to take oxygen.	**Je voudrais une escalade ambitieuse, mais je ne veux pas porter de l'oxygène.** _zhuh voo-dray oo-neh-skah-lahd aw~-bee-see-yoehz may zhuh nuh voeh pah pohr-tay duh lohk-see-zhehn_
I want to hire someone to carry my excess gear.	**Je voudrais embaucher quelqu'un qui puisse porter mon excédent de matériel.** _zhuh voo-dray aw~-boh-shay kehl-kuh~ kee pwees pohr-tay moh~-ehk-say-daw~ duh mah-tayh-ree-yehl_
We don't have time for a long route.	**Nous n'avons pas le temps de faire une longue sortie.** _noo nah-voh~ pah luh taw~ duh fayhr oon loh~g sohr-tee_
I don't think it's safe to proceed.	**Je ne pense pas qu'il soit prudent de continuer.** _zhuh nuh paw~s pah keel swah prue-daw~ duh koh~-tee-nue-ay_
Do we have a backup plan?	**Avons-nous un plan en cas de problème?** _ah-voh~-noo-zuh~ plaw~ aw~ kah duh proh-blehm_

If we're not back by tomorrow, send a search party.	**Si nous ne sommes pas revenus demain, envoyez quelqu'un à notre recherche.**
	see noo nuh sohm pah ruhv-noo duh-meh~ aw~vwah-yay kehl-kuh~ ah noh-truh ruh-shersh
Are the campsites marked?	**Les emplacements de camping sont-ils balisés?**
	layz aw~-plahs-maw~ duh kaw~-peeng soh~-teel bah-lee-zay
Can we camp off the trail?	**Est-il possible de camper en pleine nature?**
	ey-teel poh-see-bluh duh kaw~-pay aw~ plehn nah-tuehr
Is it okay to build fires here?	**A-t-on le droit de faire des feux de camp ici?**
	ah-toh~ luh dhwah duh fayhr day foeh duh kaw~ ee- see
Do we need permits?	**A-t-on besoin d'une autorisation?**
	ah-toh~ buh-zweh~ doon oh-toh-ree-zah-see-yoh~

For more camping terms, see p95.

BOATING OR FISHING

When do we sail?	**À quelle heure appareillons-nous?**
	ah keh-loehr ah-pah-ray-oh~-noo
Where are the life preservers / vests?	**Où sont les bouées / gilets de sauvetage?**
	oo soh~ lay boo-ay / zhee-lay duh sohv-tazh
Can I purchase bait?	**Puis-je acheter de l'appâts?**
	pwee-zhuh ahsh-tay duh lah-pah

Can I rent a pole?	**Puis-je louer une canne?**
	pwee-zhuh loo-ay oon kahn
How long is the voyage?	**Combien de temps dure la sortie?**
	koh~-bee-yeh~ duh taw~ duehr
	lah sohr-tee
Are we going up river or down?	**Remontons-nous ou**
	descendons-nous la rivière?
	ruh-moh~-toh~-noo oo duh-saw~-
	doh~-noo lah ree-vee-yayhr
How far out are we going?	**Jusqu'où allons-nous aller?**
	zhues-koo ah-loh~-noo-zah-lay
How fast are we going?	**On va à quelle vitesse?**
	oh~ vah ah kehl vee-tehs
How deep is the water here?	**Quelle est la profondeur de**
	l'eau ici?
	keh-lay lah proh-foh~-doehr duh
	loh ee-see
I got one!	**J'ai attrapé un poisson!**
	zhay ah-trah-pay uh~ pwah-soh~
I can't swim.	**Je ne sais pas nager.**
	zhuh nuh say pah nah-zhay
Can we go ashore?	**Pouvons-nous aller à terre?**
	poo-voh~-noo-zah-lay ah tayhr

For more boating terms, see p74.

DIVING

I'd like to go snorkeling.	**Je voudrais faire de la plongée**
	avec masque et tuba.
	zhuh voo-dray fayhr duh lah ploh~-
	zhay ah-vek mahsk ay tue-bah
I'd like to go scuba diving.	**Je voudrais faire de la plongée**
	sous-marine.
	zhuh voo-dray fayhr duh lah
	ploh~-zhay soo mah-reen

I have a NAUI / PADI certification.	**J'ai le brevet de plongeur NAUI / PADI.**
	zhay luh bruh-vay duh ploh~-zhoehr enn-ah-oo-ee / pay-ah-day-ee
I need to rent gear.	**Je voudrais louer du matériel de plongée.**
	zhuh voo-dray loo-ay due mah-tayh-ree-yehl duh ploh~-zhay
We'd like to see some shipwrecks if we can.	**Nous aimerions si possible voir des épaves.**
	noo-zeh-meh-ree-yoh~ see poh-see-bluh vwahr day-zay-pahv
Are there any good cave / reef dives?	**Y a-t-il des bonnes plongées aux grottes / récifs?**
	yah-teel day buhn ploh~-zhay oh groht / ray-seef
I'd like to see a lot of diverse sea-life.	**Je voudrais voir un milieu sous-marin diversifié.**
	zhuh voo-dray vwahr uh~ meel-yoeh soo-mah-reh~ dee-vayhr-see-fee-yay
Are the currents strong?	**Le courant est-il fort?**
	luh kooh-raw~ ey-teel fohr
How is the clarity?	**Les eaux sont-elles claires?**
	lay-zoh soh~-tehl klayhr
I want / don't want to go with a group.	**Je voudrais / je ne veux pas me joindre avec une groupe.**
	zhuh voo-dray / zhuh nuh voeh pah muh zhweh~-druh ah-vek oon groohp
Do we have to go with a group, or can we charter our own boat?	**Devons-nous nous joindre à un groupe, ou pouvons-nous louer notre propre bateau?**
	duh-voh~-noo noo zhweh~-druh ah uh~ groop oo poo-voh~-noo loo-ay noh-truh proh-pruh bah-toh

SURFING

I'd like to go surfing.	**Je voudrais aller faire du surf.** *zhuh voo-dray ah-lay fayhr due suehrf*
Are there any good beaches?	**Y a-t-il de bonnes plages à surf?** *yah-teel duh buhn plahzh ah suehrf*
Can I rent a board?	**Puis-je louer une planche?** *pwee-zhuh loo-ay oon plaw~sh*
How are the currents?	**Y a-t-il beaucoup de courant?** *yah-teel boh-koo duh koo-raw~*
How high are the waves?	**Les vagues sont de quelle hauteur?** *lay vahg soh~ duh kehl oh-toehr*
Is it usually crowded?	**Y a-t-il du monde d'habitude sur la plage?** *yah-teel due moh~d dah-bee-tued suehr lah plahzh*
Are there facilities on that beach?	**Y a-t-il des infrastructures sur la plage?** *yah-teel day-zeh~-frah-struek-tuehr suehr lah plahzh*
Is there wind surfing there also?	**Est-il possible de faire de la planche à voile?** *ey-teel poh-seeb-luh duh fayhr duh lah plaw~sh ah vwahl*

GOLFING

I'd like to reserve a tee-time, please.

Je voudrais réserver une heure de départ, s'il vous plaît.
zhuh voo-dray ray-zehr-vay oo-noehr duh day-pahr seel voo play

Do we need to be members to play your course?

Ce terrain de golf est-il réservé aux membres?
suh tuh-reh~ duh gohlf ey-teel ray-zehr-vay oh maw~-bruh

How many holes is your course?

C'est un golf à combien de trous?
seht uh~ gohlf ah koh~-bee-yeh~ duh troo

What is par for the course?

Combien est par pour ce terrain?
koh~-bee-yeh~ ay pahr poohr suh teh-reh~

I need to rent clubs.

J'ai besoin de louer des bâtons de golf.
zhay buh-zweh~ duh loo-ay day bah-toh~ duh gohlf

I need to purchase some balls.

J'ai besoin d'acheter des balles de golf.
zhay buh-zweh~ dahsh-tay day bahl duh gohlf

I need a glove.

J'ai besoin d'un gant.
zhay buh-zweh~ duh~ gaw~

I need a new hat.

J'ai besoin d'une nouvelle casquette.
zhay buh-zweh~ doon noo-vehl kahs-keht

Do you require soft spikes?	**Exigez-vous des crampons mous?** _ek-zee-zhay-voo day kraw~-poh~ moo_
Do you have carts?	**Avez-vous des voiturettes?** _ah-vay-voo day vwah-tueh-reht_
I'd like to hire a caddie.	**Je voudrais embaucher un cadet.** _zhuh voo-dray aw~-boh-shay uh~ kah-day_
Do you have a driving range?	**Avez-vous un terrain d'exercice?** _ah-vay-voo-zuh~ tuh-reh~ dayk-sayhr-sees_
How much are the greens fees?	**Combien coûte le droit d'entrée?** _koh~-bee-yeh~ koot luh dhwah daw~-tray_
Can I book a lesson with the pro?	**Puis-je prendre rendez-vous pour une leçon avec un professionnel?** _pwee-zhuh praw~-druh raw~-day-voo poohr oon leh-soh~ ah-vek uh~ proh-feh-see-yoh-nehl_
I need to have a club repaired.	**J'ai besoin de faire réparer l'un de mes bâtons.** _zhay buh-zweh~ duh fayhr ray-pah-ray luh~ duh may bah-toh~_
Is the course dry?	**L'herbe du golf est-elle sèche?** _layhrb due gohlf ey-tehl sehsh_
Are there any wildlife hazards?	**Est-ce qu'on risque de rencontrer des animaux sauvages?** _ehs koh~ reesk duh raw~-koh~-tray day-zah-nee-moh soh-vahzh_
How many total meters is the course?	**Quelle est la longueur totale du golf?** _keh-lay lah loh~-goehr toh-tahl due gohlf_
Is it very hilly?	**Le terrain est-il très onduleux?** _luh tuh-reh~-ney-teel tray-zoh~-due-loeh_

BEST SPORTS OUTFITTERS

Ballooning

The world's largest hot-air balloon operator is **Buddy Bombard's Private Europe** based in West Palm Beach, Florida (© 800/862-8537; www.bombardsociety.com). It maintains some three dozen balloons, some in the Loire Valley and Burgundy. The 5-day tours include all meals, wine tasting, and lodging in Relais & Chateaux properties. An alternative is **www.bonaventuraballoons.com** (© 800/FLY NAPA), which offers multi-day trips in Paris and Burgundy.

Barge Cruises

Gliding at a swan's pace along France's most beautiful, bucolic waterways sounds as sedentary as it gets. But the idea is not to let the world move gently around you, but to bike and hike during the day, and then return to your barge for food, wine, and sleep. Some of the best barge trips are run by **French Country Waterways, Ltd.,** based in Duxbury, Massachusetts (© 800/222-1236; www.fcwl.com). Their 1-week trips go to Burgundy and Champagne. Other outfitters include **Le Boat** (© 800/734-5491; www.leboat.com), **Go Barging** (© 800/394-8630; www.gobarging.com), and **Abercrombie & Kent** (© 800/554-7016; www.abercrombiekent.com).

Biking

The **Dordogne**, **Provence**, the **Loire Valley**—these are only some of France's top regions for biking. Keep in mind that if you bike, you don't have to rough it; you can cycle from one deluxe hotel to another, and dine on gourmet food without a twinge of guilt. Most outfitters provide maps and let you go at your own pace, so you can be as social or solitary as you want, and go at your desired speed. You can join an escorted group or ask your outfitter to customize a trip just for you and your family or friends. On some trips, your bags are carried ahead and waiting for you at your lodging at the end of the day.

Among the top outfitters are **Bike Riders** (© 800/462-2848; www.bikeriderstours.com), **Blue Marble Travel** (© 201/465-2567; www.bluemarble.org), **Mountain Travel Sobek** (© 888/831-7526; www.mtsobek.com), **Butterfield & Robinson** (© 866/551-9090, www.butterfield.com), **Backroads** (© 800/462-2848; www.backroads.com), **Classic Adventures** (© 800/777-8090; www.classicadventures.com), and **Euro-Bike & Walking Tours** (© 800/575-1540; www.eurobike.com).

One of our favorite bike rides is along **La Route du Vin** (the Wine Road) in Alsace-Lorraine, between Strasbourg and Colmar. You can rent bikes from the **Association Velo Emploi** (© 03 88 24 05 61). The Strasbourg Tourist Office has free bike maps with routes that fan out from the city, with emphasis on cycle lanes that prohibit cars. Take the 17-mile stretch that runs southwest from Strasbourg to the wine hamlet of Molsheim.

Skiing

If you want someone else to handle all the arrangements, try **World on Skis** (© 866/678-5858; www.worldonskis.com) or www.cometoski.com, based in Paris. Where should you go? **Courchevel** (www.courchevel.com) is a resort of high taste, fashion, and profile, a chic spot where luxurious chalets sit on pristine slopes. Skiers know it as part of Les Trois Vallées sometimes called "the skiing supermarket of France." There are 93 miles of ski runs and 375 of trails in Les Trois Vallées. **Courchevel 1850** is the area to go if you can afford it. **Megève** (www.megeve.com) has 190 miles of downhill runs and nearly 0 miles of cross-country trails. **Chamonix** (www.chamonix.com) is the historic capital of French skiing and the resort to choose if you're not a millionaire. A charming, old-fashioned mountain town, Chamonix is set against the breathtaking backdrop of Mont Blanc. Our fourth choice, **Val d'Isère** (www.valdisere.com), is less snobby than Courchevel and less old-fashioned than Megève. It's younger, brasher, with shorter lines.

Walking

There's no better way to experience France than on foot. Many outfitters organize walks, or help you customize your own. As with biking, there's no reason to rough it; you can walk from one historic hotel to another, and pamper yourself with hot baths and gourmet food. Most of the outfitters listed under biking (above) also organize walking trips. You can also try **Discover France** (© 800/960-2221; www.discoverfrance. com) and **Country Walkers** (© 800/464-9255; www. countrywalkers.com).

Hiking & Biking in the Fontainebleau

The **Forest of Fontainebleau** is riddled with *sentiers* (hiking trails) created by French kings and their entourages while they were hunting in the woods. A *Guide des Sentiers* is available at the tourist information center, opposite the main entrance to the chateau. Bike paths also cut through the forest. You can rent bikes at the Fontainebleau-Avon rail depot. At the station, go to the kiosk, **Location Mulot** (© 01-64-22 36-14). Bikes cost less than $20 for a half-day. *The kiosk is open weekdays 9:30am–6pm, Saturday and Sunday 10am–7pm. The train ride from the Gare de Lyon in Paris takes 45 minutes each way.*

SPECTATOR SPORTS

Football (Soccer)

France hosted and won the World Cup in soccer in 2000, which for some marked a high-point for contemporary France. Led by French president Jacques Chirac in the impressive

Stade de France stands, the country sang "We Are the Champions" as the world watched a triumphant multi-cultural France led by Algerian superstar halfback Zinedine Zidane. Football enthusiasm continues, although the French team has lost its luster. For tickets for matches at the 80,000-seat Stade de France go to **www.stadedefrance.fr**. The Paris team Paris Saint-Germain (PSG) plays at the Parc des Princes. Tickets can be purchased online at **www.psg.francebillet. com/index.do**.

Horseracing

Prix du Jockey Club and **Prix Diane-Hèrmes** take place in June in the Hippodrome de Chantilly. Thoroughbreds from as far away as Brunei and Kentucky compete in these world-famous races. Contact **www.chantilly-tourisme.com** for details. **Prix de l'Arc de Triomphe**, Hippodrome de Longchamp, Paris, is France's answer to Ascot each October. Contact **www.france-galop.com**.

Tennis

France's most celebrated tennis event, **The French Open**, is better known as **Roland Garros**, the name of the site where the classy tennis event takes place every May. Many still recall the exhilaration of watching France's most exciting player, Yannick Noah, back in 1983. Kids are let in free on the first day of the tournament—a Wednesday, when French children do not have school. To get tickets to Roland Garros, you can try your luck at: **www.fft.fr/rolandgarros/en/billetsMaq.html**. The FNAC store (www.fnac.com) and Virgin (www.virginmega.fr) also sell tickets (as well as for concerts and other cultural events). Also try the California-based company, **Advantage Tennis Tours** (© 800/341-8687; www.advantagetennis tours.com).

CHAPTER TEN

NIGHTLIFE

For coverage of movies and cultural events, see Chapter 7, Culture.

CLUB HOPPING

Would you please tell me where to find _____	**Pourriez-vous m'indiquer _____, s'il vous plaît?** *poo-vay-voo meh~-dee-kay ___ seel voo play*
a good nightclub?	**une bonne boîte de nuit** *oon buhn bwaht duh nwee*
a club with a live band?	**une boîte où une groupe joue de la musique** *oon bwaht oo oon groop zhoo duh lah mue-zeek*
a reggae club?	**une boîte où l'on joue du reggae** *oon bwaht oo loh~ zhoo due reh-gay*
a hip hop club?	**une boîte de hip-hop** *oon bwaht duh eep-ohp*
a techno club?	**une boîte de la musique techno** *oon bwaht duh lah mue-zeek tehk-noh*
a jazz club?	**une boîte de le jazz** *oon bwaht duh luh zhahz*
a country / western club?	**une boîte de la country** *oon bwaht duh lah kuhn-tree*
a gay / lesbian club?	**une boîte pour homosexuels / lesbiennes** *oon bwaht poohr oh-moh-sehk-sue-ehl / lehz-bee-yehn*

a club where I can dance?	**une boîte où l'on danse vraiment** *oon bwaht oo loh~ daw~s vray-maw~*
a club with French music?	**une boîte de la musique française** *oon bwaht duh lah mue-zeek fraw~-sehz*
the most popular club in town?	**la boîte la plus chaude du quartier** *lah bwaht lah plue shohd due kahr-tee-yay*
a singles bar?	**une boîte célibataire** *(unmarried)* *oon bwaht say-lee-bah-tayhr*
a piano bar?	**un piano-bar** *oon pee-yah-noh-bahr*
the most upscale bar?	**le bar le plus classieux / luxe** *luh bahr luh plue klah-syoeh / lueks*
What's the hottest bar these days?	**Quel est le bar le plus chaud maintenant?** *keh-lay luh bahr luh plue shohd meh~t-naw~*
What's the cover charge?	**Combien est le prix d'entrée?** *koh~-bee-yeh~ ay luh pree daw~-tray*
Do they have a dress code?	**Y a-t-il une tenue de rigueur?** *yah-teel oon teh-nue duh ree-goehr*
Is that an expensive club?	**Est-ce une boîte chère?** *es oon bwaht shayhr*
What's the best time to get there?	**Quelle est la meilleure heure d'arriver?** *keh-lay lah may-yoeh-roehr dah-ree-vay*

Do You Mind If I Smoke?

Est-ce qu'on a le droit d'y fumer?
ehs-koh~ ah luh dhwah dee fue-may

May I smoke?

Avez-vous ____, s'il vous plaît?
ah-vay-voo ____ seel voo play

Do you have ____

  une cigarette
  oon see-gah-reht

  a cigarette?

  du feu
  due foeh

  a light?

Puis-je vous offrir du feu?
pwee-zhuh voo-zoh-freer due foeh

May I offer you a light?

What kind of music do they play there?

Quel type de musique y joue-t-on?
kehl teep duh mue-zeek ee zhoo-toh~

May I smoke here?

Est-ce qu'on a le droit d'y fumer?
ehs-koh~ ah luh dhwah dee fue-may

I'm looking for ____

Je cherche ____
zhuh shayhrsh

  a good cigar shop.

  un bon magasin de cigares.
  uh~ boh mah-gah-zaw~ duh see-gahr

  a pack of cigarettes.

  un paquet de cigarettes.
  uh~ pah-kay duh see-gah-reht

I'd like ____	**Je voudrais ____**
	zhuh voo-dray
a drink, please!	**à boire, s'il vous plaît!**
	ah bwahr seel voo play
a bottle of beer, please!	**une bouteille de bière, s'il vous plaît!**
	oon boo-tay duh bee-yayhr seel voo play
a beer on tap, please.	**une bière pression, s'il vous plaît.**
	oon bee-yayhr pruh-syoh~ seel voo play
a shot of ____, please.	**un verre de ____, s'il vous plaît.**
	uh~ vayhr duh ____ seel voo play

For a full list of beverages, see p108.

Make it a double, please!	**Un double verre de ____, s'il vous plaît!**
	uh~ doo-bluh vayhr duh ____ seel voo play
May I have that with ice, please?	**Avec des glaçons, s'il vous plaît?**
	ah-vek day glah-soh~ seel voo play
I'd like to buy a drink for that girl / guy over there.	**Je voudrais offrir un verre à la jeune fille / au jeune homme là-bas.**
	zhuh voo-dray oh-freer uh~ vayhr ah lah zhoehn fee / oh zhoeh-nuhm lah-bah
How much for a bottle / glass of beer?	**Combien coûte une bouteille / un verre de bière?**
	koh~-bee-yeh~ koot oon boo-tay / uh~ vayhr duh bee-yayhr
May I have a pack of cigarettes, please?	**Puis-je avoir un paquet de cigarettes, s'il vous plaît?**
	pwee-zhuh ah-vwahr uh~ pah-kay duh seeg-ah-reht, seel voo play

Do you have a lighter or matches?	**Avez-vous un briquet ou des allumettes?**
	ah-vay-voo uh~ bree-kay oo day-zah-lue-meht
Do you smoke?	**Vous fumez?**
	voo fue-may
Would you like a cigarette?	**Voulez-vous une cigarette?**
	voo-lay-voo-zoon see-gah-reht
May I run a tab?	**Puis-je mettre cela sur une addition?**
	pwee-zhuh meht-ruh suh-lah suehr oo-nah-dee-see-yoh~
What's the cover?	**Quel est le prix à l'entrée?**
	keh-lay luh pree ah law~-tray

ACROSS A CROWDED ROOM

You look like the most interesting person in the room.	**Tu me semble comme la personne la plus intèressante ici.**
	tueh muh saw~-bluh koh~m lah payhr-suhn lah plue-zeh~-tay-ray-saw~t ee-see
Excuse me, may I buy you a drink?	**Pardon, puis-je vous offrir un verre?**
	pahr-doh~ pwee-zhuh voo-zoh-freer uh~ vayhr

You look amazing!	**Vous avez l'air fantastique!**
	voo-zah-vay layhr faw~-tahs-teek
Would you like to dance?	**Voulez-vous danser avec moi?**
	voo-lay-voo daw~-say ah-vek mwah
Do you like to dance fast or slow?	**Aimez-vous danser le rock ou le slow?**
	ey-may-voo daw~-say luh rohk oo luh sloh
Here, give me your hand.	**Alors, donne-moi la main.**
	ah-lohr duhn-mwah lah meh~
What would you like to drink?	**Qu'est-ce que vous voulez boire?**
	kehs-kuh voo voo-lay bwahr
You're a great dancer!	**Vous dansez très bien!**
	voo daw~-say tray bee-yeh~
I don't know that dance.	**Je ne sais pas cette danse.**
	zhuh nuh say pah seht daw~s
Do you like this song?	**Vous aimez cette chanson?**
	voo-zey-may seht shaw~-soh~
You have nice eyes!	**Vous avez de beaux yeux!**
	voo-zah-vay duh bohz yoeh

NIGHTLIFE

For a full list of features, see p142.

May I have your phone number?	**Puis je avoir votre numéro de téléphone?**
	pwee-zhuh ah-vwahr voh-truh nue-may-roh duh tay-lay-fohn

GETTING CLOSER

You're very attractive.	**Tu es très séduisant** *m* / **très jolie** *f*. *tueh ay tray say-dwee-zaw~ / tray zhoh-ee*
I like being with you.	**Je me sens bien avec toi.** *zhuh muh saw~ bee-yeh~ ah-vek twah*
I like you.	**Tu me plaît beaucoup.** *tueh muh play boh-koo*
I want to hold you.	**Je veux te serrer dans les bras.** *zhuh voeh tuh suh-ray daw~ lay brah-s*
Kiss me.	**Embrassez-moi.** *aw~-brah-say mwah*
May I give you a kiss?	**Puis-je t'embrasser?** *pwee-zhuh taw~-brah-say*
Would you like a massage / a back rub?	**Veux-tu un massage / que je te masse le dos?** *voeh-tueh uh~ mah-sazh / kuh zhuh tuh mahs luh doh*

SEX

Would you like to come inside?	**Veux-tu entrer?**
	voeh-tueh aw~-tray
May I come inside?	**Puis-je entrer?**
	pwee-zhuh aw~-tray
Let me help you out of that.	**Laissez-moi l'enlever pour toi.**
	leh-say mwah law~-luh-vay poohr twah
Would you help me out of this?	**Peux-tu m'aider à l'enlever?**
	poeh-tueh may-day ah law~-luh-vay
You smell so good.	**Tu sens si bon.**
	tueh saw~ see boh~
You're handsome / beautiful.	**Tu es très beau** *m* / **très belle** *f*.
	tueh ay tray boh / tray bell
May I?	**Puis-je?**
	pwee-zhuh
OK?	**Tu es d'accord?**
	tueh ay dah-kohr
Like this?	**Comme cela?**
	kohm suh-lah
How?	**Comment?**
	koh-maw~

HOLD ON A SECOND

Please, don't do that.	**S'il te plaît, arrête de faire cela.**
	seel tuh play ah-reht duh fayhr suh-lah
Stop, please.	**S'il te plaît, arrête.**
	seel tuh play ah-reht
Do you want me to stop?	**Tu veux que j'arrête?**
	tueh voeh kuh zhah-reht
Let's just be friends.	**Soyons amis, sans plus.**
	swah-yoh~-zah-mee saw~ plues

For a full list of features, see p142.
For a full list of body parts, see p236.

NIGHTLIFE

Do you have a condom?	**Est-ce que tu as un préservatif?** *ehs-kuh tueh ah uh~ prey-zehr-vah-teef*
Are you on birth control?	**Est-ce que tu prends la pillule?** *ehs-kuh tueh praw~ lah peel-uel*
Hold on, I have a condom here.	**Attends, laisse-moi prendre un préservatif.** *ah-taw~ lehs-mwah praw~druh uh prey-zehhr-vah-teef*
You don't have anything you want to tell me first, do you?	**Y a-t-il quelque chose dont tu voudrais me parler?** *yah-teel kehl-kuh shohz doh~ tueh voo-dray muh pahr-lay*

BACK TO IT

That's it!	**Oui, comme ça!** *wee kohm sah*
That's not it!	**Non, pas comme ça!** *noh~ pah kohm sah*
Here.	**Voici.** *vwah-see*
There.	**Voilà.** *vwah-lah*
More!	**Continue comme ça!** *koh~-tee-nue kohm sah*
Harder!	**Plus fort!** *plue fohr*
Faster!	**Plus vite!** *plue veet*
Deeper!	**Va plus loin!** *vah plue lweh~*
Slower!	**Moins vite!** *mweh~ veet*
Easier!	**Plus doucement!** *plue doos-maw~*

COOLDOWN

You're great!	**Tu as été formidable!**
	tueh ah ay-tay fohr-mee-dah-bluh
That was great.	**C'était magnifique.**
	seh-tay mah-nyee-feek
Would you like _____	**Tu veux _____**
	tueh voeh
a drink?	**quelque chose à boire?**
	kehl-kuh shohz ah bwahr
a snack?	**manger quelque chose?**
	maw~-zhay kehl-kuh shohz
a shower?	**prendre une douche?**
	praw~-druh oon doosh
May I stay here?	**Puis-je passer la nuit ici?**
	pwee-zhuh pah-say lah nwee ee-see
Would you like to stay here?	**Veux-tu passer la nuit ici?**
	voeh-tueh pah-say lah nwee ee-see
I'm sorry, I have to go now.	**Je suis désolé(e), je dois m'en aller maintenant.**
	zhuh swee day-zoh-lay zhuh dwah maw~-nah-lay meh~-t-naw~
Where are you going?	**Où vas-tu?**
	oo vah-tueh
I have to work early.	**Je dois me lever tôt pour mon travail.**
	zhuh dwah muh leh-vay toh poohr moh~ trah-vie
I'm flying home in the morning.	**Je prends l'avion demain matin.**
	zhuh praw~ lah-vee-yon duh-meh~ mah-teh~
I have an early flight.	**Mon vol part très tôt.**
	moh~ vohl pahr tray toh

I think this was a mistake.	**Nous n'aurions pas dû.**
	noo noh-ree-yoh~ pah due
Will you make me breakfast?	**Peux-tu me préparer un petit déjeuner?**
	poeh-tueh muh pray-pah-ray uh~ puh-tee day-zhoeh-nay
Stay, I'll make you breakfast.	**Reste, je te sert de petit déjeuner.**
	rehst zhuh tuh sayhr duh puh-tee day-zhoeh-nay

IN THE CASINO

How much is this table?	**Combien sont les mises à cette table?**
	koh~-bee-yeh~ soh~ lay meez ah seht tah-bluh
Deal me in.	**Donnez-moi des cartes, s'il vous plaît.**
	doh-nay mwah day kahrt seel voo play
Put it on red!	**Sur le rouge, s'il vous plaît!**
	suehr luh roozh seel voo play
Put it on black!	**Sur le noir, s'il vous plaît!**
	suehr luh nwahr seel voo play
Let it ride!	**Je garde ma mise sur la table!**
	zhuh gahrd mah meez suehr lah tah-bluh
21!	**Vingt-et-un!**
	veh~-tay-uh~
Snake-eyes!	**Paire d'as!**
	payhr dahs
Seven.	**Sept.**
	seht

For a full list of numbers, see p7.

Damn, eleven.	**Mince, c'est le onze.** *meh~s say loh~z*
I'll pass.	**Passe.** *pahs*
Hit me!	**Donne!** *duhn*
Split.	**Le split.** *luh spleet*
Are the drinks complimentary?	**Les boissons sont-elles gratuites?** *lay bwah-soh~ soh~-tehl grah-tweet*
May I bill it to my room?	**Puis-je mettre cela sur ma note?** *pwee-zhuh meh-truh seh-lah suehr mah noht*
I'd like to cash out.	**Je voudrais faire les comptes.** *zhuh voo-dray fayhr lay koh~t*
I'll hold.	**Je reste.** *zhuh rehst*
I'll see your bet.	**Je relance ta mise.** *zhuh ruh-law~s tah meez*
I call.	**J'abandonne.** *zhah-baw~-duhn*
Full house!	**Full!** *fuehl*
Royal flush!	**Quinte flush royale!** *keh~t fluesh rwah-yahl*
Straight!	**Quinte!** *keh~t*

FRENCH MUSIC

The French music scene is both lively and eclectic, ranging from traditional popular *chansons* and jazz to cutting edge hip-hop and rap. For a listing of what's on and whose playing, consult **www.infoconcert.com.** For French music via Internet radio, try: **Europe2** (www.europe2.fr) for popular music; **FIP** (www.radio-france.fr), for excellent jazz programming; **FG** (www.radiofg.fr), a gay radio station, for house and techno music; **Nova** (www.novaplanet.com), the radio version of Nova Magazine, which appeals to hip Parisians; **NRJ** (www.nrj.fr), one of the most popular music stations for French youth; **Skyrock** (www.skyrock.com), the most popular radio among French youth; and **Radio Latina** (www.radiolatina.fr), the leading station for salsa and Latin music in France.

For escorted music tours through France, **Dailey-Thorp** (© 800/998-4677; www.daileythorp.com) coordinates luxurious hotel stays with major classical music and opera events.

To land tickets to concerts, theater, and other events in France try **Global Tickets** (© 800/223-6108; www.globaltickets. com/GTS/INDEX.htm). Other options include **Classic Tic** (www.classictic.com), and **Western States Ticket Service** (© 800/326-0331; www.wstickets.com).

GREAT FRENCH FILMS & DIRECTORS

The Lovers (1958), Louis Malle

The 400 Blows (1959), François Truffaut

Hiroshima Mon Amour (1959), Alain Resnais

Breathless (1960), Jean-Luc Godard

Jules and Jim (1962), François Truffaut,

Claire's Knee (1971), Eric Rohmer

The Last Metro (1980), François Truffaut

My Dinner with André (1981), Louis Malle

Jean de Florette (1986), Claude Berri

Hate (1986), Mathieu Kassovitz
Au Revoir les Enfants (1987), Louis Malle
Le Grand Bleu (1988), Luc Besson
Three Colors Trilogy (1990s), Krysztof Kieslowski
Amélie (2001), Audrey Tatou

MUSIC & FILM FESTIVALS

May

Movie madness turns the **Cannes Film Festival** (www.festival-cannes.org) into a media circus. Admission to the films is by invitation only, but there are other movies and, of course, lots of people-watching. *Plan far ahead.*

June

From a music lover's point of view, the best day to visit France is June 21, the **Fête de la Musique**, launched in the 1980s by Jacques Lang, France's flamboyant Minister of Culture and political celebrity. The bars, cafés, public squares, and side-walks throughout the entire country are filled with outbursts of musical expression—ranging from the work of superstars such as James Brown playing at La Republique in Paris, to neighborhood garage bands jamming on street corners. Everything musical is encouraged and permitted on this evening, and you'll best understand France's commitment to culture by participating. *June 21.*

A cast of 2,500 actors, dozens of horses, and laser shows cel-ebrate the achievements of the Middle Ages at the **Chateau du Puy du Fou** (www.puydufou.com) in Les Epesses, Brittany. *Early June through early September.*

July

The **Colmar International Music Festival** (www.festival-colmar.com) is a series of classical concerts in public buildings in Colmar, one of the most folkloric towns in Alsace. *First 2 weeks in July.*

One of southern France's most important lyric festivals (oratorios, operas, and choral works), **Les Chorégies d'Orange** (www.choregies.asso.fr) takes place in Orange. Concerts are in the best-preserved amphitheater in France. *Through early August.*

Fête Chopin (www.frederic-chopin.com) in Paris, presents most everything you want to hear by this Polish exile, who lived most of his life in Paris. *Early July.*

Festival d'Avignon (www.festival-avignon.com) has a reputation for exposing new talent to critical scrutiny and acclaim. The focus is on the avant-garde in theater, dance, and music. Many of the performances take place in either the 14th-century courtyard of the Palais des Papes or the medieval cloister. *Last 3 weeks in July.*

For 4 weeks music rules the **Arènes de Lutèce** and the **Cour d'Honneur** (www.quartierdete.com) at the Sorbonne, both in Paris's Latin Quarter. The dozen or so concerts by major European orchestras are grander than the outdoor setting. *Mid-July to Mid-August.*

The **Nice Music Festival** (© 0892-683-622) is the most prestigious jazz festival in Europe. Concerts begin in the afternoon and continue at night (sometimes all night) on a hill above the city. *Mid-July.*

The month-long **Festival d'Aix-en-Provence** (www.festival-aix.com) serves up everything from Gregorian chants to music created on synthesizers. Recitals are in the medieval cloister. Expect heat, crowds, traffic, and glorious music. *July.*

During the **St-Guilhem Music Season** (www.saint-guilhem-le-desert.com) near Montpellier, Languedoc, a monastery plays host to a month of baroque organ and choral music.

August

Celtic verse and lore are celebrated in the Celtic heart of France in the *Festival Interceltique de Lorient* (www.festival-interceltique.com) in Brittany. The 150 or so concerts include classical and folkloric music, dance, song, and art. There are also traditional pardons (religious processions). *Early August.*

The *International Festival of Folklore and Wine* (www.fetesdelavigne.com) takes place in Dijon, Beaune, and some 20 other towns. Dance troupes from around the world perform in celebration of the wines of Burgundy. *Late August–early September.*

September

At the *Villette Jazz Festival* (www.villette.com) some 50 concerts are held in churches and concert halls in the Paris suburb of Villette. Past festivals have included Herbie Hancock, Shirley Horn, and other greats. *Through September.*

One of France's most famous festivals is the Festivale d'Automne (www.festival-automne.com) in Paris. It's also one of the most eclectic, focusing mainly on modern music, dance, and art. *Mid-September to late December.*

October

At the *Perpignan Jazz Festival* (www.jazzebre.com) musicians from around the world jam in what many consider Languedoc's most appealing season.

November

Paris's *Festival of Sacred Art* (www.mondial-automobile.com) is a dignified series of concerts in five of the oldest and most venerable churches. *Mid-November through December.*

NIGHTLIFE

CHAPTER ELEVEN

HEALTH & SAFETY

This chapter covers the terms you'll need to maintain your health and safety—including the most useful phrases for the pharmacy, doctor's office, and police station.

AT THE PHARMACY

Would you please fill this prescription?	**Pouvez-vous exécuter cette ordonnance, s'il vous plaît?** *poo-vay-voo-zehk-say-kue-tay seht ohr-duh-naw~s seel voo play*
Do you have anything for a cold?	**Avez-vous quelque chose contre le rhume?** *ah-vay-voo kehl-kuh shohz koh~-truh luh ruem*
I have a cough.	**Je tousse.** *zhuh toos*
I need something to help me sleep.	**J'ai besoin de quelque chose pour m'aider à dormir.** *zhay buh-zweh~ duh kehl-kuh shohz poohr may-day ah dohr-meer*
I need something to help me relax.	**J'ai besoin de quelque chose pour m'aider à me détendre.** *zhay buh-zweh~ duh kehl-kuh shohz poohr may-day ah muh day-taw~-druh*
I want to buy ____	**Je voudrais acheter ____** *zhuh voo-dray ahsh-tay*
condoms.	**des préservatifs.** *day prey-zayhr-vah-teef*
an antihistimine.	**de l'antihistamique.** *duh law~-tee-ees-tah-meek*
antibiotic cream.	**de l'antibiotique.** *duh law~-tee-bee-oh-teek*

232

aspirin.	**de l'aspirine.**
	duh lah-spreen
nonaspirin pain reliever.	**de l'analgésique.**
	duh law~-nahl-zhay-zeek
medicine with codeine.	**du médicament avec du codéine.**
	due may-deek-maw~ ah-vehk
	due koh-deen
insect repellant.	**de l'insectifuge.**
	duh leh~-sehk-tee-fuezh
I need something for _____	**J'ai besoin de quelque chose pour**
	_____
	zhay buh-zweh~ duh kehl-kuh
	shohz poohr
corns.	**le cor au pied.**
	luh kohr oh pee-yay
congestion.	**la congestion.**
	lah koh~-zhay-stee-yoh~
warts.	**la vernie.**
	lah vayhr-nee
constipation.	**la constipation.**
	lah koh~-stee-pah-see-yoh~
diarrhea.	**la diarrhée.**
	lah dee-yah-ray
indigestion.	**l'indigestion.**
	leh~-dee-zhay-stee-yoh~
nausea.	**la nausée.**
	lah noh-zay
motion sickness.	**le mal de transports.**
	luh mahl duh traw~-spohr
seasickness.	**le mal de mer.**
	luh mahl duh mayhr
acne.	**l'acné.**
	lahk-nay
I need a band-aid.	**J'ai besoin d'un pansement.**
	zhay buh-zweh~ duh~ paw~-s-maw~

AT THE DOCTOR'S OFFICE

I would like to see ____	**Je voudrais consulter ____**
	zhuh voo-dray koh~-suel-tay
a doctor.	**un médecin.**
	uh~ may-duh-seh~
a chiropractor.	**un chiropracticien.**
	uh~ kee-roh-prahk-tees-yeh~
a gynecologist.	**un gynécologue.**
	uh~ zhee-nay-koh-lohg
an eye specialist / an ear, nose, and throat (ENT) specialist.	**un oculiste / un oto-rhino-laryngologiste (ORL).**
	un~-noh-kue-leest / uh~-noh-toh-ree-noh-lah-ree-goh-loh-zheest (oh-ayhr-ehl)
a dentist.	**un dentiste.**
	uh~ daw~-teest
an optometrist.	**un optométriste.**
	uh~ ohp-toh-may-treest
a dermatologist.	**un dermatologue.**
	uh~ dayhr-mah-toh-lohg
Do I need an appointment?	**Ai-je besoin d'un rendez-vous?**
	ay-zhuh buh-zweh~ duh~ raw~-day-voo
I have an emergency.	**C'est une urgence.**
	seh-toon oohr-zhaw~s
I need an emergency prescription refill.	**J'ai besoin de faire renouveler mon ordonnance d'urgence.**
	zhay buh-zweh~ duh fayhr ruh-noov-lay moh~-nohr-doh-naw~s duehr-zhaw~s
Please call the doctor.	**Appelez un médecin, s'il vous plaît.**
	ah-play uh~ may-duh-seh~ seel voo play
I need an ambulance.	**Faites venir une ambulance.**
	feht veh-neer oon aw~-bue-law~s

SYMPTOMS

My _____ hurts.	**J'ai mal au m / à la f / aux pl _____.**
	zhay mahl oh / ah lah / oh
My _____ is stiff.	**Le m / La f _____ est raide.**
	luh / lah _____ ay rehd
I think I'm having a heart attack.	**Je crois que je vais faire une crise cardiaque.**
	zhuh kwah kuh zhuh vay fayhr oon kreez kahr-dee-yahk
I can't move.	**Je ne peux pas bouger.**
	zhuh nuh poeh pah boo-zhay
I fell.	**Je suis tombé(e).**
	zhuh swee toh~-bay
I fainted.	**J'ai perdu connaissance.**
	zhay payhr-due koh~-nay-saw~s
I have a cut on my _____.	**Je me suis coupé(e) le m / la f _____.**
	zhuh muh swee koo-pay luh / lah
I have a headache.	**J'ai mal à la tête.**
	zhay mahl ah lah teht
My vision is blurry.	**Je vois trouble.**
	zhuh vwah troo-bluh
I feel dizzy.	**J'ai des vertiges.**
	zhay day vayhr-teezh
I think I'm pregnant.	**Je crois que je suis enceinte.**
	zhuh kwah kuh zhuh swee-zaw~-sehnt
I don't think I'm pregnant.	**Je ne crois pas que je suis enceinte.**
	zhuh nuh kwah pah kuh zhuh swee-zaw~-sehnt
I'm having trouble walking.	**J'ai du mal à marcher.**
	zhay due mahl ah mahr-shay
My back hurts.	**J'ai mal au dos.**
	zhay mahl oh doh

- les épaules
- les mains
- les doigts
- les bras
- la poitrine
- le torse
- l'estomac
- la taille
- le pénis
- les mollets
- les pieds
- les orteils

- le cou
- les seins
- le nombril
- la hanche
- les poignets
- le derrière
- le vagin
- les fesses
- les jambes
- les chevilles

I can't get up.	**Je ne peux pas me lever.** *zhuh nuh poeh pah muh luh-vay*
I was mugged.	**J'ai été attaqué(e) par des voleurs.** *zhay ay-tay ah-tah-kay pahr day voh-loehr*
I was raped.	**J'ai été violé(e).** *zheh-tay vee-yoh-lay*
A dog attacked me.	**J'ai été attaqué(e) par un chien.** *zhay ay-tay ah-tahk-ay pahr uh shee-yeh~*
A snake bit me.	**J'ai été mordu(e) par un serpent.** *zhay ay-tay mohr-due pahr uh~ sayhr-paw~*
I can't move my _____ without pain.	**Cela fait mal lorsque je bouge le *m* / la *f* _____.** *suh-lah fay mahl lohr-skuh zhuh boozh luh / lah*
I think I sprained my ankle.	**Je crois que j'ai la cheville foulée.** *zhuh kwah kuh zhay lah shuh-vee foo-lay*

MEDICATIONS

I need morning-after pills.	**J'ai besoin des pilules de lendemain.** *zhay buh-zweh~ day peel-uel duh law~-d-meh~*
I need birth control pills.	**J'ai besoin des pilules contraceptives.** *zhay buh-zweh~ day peel-uel koh~-trah-sehp-teev*
I lost my eyeglasses and need new ones.	**J'ai perdu mes lunettes et j'en ai besoin de nouvelles.** *zhay payhr-due may lue-neh-tay zhaw~-nay buh-zweh~ duh noo-vehl*
I lost a contact lens.	**J'ai perdu une lentille de contact.** *zhay payhr-due oon law~-tee duh koh~-tahkt*
I need erectile dysfunction pills.	**J'ai besoin des pilules d'érectile-dysfonctionnent.** *zhay buh-zweh~ day peel-uel day-rukh-teel dees-foh~k-see-yoh~-n-maw~*
It's cold in here!	**Il fait froid ici!** *eel fay fwah ee-see*
I am allergic to ____	**Je suis allergique ____** *zhuh swee-zah-layhr-zheek*
penicillin.	**à la pénicilline.** *ah lah pay-nee-see-leen*
antibiotics.	**aux antibiotiques.** *oh-zaw~-tee-bee-yoh-teek*
sulfa drugs.	**aux sulfamides.** *oh suel-fah-meed*
steroids.	**aux stéroïdes.** *oh stay-roh-eed*
I have asthma.	**Je suis asthmatique.** *zhuh swee-zahst-mah-teek*

DENTAL PROBLEMS

I have a sore tooth.	**J'ai mal à une dent.**
	zhay mahl ah oon daw~
I chipped a tooth.	**J'ai une dent d'ébréchée.**
	zhay oon daw~ day-bray-shay
My bridge came loose.	**Mon bridge s'est défait.**
	moh~ breedzh say day-fay
I lost a crown.	**J'ai perdu une couronne.**
	zhay payhr-due oon koo-rohn
I lost a denture plate.	**J'ai perdu une plaque de prothèse.**
	zhay payhr-due oon plak duh proh-tehz

DEALING WITH POLICE

I'm sorry, did I do something wrong?	**Pardon, j'ai fait quelque chose de mal?**
	pahr-doh~ zhay fay kehl-kuh shohz duh mahl
I am _____	**Je suis _____**
	zhuh swee
American.	**américain** *m* / **américaine** *f.*
	ah-may-ree-kah / ah-may-ree-kehn
Canadian.	**canadien** *m* / **canadienne** *f.*
	kah-nah-dee-eh~ / kah-nah-dee-ehn
Irish.	**irlandais** *m* / **irlandaise** *f.*
	eer-law~-day / eer-law~-dehz
English.	**anglais** *m* / **anglaise** *f.*
	aw~-glay / aw~-glehz
Australian.	**australien** *m* / **australienne** *f.*
	oh-strah-lee-eh~ / oh-strah-lee-ehn
New Zealander.	**néo-zélandais** *m* / **néozélandaise** *f.*
	nay-oh-zay-law~dey / nay-oh-zay-law~-dehz

For more languages and nationalities, see the English / French dictionary.

Listen Up: Police Lingo

Permis de conduire et carte grise, s'il vous plaît.	Your license, registration, and insurance, please.
payhr-mee duh koh~-dweer ay kahrt greez seel voo play	
L'amende est de ____ euros, et vous pouvez me la régler directement.	The fine is ____, and you can pay me directly.
lah-maw~d ay duh ____ oehr-oh ay voo poo-vay muh lah reh-glay dee-rehkt-maw~	
Votre passeport, s'il vous plaît?	Your passport please?
voh-truh pahs-pohr seel voo play	
Où allez-vous?	Where are you going?
oo ah-lay-voo	
Pourquoi êtes-vous si pressé(e)?	Why are you in such a hurry?
poohr-kwah eht-voo see prehs-say	

The car is a rental.	**C'est une voiture de location.**
	seh-toon vwah-tuehr duh loh-kah-see-yoh~
Am I supposed to pay the fine to you?	**Dois-je vous régler directement l'amende?**
	dwah-zhuh voo reh-glay dee-rehkt-maw~ lah-maw~d
Do I have to go to court? When?	**Dois-je passer en justice? Quand?**
	dwah-zhuh pah-say aw~ zhue-stees; kaw~

I'm sorry, my French isn't very good.	**Je suis désolé(e), je ne parle pas bien le français.**
	zhuh swee day-zoh-lay zhuh nuh pahrl pah bee-yeh~ luh fraw~-say
I need an interpreter.	**J'ai besoin d'un interprète.**
	zhay buh-zweh~ duh~-neh~- tayhr-preht
I'm sorry, I don't understand the ticket.	**Désolé(e), je ne comprends pas pourquoi vous voulez me donner une amende.**
	day-zoh-lay zhuh nuh koh~- praw~pah poohr-kwah voo voo- lay muh duh-nay oon ah-maw~d
May we call the embassy?	**Pouvons-nous appeler l'ambassade de notre pays?**
	poo-voh~-noo-zah-play law~-bah- sahd duh noh-truh pay-ee
I was robbed.	**J'ai été victime d'un vol.**
	zhay ay-tay veek-teem duh~ vohl
I was mugged.	**J'ai été attaqué(e).**
	zhay ay-tay ah-tah-kay
I was raped.	**J'ai été violé(e).**
	zhay ay-tay vee-yoh-lay
May I make a report?	**Puis-je faire une déclaration?**
	pwee-zhuh fayhr oon day-klah- rah-see-yoh~
Somebody broke into my room.	**Quelqu'un s'est introduit dans ma chambre.**
	kehl-kuh~ say-teh~-tro-dwee daw~ mah shaw~-bruh
Someone stole my purse / wallet.	**Quelqu'un m'a volé mon sac à main / portefeuille.**
	kehl-kuh~ mah voh-lay moh~ sahk ah meh~ / pohrt-foeh-yuh

HEALTH

The French national health system is one of the best in the world, with public health focusing more on prevention than on emergency medicine. Pharmacists are extremely knowledgeable and pharmacies are available even in small towns and rural areas. It's advisable to bring prescriptions for any medication you are taking, as well as generic names, as local chemists may not be familiar with American brands. *Eau de robinet* (tap water) is almost always safe to drink, although the French drink a lot of bottled water in restaurants and at work. In fact, most people order a *carafe d'eau* when eating in restaurants or cafes.

SAFETY

Safety at the Airport   Airport theft is not unknown, so put a lock on your luggage. Put something colorful—a sticker, a piece of string—on your bags, to distinguish them from hundreds of others. Don't wear expensive jewelry. Stash your money in at least two places. Get cash as you go along; with the proliferation of ATMs, there's no reason to carry all your cash with you.

Be sure to bring extra contact lenses or prescription glasses. Pack them, and medicines, in your carry-on luggage.

Safety on the Roads   The key to driving safely in France is to remain calm. Traffic moves quickly and there are roundabout intersections in the cities. In France, one yields in most cases to cars on your right.

Priorité à droit   Remember this at all times. When you have the right of way, take it. On the highway, pass on the left and keep to the right. The French rarely honk, but if they're not happy they'll flash their high beams.

Be on the lookout for police control points. These are usually inoffensive and a matter of routine security. Show respect for the authority of the police or they will find a few things that merit a *PV* or *contravention* (fine). Don't talk on your cellphone while driving. That's a sure way of getting pulled over. And use your seat belts. This too is seriously controlled.

It is preferable to have an international drivers permit (IDP) in addition to your regular North American drivers license. Apply for one in person at your local AAA. Be careful not to attempt to buy one elsewhere online; there have been numerous scam sites claiming to sell the IDP.

THEFT

Wallets are safer in a front pocket. Keep your credit card numbers, and the numbers you need to call should they get lost, in a separate place. Consider bringing two credit cards in case you lose one or one doesn't work. If you're driving, lock your belongings in the trunk, out of sight (don't rent a wagon or SUV without an enclosed trunk; they're an invitation to thieves).

Carry photocopies of important documents with you when you travel, but do not keep them in the same place as the originals. If your credit cards are lost or stolen, report the incident to the relevant card companies. Here are the local phone numbers for major credit cards:

- **Visa**   ℂ **08 36 69 08 80** or **01 42 77 11 90**
- **MasterCard**   ℂ **08 36 69 08 80** or **01 45 67 84 84**
- **American Express**   ℂ **01 47 77 72 00**
- **Diners Club**   ℂ **01 49 06 17 50**

INSURANCE

Check your existing insurance policies before you buy travel insurance to cover trip cancellation, lost luggage, medical expenses, or rental car accidents; you're likely to have partial or complete coverage already. Popular companies include **Access America** (✆ 800/284-8300; www.accessamerica.com); **Travel Assistance International** (✆ 800/821-2828; www.travelassistance.com); **Travel Guard International** (✆ 800/826-4919; www.travelguard.com); **Travel Insured International** (✆ 800/243-3174; www.travelinsured.com); and **Travelex Insurance Services** (✆ 800/228-9892; www.travelex-insurance.com).

Trip-Cancellation Insurance This comes in three forms: first, when a pre-paid tour gets cancelled, and there's no refund; second, when you or a family member gets sick or dies, and you can't travel (this may not cover a pre-existing condition); and third, when bad weather makes travel impossible. Some insurers cover events such as jury duty; local natural disasters, even job loss. A few provide for cancellations due to terrorist activities.

In this unstable world, trip-cancellation insurance makes sense, particularly if you're making reservations months in advance—who knows what state the world will be in 6 months or a year from now? Be sure to check the fine print before signing on, and only buy trip-cancellation insurance from a travel insurance company (not from the company that sells you the trip). A good resource is **Travel Guard Alert**, a list of companies considered high risk by Travel Guard International (see above). Protect yourself further by buying insurance with a credit card—by law, consumers can get their money back on goods and services not received if they report the loss within 60 days after the charge is listed on their credit card statement.

Medical Insurance Most health insurance policies cover you if you get sick away from home—but check, particularly if you're insured by an HMO. With the exception of certain HMOs and Medicare/Medicaid, your medical insurance should cover medical treatment—even hospital care—overseas. However, most out-of-country hospitals make you pay your bills up front and send you a refund after you've returned home and filed the necessary forms. Members of **Blue Cross/Blue Shield** can now use their cards at select hospitals in most major cities worldwide. Call ✆ **800/810-BLUE** or log on to www.bluecares.com for a list of hospitals. Some credit cards (**American Express** and certain gold and platinum **Visas** and **MasterCards**, for example) offer automatic flight insurance against death or dismemberment. Check whether your medical insurance covers you for emergency medical evacuation. If you have to buy a one-way, same-day ticket home and forfeit your nonrefundable round-trip ticket, you may be out big money.

Lost-Luggage Insurance   On international flights baggage insurance is limited to $9.07 per pound, up to $635 per checked bag. For valuable items, purchase "excess valuation" coverage from the airline, up to $5,000. Take any valuables or irreplaceable items with you in your carry-on luggage. If you file a lost luggage claim, be prepared to answer detailed questions about the baggage contents, and file a claim immediately, as most airlines enforce a 21-day deadline. Make a list estimating the value of items insured before you leave home. Once you've filed a complaint, follow up, as there are no laws governing the length of time it takes for a carrier to reimburse you.

If you arrive at a destination without your bags, ask the airline to forward them to your hotel or next destination. If a bag is delayed or lost, the airline may reimburse you for reasonable expenses, such as a toothbrush or a set of clothes, but they're not legally obligated to.

CHAPTER TWELVE

CULTURE GUIDE

FRENCH ART

Prehistoric, Celtic & Classical (25,000 B.C.–A.D. 500)   After England's Stonehenge, Europe's most famous prehistoric remains are France's Paleolithic cave paintings. Created 15,000 to 20,000 years ago, they depict mostly hunting scenes and abstract shapes. Whether the paintings served in religious rites or were simply decorative is anybody's guess. Important examples of ancient art include:

- **Cave art.** The caves at Lascaux, the Sistine Chapel of prehistoric art, have been closed since 1963, but experts have created a replica, Lascaux II. To see the real stuff, visit Les Eyzies-de-Tayac, which boasts four caves (Font de Gaume is the best). In the neighboring Lot Valley, outside Cahors, is the Grotte du Pech-Merle, with France's oldest cave art (about 20,000 years old).

- **Celtic and classical art**. Little remains of the art of Celtic (ca. 1,000 B.C.–A.D. 125) and Roman (A.D. 125–500) Gaul. Surviving items—small votive bronzes, statues, jewelry, and engraved weapons and tools—are spread across France's archaeology museums. Burgundy preserves the most of Celtic Gaul, including sites at Dijon, Châtillon-sur-Seine, Alise-Ste-Reine, and Auxerre. To see artifacts of Roman Gaul, visit the southern towns of Nîmes, Arles, Orange, St-Rémy-de-Provence, and Vienne. You'll also find some sculptures in Paris's Musée de Cluny.

- **Romanesque** (900–1100)   Artistic expression in early medieval France was largely church-related. Because Mass was in Latin, images were used to communicate the Bible's lessons to the mostly illiterate people. *Bas-reliefs* (sculptures

that project slightly from a flat surface) were used to illus-
trate key tales that inspired faith in God and fear of sin (th
Last Judgment was a favorite). These reliefs were wrappe
around column capitals and fitted into the *tympanums*, c
arched spaces above doorways (the complete door, tym
panum, arch, and supporting pillars assemblage is the por
tal). Worshipers were also interested in specialized saint
associated with everyday matters, such as crops, marriage
animals, and health. Chapels were built to house silver an
gold reliquaries displaying bits of saints to which wor
shipers could pray. Saintly statues also began appearing o
facades, though this became more of a Gothic conventior

The best examples of Romanesque art include:

- **Sculptures and statues**. The best surviving examples ar
  a Last Judgment tympanum by Gislebertus at St-Lazare i
  Autun; 76 Romanesque cloister capitals and one of France'
  best-carved 11th-century portals at St-Pierre Abbey i
  Moissac near Montauban; the tympanum over the inne
  main portal of huge Ste-Madeleine in Vézelay; reliefs c
  Christ and the Evangelists by Bernard Guildin in the cryp
  of St-Semin in Toulouse; and the wonderfully detaile
  facade frieze and statues of St-Pierre in Angoulême.

- **Wall paintings and frescoes**. You'll find examples a
  Notre-Dame in Le Puy (ca. 1000), St-Savin near Poitier
  (1100), and Berzé-la-Ville (1100) near Cluny.

- **Bayeaux Tapestry** (1066–1077). The most notable exam
  ple of Romanesque artistry is the *Bayeaux Tapestry*, 69n
  (226 ft.) of embroidered linen telling the story of William th
  Conqueror's defeat of the English.

Gothic (1100–1400) Late medieval French art remained largel
ecclesiastical. Church facades and choir screens were festoone
with statues and carvings, and the French became masters c

stained glass. Many painterly conventions began on window-panes or as elaborate designs in illuminated manuscript margins, which developed into altarpieces of the colorful, expressive International Gothic style of posed scenes and stylized figures.

In Gothic painting and sculpture, figures tended to be more natural than in the Romanesque, but they were also highly stylized, flowing, and rhythmic. The features and gestures were usually exaggerated for symbolic or emotional emphasis.

The best examples of Gothic art include:

- **Sculpture and statues.** The best-preserved examples are at the cathedrals of Chartres, Amiens, and Reims (see "Architecture 101," below), and at Strasbourg, which boasts one of the most elaborate Gothic portals and rose windows in France.

- **Stained glass**. All of the above churches (especially Chartres) contain some of the most stunning stained glass in Europe—though first prize goes to Paris's Ste-Chapelle.

- **Painting**. Burgundy was the first French area to embrace the High Gothic painting style of its Flemish neighbors. The great van der Weyden left works in Dijon and Beaune as well as at the Louvre. The Dutch Limbourg Brothers' *Les Très Riches Heures* (1413–16, finished after their deaths), now in Château de Chantilly, is considered a touchstone of the International Gothic style. Enguerrand Quarton was the most important French painter of the period. His only documented paintings are *Virgin of Mercy* (1452) at Chantilly and a work at the Musée de l'Hospice in Villeneuve-lèz-Avignon, but most scholars also attribute to him the Louvre's *Villeneuve Pietà* (1460).

- **Unicorn Tapestries** (1499–1514). Now in Paris's Musée de Cluny, these tapestries shine brightly as a statement of medieval sensibilities while borrowing some burgeoning Renaissance conventions.

The Renaissance & Baroque (1450–1800)   Renaissance means "rebirth"—in this case, that of classical ideals. Humanist thinkers rediscovered the wisdom of ancient Greece and Rome, while artists strove for naturalism, using newly developed techniques such as linear perspective. The French had little to do with this movement, which started in Italy and was picked up only in Germany and the Low Countries. However, many Renaissance treasures are in French museums, thanks to collectors such as François I.

Not until the 17th-century baroque did a few French masters emerge. This period is hard to pin down. In some ways a result of the Catholic Counter-Reformation, it reaffirmed spirituality in a simplified, monumental, and religious version of Renaissance ideals. In other ways, it delved even deeper into classical modes and a kind of superrealism based on using peasants as models and the *chiaroscuro* (contrast of light and dark) of the Italian painter Caravaggio.

Some view those two baroque movements as extensions of Renaissance experiments and find the true baroque in later, complex compositions—explosions of dynamic fury, movement, color, and figures—that are well balanced but in such cluttered abundance as to appear untamed. Rococo is this later baroque art gone awry: frothy and chaotic.

Paris's Louvre abounds with Renaissance works by Italian, Flemish, and German masters, including Michelangelo (1475–1564) and Leonardo da Vinci (1452–1519). Leonardo's *Mona Lisa* (1503–05), perhaps the world's most famous painting, hangs there. Great baroque and rococo artists include:

- **Nicolas Poussin** (1594–1665). While his mythological scenes presaged the Romantic movement, on a deeper level his balance and predilection to paint from nature had closer connection to (and greater influence on) Impressionists like Cézanne. Find his works in the Louvre and in Nancy.

- **Antoine Watteau** (1684–1721). A rococo painter of colorful, theatrical works now in the Louvre, Watteau began the short-lived *fête galante* style of china-doll figures against stylized landscapes of woodlands or ballrooms.

- **François Boucher** (1703–70). Louis XV's rococo court painter, Boucher studied Watteau and produced decorative landscapes and genre works, now at the Louvre.

- **Jean-Honoré Fragonard** (1732–1806). Boucher's student and master of rococo pastel scenes, Fragonard painted pink-cheeked, wispy, genteel lovers frolicking among billowing trees. His famous *The Bathers* hangs in the Louvre. More work is in Amiens's Musée de Picardie.

Neoclassical & Romantic (1770–1890)   As the baroque got excessive and the rococo got cute, and as the somber Counter-Reformation got serious about imposing limits on religious art, several artists, such as Jacques-Louis David, looked to the ancients. Viewing new excavations of Greek and Roman sites (Pompeii, Paestum) and statuary became integral parts of the Grand Tour through Italy, while the Enlightenment (and growing revolutionary) interest in Greek democracy beat an intellectual path to the distant past. This gave rise to a neoclassical style that emphasized symmetry, austerity, clean lines, and classical themes, such as depictions of historical or mythological scenes.

The Romantics, on the other hand, felt that both the ancients and the Renaissance had gotten it wrong and that the Middle Ages were the place to be. They idealized tales of chivalry and held a deep respect for nature, human rights, and the nobility of peasantry, as well as a suspicion of progress. Their paintings were heroic, historic, and (melo-) dramatic.

The greatest artists and movements of the era include:

- **Jacques-Louis David** (1744–1825). David dropped the baroque after study in Rome exposed him to neoclassicism, which he brought back to Paris and displayed in such paintings as *The Oath of the Horatii* (1784) and *Coronation of Napoléon and Joséphine* (1805–08), both in the Louvre.

- **Jean-Auguste-Dominique Ingres** (1780–1867). Ingres trained with David, from whom he broke to adapt a more Greek style. He became a defender of the neoclassicists and the Royal French Academy, and opposed the Romantics. His *Grand Odalisque* (1814) hangs in the Louvre.

- **Théodore Géricault** (1791–1824). One of the early Romantics, Géricault painted *The Raft of the Medusa* (1819), which served as a model for the movement. This large, dramatic history painting hangs in the Louvre.

- **Eugène Delacroix** (1798–1863). Painted in the Romantic style, his *Liberty Leading the People* (1830), in the Louvre, reveals experimentation in color and brush stroke.

- **The Barbizon School**. This group of landscape painters, founded in the 1830s by Théodore Rousseau (1812–67), painted from nature at Barbizon, where the Musée Ganne is devoted to Rousseau's works. The paintings of Jean-François Millet (1814–75), who depicted classical scenes and peasants, hang in his studio nearby and in Paris's Musée d'Orsay. You'll find works by Jean-Baptiste-Camille Corot (1796–1875), a sort of idealistic proto-Impressionist, in the Louvre.

Impressionism (1870–1920)   Formal, rigid neoclassicism and idealized Romanticism rankled some late-19th-century artists interested in painting directly from nature. Seeking to capture the fleeting impression of light reflecting off objects, they adopted a free, open style characterized by deceptively loose compositions; swift, visible brushwork; and often, light colors. For subjects, they turned away from the historical depictions of previous styles to landscapes and scenes of daily life. Unless specified below, you'll find some of their best works in Paris's Musée d'Orsay.

Impressionist greats include:

- **Edouard Manet** (1832–83). His groundbreaking *Picnic on the Grass* (1863) and *Olympia* (1863) weren't Impressionism proper, but they helped inspire the movement with their realism, visible brush strokes, and thick outlines.

- **Claude Monet** (1840–1926). The Impressionist movement began with an 1874 exhibition in which Monet showed his loose, Turner-inspired *Impression, Sunrise* (1874), now in the Musée Marmottan. One critic focused on it to lambaste the whole exhibition, deriding it all as "Impressionist." Far from being insulted, the show's artists adopted the word for their movement. Monet's *Water Lilies* hangs in the basement of Paris's Musée de l'Orangerie. You can visit his studio and gardens at Giverny, north of Paris.

- **Pierre-Auguste Renoir** (1841–1919). Originally Renoir was a porcelain painter, which helps explain his figures' ivory skin and chubby pink cheeks.

- **Edgar Degas** (1834–1917). Degas was an accomplished painter, sculptor, and draftsman—his pastels of dancers and bathers are memorable.

- **Auguste Rodin** (1840–1917). The greatest sculptor of the Impressionist era, Rodin crafted remarkably expressive bronzes, refusing to idealize the human figure as had his neoclassical predecessors. The Musée Rodin, his former Paris studio, contains, among other works, his *Burghers of Calais* (1886), *The Kiss* (1886–98), and *The Thinker* (1880).

Post-Impressionism (1880–1930) Few experimental French artists of the late 19th century were considered Impressionists, though many were friends with those in the

CULTURE GUIDE

movement. The smaller movements or styles are usually lumped together as "post-Impressionist."

Again, you'll find the best examples of their works at Paris's Musée d'Orsay, although the pieces mentioned below by Matisse, Chagall, and the Cubists are in the Centre Pompidou. Important post-Impressionists include:

- **Paul Cézanne** (1839–1906). Cézanne adopted the short brush strokes, landscapes, and light color palette of his Impressionist friends, but his style was more formal and deliberate. He sought to give his art monumentality and permanence, even if the subjects were still lifes (*Nature Morte: Pommes et Oranges,* 1895–1900), portraits (*La Femme a la Cafetière,* 1890–95), and landscapes (*La Maison du Pendu Auvers-sur-Oise,* 1873).

- **Paul Gauguin** (1848–1903). Gauguin could never settle himself or his work, trying Brittany, where he developed synthetism (black outlines around solid colors), and hopping around the South Pacific, where he was inspired by local styles and colors, as in *Femmes de Tahiti sur la Plage* (1891).

- **Georges Seurat** (1859–91), **Paul Signac** (1863–1935), and **Camille Pissaro** (1830–1903). These artists developed divisionism and its more formal cousin, pointillism. Rather than mixing yellow and blue together to make green, they applied tiny dots of yellow and blue right next to one another so that the viewer's eye mixed them together to make green. Seurat's best work in the Orsay is *Le Cirque* (1891), though the lines are softer and subjects more compelling in the nude studies called *Les Poseuses* (1886–87).

- **Henri de Toulouse-Lautrec** (1864–1901). He's most famous for his work with thinned-down oils, which he used to create paintings and posters of wispy, fluid lines, anticipating Art Nouveau. He often depicted the bohemian life of Paris (dance halls, cafes, and top-hatted patrons at fancy parties), as in the barely sketched *La Danse Mauresque* (1895). The pastel *Le Lit* (1892) shows his quieter, more intimate side.

- **Vincent van Gogh** (1853–1890). A Dutchman, van Gogh spent most of his career in France. He combined divisionism, synthetism, and a touch of Japanese influence and painted with thick, short strokes. Never particularly accepted by any artistic circle, he is the most popular painter in the world today, even though he sold only one painting in his life. The Orsay contains such works as *Le Chambre de Van Gogh à Arles* (1889), a self-portrait (1887), a portrait of his psychiatrist Docteur Paul Gachet (1890), and *La Méridienne* (1889–90).

- **Henri Matisse** (1869–1954). Matisse took a hint from synthetism and added wild colors and strong patterns to create Fauvism (a critic described those who used the style as *fauves*, meaning "wild beasts"), such as *Interior, Goldfish Bowl* (1914). He continued exploring these themes even when most artists were turning to cubism. When his health failed, he assembled brightly colored collages of paper cutouts (such as the Pompidou's *Sorrow of the King,* 1952). You'll find several of his works in the Musée Matisse in Nice. His masterpiece, the Chapelle du Rosaire (1949–51), a chapel he designed and decorated, is near Vence.

- **Georges Braque** (1882–1963) and **Pablo Picasso** (1881–1973). French-born Braque and Spanish-born Picasso painted objects from all points of view at once, rather than using tricks like perspective to fool viewers into seeing three dimensions (in the Pompidou, Braque's *Man with Guitar,* 1914, and Picasso's 1907 study for *Les Demoiselles d'Avignon*). The result was called cubism and was expanded upon by the likes of Fernand Léger (1881–1955; *Wedding,* 1911) and the Spaniard Juan Gris (1887–1927; *Le Petit Déjeuner,* 1915).

Braque developed the style using collage (he added bits of paper and cardboard to his images), while Picasso moved on to other styles. You can see work from all of Picasso's periods at museums dedicated to him in Paris, Antibes, and Vallauris, where Picasso revived the ceramics industry.

- **Marc Chagall** (1889–1985). This Hasidic Jewish artist is hard to pin down. He traveled widely in Europe, the United States, Mexico, and Israel; his painting started from cubism and picked up inspiration everywhere to fuel a brightly colored, allegorical, often whimsical style. You'll find a museum devoted to him in Nice, several of his stained-glass windows in the Cathédrale Notre-Dame d'Amiens, his painted ceiling in Paris's Opéra Garnier, and *To Russia*, the *Asses* and the *Others* (1911) in the Pompidou.

ARCHITECTURE 101

While each architectural era has its distinctive features, some elements, floor plans, and terms are common to many of the eras. From the Romanesque period on, most churches consist of either a single wide aisle or a central nave flanked by two narrow aisles. The aisles are separated from the nave by a row of columns or, more accurately, by square stacks of masonry called piers, connected by arches. Sometimes in structures from the Romanesque and Gothic eras, you'll see a second level, the clerestory, above these arches (and hence above the low roof over the aisles) punctuated by windows.

This main nave and aisle assemblage is usually crossed by a perpendicular corridor called a transept, placed near the far, east end of the church so that the floor

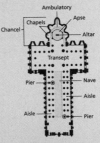

Church Floor Plan

plan looks like a Latin Cross (shaped like a crucifix). The shorter, east arm of the nave is called the chancel; it often houses the stalls of the choir and the altar. If the far end of the chancel is rounded off, it is termed an apse. An ambulatory is a curving corridor outside the altar and the choir area, separating them from the ring of smaller chapels radiating off the chancel and apse.

Some churches, especially those built after the Renaissance, when mathematical proportion became important, have a Greek Cross plan, with each axis the same length–like a giant plus sign (+).

Very few buildings (especially churches) were built in one particular style. Massive, expensive structures often took centuries to complete, during which time tastes would change and plans would be altered.

Ancient Roman (125 B.C.–A.D. 450) Provence was Rome's first transalpine conquest, and the legions of Julius Caesar quickly subdued the Celtic tribes across France, converting it into Roman Gaul. Roman architectural innovations include:

- The load-bearing arch
- The use of concrete, brick, and stone

Nîmes preserves from the 1st century B.C. a 20,000-seat amphitheater, a Corinthian temple called the "Square House," a fine archaeology museum, and the astounding pont du Gard, a 47m (158-ft.) long, three-story aqueduct made of cut stones fitted together without mortar.

From the Augustan era of the 1st century A.D., Arles preserves a 25,000-seat amphitheater, a rebuilt theater, and a decent museum. The nearby Glanum excavations outside St-Rémy-de-Provence (which houses its archaeology museum) offer a complete,

Pont du Gard, Nîmes

albeit highly ruined, glimpse of an entire Roman provincial town, from a few pre-Roman Gallic remnants and a 20 B.C. arch to the last structures sacked by invading Goths in A.D. 480.

Romanesque (800–1100)   Romanesque churches were large, with a wide nave and aisles to accommodate the faithful who came to hear Mass and worship at the altars of various saints. To support the weight of all that masonry, the walls had to be thick and solid (meaning they could be pierced by only a few small windows) and had to rest on huge piers, giving Norman churches a dark, somber feeling. Some of the features of this style include:

- **Rounded arches.** These load-bearing architectural devices allowed architects to open up wide naves and spaces, channeling the weight of the stone walls and ceiling across the curve of the arch and into the ground through the columns or pilasters.
- **Thick walls.**
- **Infrequent and small windows.**
- **Huge piers.**

The Cathédrale St-Bénigne in Dijon was the first French Romanesque church, but of that era only the crypt remains. The Cathédrale St-Pierre in Angoulême has a single large nave, a rounded apse with small radiating chapels, and a pair of transept miniapses.

Gothic (1100–1500)   By the 12th century, engineering developments freed architecture from the heavy, thick walls of the Romanesque and allowed ceilings to soar, walls to thin, and windows to proliferate. The Gothic was France's greatest homegrown architectural style, copied throughout Europe.

Instead of dark, relatively unadorned Romanesque interiors that forced the eyes of the faithful toward the altar, the

Gothic interior enticed the churchgoers' gaze upward to high ceilings filled with light. The priests still conducted Mass in Latin, but now peasants could "read" the stories told in stained-glass windows.

The squat, brooding exteriors of the Romanesque fortresses of God were replaced by graceful buttresses and soaring spires, which rose from town centers like beacons of religion. Some identifiable Gothic features include:

- **Pointed arches**. The most significant development of the Gothic era was the discovery that pointed arches could carry far more weight than rounded ones.

- **Cross vaults**. Instead of being flat, the square patch of ceiling between four columns arches up to a point in the center, creating four sail shapes, sort of like the underside of a pyramid. The X separating these four sails is often reinforced with ridges called ribbing.

Cross Vault

- **Flying buttresses.** These free-standing exterior pillars connected by graceful, thin arms of stone help channel the weight of the building and its roof out and down into the ground. Not every Gothic church has evident buttresses.

- **Stained glass**. The multitude and size of Gothic windows allowed them to be filled with Bible stories and symbolism portrayed in colorful patterns of stained glass. The use of stained glass was more common in the later Gothic periods.

- **Rose windows.** These huge circular windows, often the centerpieces of facades, are filled with elegant tracery and "petals" of stained glass.

Flying Buttress

Cross Section of Gothic Church

- **Tracery**. Lacy spider webs of carved stone curlicues grace the pointed ends of windows and sometimes the spans of ceiling vaults.
- **Spires**. These pinnacles of masonry seem to defy gravity and reach toward heaven.
- **Gargoyles**. These are drain spouts disguised as wide-mouthed creatures or human heads.
- **Choir screen.** Serving as the inner wall of the ambulatory and the outer wall of the choir section, the choir screen is often decorated with carvings.

The Basilique St-Denis (1140–44), today in a Paris suburb, was the world's first Gothic cathedral. The statuary, spire, and some 150 glorious stained-glass windows of the Cathédrale Notre-Dame de Chartres (1194–1220) make it a must-see, while the Cathédrale Notre-Dame de Reims (1225–90) sports more than 2,300 exterior statues and stained glass from 13th-century rose window originals to 20th-century windows by Marc Chagall. The Cathédrale Notre-Dame d'Amiens (1220–36) is pure Gothic, its festival of statues and reliefs built with remarkable speed.

Paris's **Notre-Dame Cathedral** (1163–1250) has good buttresses, along with a trio of France's best rose windows, portal carvings, a choir screen of carved reliefs, and spiffy gargoyles (many of which are actually 19th-century neo-Gothic). The *sine qua non* of stained glass is Paris's Ste-Chapelle (1240-50).

*Cathédrale
Notre-Dame de
Chartres*

Renaissance (1500–1630)   In architecture as in painting, the Renaissance came from Italy and was only slowly Frenchified. And as in painting, its rules stressed proportion, order, classical inspiration, and precision to create unified, balanced structures. Some identifiable Renaissance features include:

- A sense of **proportion**.
- A reliance on **symmetry**.
- The use of **classical orders**. This specifies three types of column capitals: **Doric**, **Ionic**, and **Corinthian**.
- **Steeply pitched roofs.** They often feature dormer windows (upright windows projecting from a sloping roof).

The Loire Valley and Burgundy are home to many Renaissance châteaux. Foremost is the Loire's

Château de Chambord

Château de Chambord, started in 1519, probably according to plans by Leonardo da Vinci (who may have designed its double helix staircase). In contrast, the Château de Chenonceau, home to many a French king's wife or mistress, is a fanciful fairy tale built in the middle of a river. The best example in Burgundy is the Château de Tanlay, east of Chablis.

Classicism & Rococo (1630–1800) While Italy and Germany embraced the opulent baroque, France took the fundamentals of Renaissance classicism even further, becoming more imitative of ancient models. This represents a change from the Renaissance preference of finding inspiration in the classic era.

During the reign of Louis XIV, art and architecture were subservient to political ends. Buildings were grandiose and severely ordered on the Versailles model. Opulence was saved for interior decoration, which increasingly (especially from 1715–50, after the death of Louis XIV) became a detailed and self-indulgent rococo (*rocaille* in French). Externally, rococo is noticeable only in a greater elegance and delicacy.

Rococo tastes didn't last long, and soon a neoclassical movement was raising structures, such as Paris's Pantheon (1758), that were even more strictly based on ancient models than the earlier classicist designs had been. Some identifiable features of classicism include:

- Highly **symmetrical**, **rectangular** structures based on the classical orders.
- **Projecting central sections** topped by **triangular pediments**.
- **Mansard roofs.** A defining feature and true French trademark developed by **François Mansart** (1598–1666) in the early 15th century; a mansard roof has a double slope, the lower longer and steeper than the upper.

Mansard Roof

- **Dormer windows.**
- *Oeil-de-bouef* **("ox-eyes").** These small, round windows poke out of the roof's slope.

Mansart built town houses, châteaux, and churches (Val-de-Grâce in Paris; the Palais du Tau in Reims) and laid out Dijon's Place de la Libération. But the Parisian architect is chiefly remembered for his steeply sloping namesake, "mansard" roofs.

Louis Le Vau (1612–70) was the chief architect of the Louvre from 1650 to 1670 and of the Château de Vaux-le-Vicomte (1656–61) outside Paris. This latter gig put him and his collaborators—including Mansart, interior decorator Charles Le Brun (1619–90), and the unparalleled landscape gardener André Le Nôtre (1613–1700)—on Louis XIV's radar and landed them the

Château de Versailles

commission to rebuild Versailles (1669–85). Versailles is Europe's grandest palace.

Rococo architecture is tough to find. In Paris, seek out Delamair's Marais town house, the Hôtel de Soubise (1706–12), and the prime minister's residence, the Hôtel Matignon (1721), by Courtonne. For rococo decor, check out the Clock Room in Versailles.

The 19th Century   Architectural styles in 19th-century France began in a severe classical mode. Then they dabbled with medieval revival, delved into modern urban restructuring, and ended with an identity crisis torn between industrial-age advancements and Art Nouveau organic. The 19th century saw several distinct styles, including:

- **First Empire.** Elegant neoclassical furnishings—distinguished by strong lines often accented with a simple curve—during Napoleon's reign. Napoleon spent his imperial decade (1804–14) refurbishing the Palais de Fontainebleau in First Empire style. The ultimate paean to the classical was the Arc de Triomphe (1836), Napoleon's imitation of a Roman triumphal arch.

- **Second Empire.** Napoleon III's reign saw the eclectic Second Empire reinterpret classicism in a dramatic mode. Baron Haussmann (1809–91), who cut broad boulevards through the city's medieval neighborhoods, restructured Paris. In the Second Empire, Napoleon III commissioned Baron Haussmann in 1852 to remap Paris according to modern urban-planning theories—clearing out the tangles of medieval streets to lay out wide boulevards radiating off grand squares (the Etoile anchored by the Arc de Triomphe is his classic).

- **Third Republic/early industrial.** Expositions in Paris in 1878, 1889, and 1900 were the catalysts for constructing huge glass-and-steel structures that showed off modern techniques and the engineering prowess of the Industrial Revolution. This produced such Parisian monuments as the Eiffel Tower (Tour Eiffel) and Basilique du Sacré-Coeur.

Tour Eiffel

* **Art Nouveau.** Architects and decorators rebelled against the Third Republic era of mass production by stressing the uniqueness of craft. They created asymmetrical, curvaceous designs based on organic inspiration (plants and flowers) in wrought iron, stained glass, tile, and wallpaper.

In 1889, the French wanted to show how far they had come since the Revolution. They hired **Gustave Eiffel** (1832–1923) to build the world's tallest structure, a temporary 315m-high (1,051-ft.) tower made of riveted steel girders. Everyone agreed it was tall; most thought it was ugly. Its usefulness as a radio transmitter saved Eiffel's tower from being torn down.

Art Nouveau was less an architectural mode than a decorative movement, though you can still find some of the original Art Nouveau Métro entrances designed by Hector Guimard (1867–1942) in Paris. (A recently renovated entrance is at the Porte Dauphine station on the no. 2 line.)

The 20th Century   France commissioned some ambitious architectural projects in the last century, most of them the grand projects of the late **François Mitterrand**. Most were considered controversial, outrageous, or even offensive. Other than a concerted effort to break convention and look stunningly modern, nothing unifies the look of this architecture—except that foreigners designed much of it.

Britain's **Richard Rogers** (b. 1933) and Italy's **Renzo Piano** (b. 1937) turned architecture inside out—literally—to craft the

Centre Pompidou, Paris

eye-popping **Centre Pompidou** (1977), Paris's modern art museum. Exposed pipes, steel supports, and plastic-tube escalators wrap around the exterior.

Chinese-American maestro **I. M. Pei** (b. 1917) was called in to cap the Louvre's new underground Métro entrance with glass pyramids (1989), placed smack in the center of the Palais du Louvre's 17th-century courtyard.

In 1989, Paris's opera company moved into the curvaceous, dark glass mound of space of the **Opéra Bastille** (1989), designed by Canadian **Carlos Ott**. (Unfortunately, the acoustics have been lambasted.)

CULTURE GUIDE

DICTIONARY KEY

n	noun	*m*	masculine
v	verb	*f*	feminine
adj	adjective	*s*	singular
prep	preposition	*pl*	plural
adv	adverb	*interj*	interjection

All verbs are listed in infinitive (to + verb) form, cross-referenced to the appropriate conjugations page. Adjectives are listed first in masculine form, followed by the feminine ending.

For food terms, see the Menu Reader and the Grocery section in Chapter 4, Dining.

A

able, to be able to (can) *v* pouvoir **p34**

above *adv* au-dessus de

accept, to accept *v* accepter **p24**

  Do you accept credit cards? *Acceptez-vous les cartes de crédit?*

accident *n* l'accident *m*

  I've had an accident. *J'ai eu un accident.*

account *n* le compte *m*

  I'd like to transfer to / from my checking / savings account. *Je désire transférer des fonds sur / de mon compte courant / épargne.*

acne *n* l'acné *f*

across *prep* en face de / de l'autre côté de

  across the street *de l'autre côté de la rue*

actual *adj* réel / réelle

adapter plug *n* l'adaptateur *m*

address *n* l'adresse *f*

  What's the address? *Quelle est l'adresse?*

admission fee *n* le prix d'entrée

in advance *adv* à l'avance

African American *n adj* afro-américain(e)

afternoon *n* l'après-midi *m*

  in the afternoon *durant l'après-midi*

age *n* l'âge *m*

  What's your age? *Quel âge avez-vous?*

agency *n* l'agence *f*

  car rental agency *l'agence de location de voitures*

agnostic *n adj* agnostique

air conditioning *n* la climatisation *f*

  Would you lower / raise the air conditioning? *Pouvez-vous baisser / monter la climatisation?*

airport n l'aéroport m
I need a ride to the airport. *Je désire aller à l'aéroport.*
How much does the trip to the airport cost? *Combien coûte le trajet jusqu'à l'aéroport?*

airsickness bag n le sac vomitoire m

aisle (in store) n le rayon m
Which aisle is it in? *Dans quel rayon cela se trouve-t-il?*

alcohol n l'alcool m
Do you serve alcohol? *Vendez-vous de l'alcool?*
I'd like nonalcoholic beer. *Je voudrais une bière sans alcool.*

all n tout m
all of the time tout le temps
all adj tout(e) / tous pl

allergic adj allergique
I'm allergic to ____. *Je suis allergique à ____.*

altitude n l'altitude f
aluminum n l'aluminium m
ambulance n l'ambulance f
American n adj américain(e)
amount n le montant m
angry adj fâché(e)
animal n l'animal m
another adj autre
answer n la réponse f
answer, to answer v répondre (à) p25

Answer me, please. *Répondez-moi, s'il vous plaît!*

antibiotic n l'antibiotique m
I need an antibiotic. *J'ai besoin d'un antibiotique.*

antihistamine n l'antihistaminique m

anxious adj impatient(e)
any adj n'importe lequelle m / laquelle f
anything n n'importe quoi
anywhere adv n'importe où
April n l'avril m
appointment n le rendez-vous m

Do I need an appointment? *Est-ce que j'ai besoin d'un rendez-vous?*

are v See être (to be) p27.
Argentinian n adj argentin(e)
arm n le bras m
arrive, to arrive v arriver p24
arrival(s) n l'arrivée f / les arrivées f pl
art n l'art m

exhibit of art l'exposition d'art
art museum le musée d'art

artist n l'artiste m f
Asian n adj asiatique
ask, to ask v demander p24 (request) / poser (ask) p24

to ask for a drink demander une boisson
to ask a question poser une question

ENGLISH—FRENCH

aspirin n l'aspirine f
assist, to assist v aider **p24**
assistance n l'assistance f
asthma n l'asthme m

I have asthma. Je fais de
l'asthme.

atheist adj athée
ATM n le distributeur
automatique de billets
(DAB) m / la billetterie
automatique f

I'm looking for an ATM. Je
cherche un distributeur
automatique de billets.

attend, to attend v participer
(à) / assister (à) **p24**
audio adj audio
August n le août m
aunt n la tante f
Australia n l'Australie f
Australian n adj australien m
/ australienne f
autumn n l'automne m
available adj disponible

B

baby n le bébé m
baby adj pour bébés

Do you sell baby food?
Vendez-vous des aliments
pour bébés?

babysitter n le / la baby-sitter

Do you have babysitters
who speak English? Avez-
vous des baby-sitters qui
parlent anglais?

baby stroller n la poussette f
back n le dos m

My back hurts. J'ai mal au
dos.

back rub n le massage dorsal m
backed up (toilet) adj
bouchées f pl

The toilet is backed up. Les
toilettes sont bouchées.

bag n le sac m

airsickness bag le sac vomitoire

My bag was stolen. On a
volé mon sac.

I lost my bag. J'ai perdu
mon sac.

bag, to bag v emballer **p24**
baggage n le bagage m
baggage adj des bagages m pl

baggage claim la récupération des bagages

bait n l'appât m
balance (bank account) n le
solde m
balance, to balance v se bal-
ancer **p24, 38**
balcony n le balcon m
ball (sport) n le ballon m / la
balle f
ballroom dancing n la danse
de salon f
band (musical ensemble) n le
groupe m
band-aid n le pansement
(adhésif) m

bank n la banque f

    Can you help me find a bank? Pouvez-vous m'indiquer une banque?

bar n le bar m

barber n le coiffeur m

bass (instrument) n la basse f

bath n le bain m

bathe, to bathe v (se) baigner p24, 38

bathroom (restroom) n les toilettes f pl / les WC m pl

    Where is the nearest public bathroom? Où sont les toilettes publiques les plus proches?

bathtub n la baignoire f

battery n la pile (for flashlight) f / la batterie (for car) f

be, to be v être p27

beach n la plage f

beard n la barbe m

beautiful adj beau m / belle f

bed n le lit m

    pull-out bed le canapé-lit

    bed-and-breakfast (B & B) la chambre d'hôte / le bed-and-breakfast

bee n l'abeille f

    I was stung by a bee. J'ai été piqué(e) par une abeille.

beer n la bière f

    draft beer la bière pression

begin, to begin v commencer (à) p24

behave, to behave v se tenir p24, 38

behind prep derrière

beige adj beige

Belgian n adj belge

Belgium n la Belgique f

below prep en dessous de

belt n la ceinture (clothing) f

bet, to bet v miser / parier (sur) p24

best adj le / la meilleur(e)

best adv le mieux pl

better adv mieux

big adj grand(e)

bilingual adj bilingue

bill n le billet (currency) m / la note / la facture (tab) f

bill, to bill v facturer p24

biography n la biographie f

biracial adj biracial(e)

bird n l'oiseau n

birth control (pill) n la pillule f

    I need more birth control pills. J'ai besoin d'une ordonnance pour la pillule.

bit (small amount) n un peu m

black adj noir(e)

blanket n la couverture f

bleach n l'eau de Javel f

blind (visually impaired) adj aveugle / malvoyant(e)

block, to block v bloquer p24

blond(e) adj blond(e)

blouse n le chemisier m

blue adj bleu(e)

blurred vision n la vision trouble f

board (transportation) *n le bord m*

on board *à bord*

board, to board *v embarquer* **p24**

boarding pass *n la carte d'embarquement f*

boat *n le bateau m*

bomb *n la bombe f*

book *n le livre m*

bookstore *n la librairie f*

boss *n le / la patron(e) m f*

bottle *n la bouteille f / le biberon* **(baby)** *m*

May I heat this bottle someplace? *Puis-je réchauffer ce biberon quelque part?*

box (seat) *n la loge m*

box office *n le guichet m*

boy *n le garçon m*

boyfriend *n le petit ami m*

braid *n la tresse f*

braille, American *n le braille américain m*

brake, to brake *v freiner* **p24**

brandy *n l'eau-de-vie f / le cognac m*

bread *n le pain m*

break *n la cassure f*

break, to break *v (se) casser* **p24, 38**

breakfast *n le petit déjeuner m*

What time is breakfast? *À quelle heure est le petit déjeuner?*

bridge *n le pont* **(across a river)** *m / le bridge* **(dental structure)** *m*

briefcase *n la serviette f*

bright *adj lumineux m / lumineuse f*

broadband *n adj (à) large bande f*

bronze (color) *adj mordoré*

brother *n le frère m*

brown *adj marron*

brunette *n le / la brun(e) m f*

Buddhist *n adj bouddhiste*

budget *n le budget m*

buffet *n le buffet m*

bug *n l'insecte m*

burn, to burn *v brûler* **(fire)** */ graver* **(disk) p24**

Can I burn a CD here? *Puis-je graver un CD ici?*

bus *n le car* **(school bus, motorcoach)** *m / l'autobus* **(city bus)** *m / la navette* **(shuttle bus)** *f*

Where is the bus stop? *Où se trouve l'arrêt d'auto-bus?*

Which bus goes to ____? *Quel autobus va à ____?*

business *n l'entreprise* **(a business)** *f / les affaires* **(in general)** *f pl*

Here's my business card. *Voici ma carte de visite.*

business center *le centre d'affaires*

busy *adj* **plein** (restaurant) *m* / **occupée** (phone line) *f*

but *conjunction* **mais**

butter *n* **le beurre** *m*

buy, to buy *v* **acheter p24**

C

café *n* **le café** *m*

Internet café **le cybercafé**

call, to call *v* **(s')appeler p24, 39**

camp, to camp, to go camping *v* **camper p24**

Do we need a camping permit? *Avons-nous besoin d'une autorisation de camper?*

camper (motor home) *n* **le camping-car** *m*

campsite *n* **le terrain de camping** *m*

can *n* **la boîte de conserve** *f*

can (to be able to) *v* **pouvoir p34**

Canada *n* **le Canada** *m*

Canadian *n adj* **canadien** / **canadienne**

cancel, to cancel *v* **annuler p24**

My flight was canceled. *Mon vol a été annulé.*

canvas *n* **la toile** *f*

cappuccino *n* **le cappucino** *m*

car *n* **la voiture** *f*

car rental agency *l'agence de location de voitures*

I need to rent a car. *Je voudrais louer une voiture.*

card *n* **la carte** *f*

Do you accept credit cards? *Acceptez-vous les cartes de crédit?*

May I have your business card? *Puis-je avoir votre carte de visite?*

car seat (child's safety seat) *n* **le siège auto** *m*

Do you rent car seats for children? *Louez-vous des sièges auto pour enfants?*

car sickness *n* **le mal des transports** *m*

cash *n* **les espèces** *f*

cash only *espèces uniquement*

cash, to cash *v* **encaisser p24**

to cash out (gambling) *v* **toucher les gains p24**

cashmere *n* **le cachemire** *m*

casino *n* **le casino** *m*

cat *n* **le / la chat(e)** *m f*

Catholic *adj* **catholique**

cavity (tooth) *n* **la carie** *f*

I think I have a cavity. *Je pense que j'ai une carie.*

CD *n* **le CD** *m*

CD player *n* **le lecteur de CD** *m*

celebrate, to celebrate *v* **fêter p24**

cell phone *n* **le téléphone portable** *m*

centimeter *n* **le centimètre** *m*

chamber music *n* **la musique de chambre** *f*

change (money) n la monnaie f

I'd like change, please. *Je voudrais de la monnaie, s'il vous plaît.*

This isn't the correct change. *Ce n'est pas la monnaie exacte. See for numbers.*

change, to change v changer (de) / langer (a baby diaper) p24

changing room n la cabine d'essayage f

charge, to charge v mettre (money) p25 / recharger (battery) p24

charmed adj enchanté(e)

charred (meat) adj très cuite (viande)

charter, to charter (transportation) v affréter p24

cheap adj pas cher / pas chère

check n le chèque (money) m / l'addition (tab) f

Do you accept travelers' checks? *Acceptez-vous les chèques de voyage?*

Check, please! *L'addition, s'il vous plaît!*

check, to check v vérifier p24

checked (pattern) adj à carreaux m

check-in n l'enregistrement m

What time is check-in? *À quelle heure est l'enregistrement?*

check-out n la libération de la chambre f

What time is check-out? *À quelle heure doit-on libérer la chambre?*

check out, to check out (of hotel) v libérer la chambre p24

cheese n le fromage m

chicken n le poulet (meat) m

child n l'enfant m f

children n les enfants m f

Are children allowed? *Les enfants sont-ils acceptés?*

Do you have children's programs? *Avez-vous des spectacles pour enfants?*

Do you have a children's menu? *Avez-vous un menu pour enfants?*

China n la Chine f

Chinese n adj chinois(e)

chiropractor n le chiropracticien m / la chiropracticienne f

Christian adj chrétien m / chrétienne f

church n l'église f

cigar n le cigare m

cigarette n la cigarette f

pack of cigarettes *le paquet de cigarettes*

cinema n le cinéma m

city *n* la ville *f*

claim *n* la réclamation *f*

I'd like to file a claim. *Je voudrais faire une réclamation.*

clarinet *n* la clarinette *f*

class *n* la classe *f*

business class *la classe affaires*

economy class *la classe économique*

first class *la première classe*

classical (music) *adj* de musique classique *f*

clean *adj* propre

clean, to clean *v* nettoyer **p24**

Please clean the room today. *Veuillez nettoyer la chambre aujourd'hui.*

clear, to clear *v* enlever **p24**

clear *adj* clair(e)

climbing *n* l'escalade *f* / la varappe (rock climbing) *f*

climb, to climb *v* escalader (mountain) **p24** / monter (stairs) **p24**

close, to close *v* fermer **p24**

close (near) *adj* près de, proche de

closed *adj* fermé(e)

cloudy *adj* couvert(e)

clover *n* le trèfle *m*

go clubbing, to go clubbing *v* sortir en boîte **p36**

coat *n* le manteau *m*

coffee *n* le café (espresso) *m*

iced coffee *le café glacé*

cognac *n* le cognac *m*

coin *n* la pièce *f*

cold *n* le rhume *m*

I have a cold. *J'ai un rhume.*

cold *adj* froid(e)

I'm cold. *J'ai froid.*

collect *adj* en PCV

I'd like to place a collect call. *Je voudrais faire un appel en PCV.*

collect, to collect *v* ramasser / collectionner **p24**

college *n* l'université *f*

color *n* la couleur *f*

color, to color *v* colorer **p24**

come, to come *v* venir **p36**

computer *n* l'ordinateur *m*

concert *n* le concert *m*

condition *n* l'état *m*

in good / bad condition *en bon / mauvais état*

condom *n* le préservatif *m*

Do you have a condom? *As-tu un préservatif sur toi?*

not without a condom *pas sans préservatif*

confirm, to confirm *v* confirmer **p24**

I'd like to confirm my reservation. *Je voudrais confirmer ma réservation.*

confused *adj* confus(e)

congestion *n* la congestion (respiratory) *f* / l'embouteillage (traffic) *m*

connection speed *n* la vitesse de connexion *f*

ENGLISH–FRENCH

constipated adj constipé(e)
I'm constipated. Je suis constipé(e).

contact lens n la lentille de contact f

continue, to continue v continuer **p24**

convertible (car) n la voiture décapotable f / le cabriolet m

cook, to cook v cuisiner **p24**
I'd like a room where I can cook. Je voudrais une chambre où il est possible de cuisiner.

cookie n le petit gâteau m

copper adj cuivre (color)

cork n le bouchon m

corkscrew n le tire-bouchon m

corner n le coin m
on the corner au coin

correct, to correct v corriger **p24**

correct adj bon m / bonne f
Am I on the correct train? Suis-je dans le bon train?

cost, to cost v coûter **p24**
How much does it cost? Combien est-ce que cela coûte?

costume n le déguisement m

cotton n le coton m

cough n la toux f

cough, to cough v tousser **p24**

counter (in bar) n le comptoir m

country-and-western n la country f

country-and-western adj country

court n la justice (legal) f / le court (sports) m

courteous adj courtois(e)

cousin n le / la cousin(e) m f

cover charge (in bar) n l'entrée f

cow n la vache f

crack (in glass object) n la fissure f

craftsperson n l'artisan(e) m f

cream n la crème f

credit card n la carte de crédit f
Do you accept credit cards? Acceptez-vous les cartes de crédit?

crib n le lit d'enfant m

crown (dental) n la couronne f

curb n la bordure de trottoir f

curl n la boucle f

curly adj bouclé(e)

currency exchange n le change m
Where is the nearest currency exchange? Où se trouve le bureau de change le plus proche?

current (water) n l'eau courante f

customs n la douane f

cut (wound) n la coupure f / l'entaille f
I have a bad cut. Je me suis fait une vilaine entaille.

cut, to cut v couper **p24**

cybercafé n le cybercafé m

Where can I find a cyber-café? Où puis-je trouver un cybercafé?

D

damaged adj abîmé(e)

Damn! expletive Mince!

dance, to dance v danser p24

danger n le danger m

dark n le noir m

dark adj sombre

daughter n la fille f

dawn n l'aube f

at dawn à l'aube

day n le jour m

the day before yesterday avant-hier

these last few days ces derniers jours

deaf adj sourd(e) / malentendant(e) (hearing-impaired)

deal (issue) n l'affaire f

deal, to deal (cards) v donner p24

Deal me in. Tu peux compter sur moi!

December n le décembre m

declined adj rejeté(e)

Was my credit card declined? Ma carte de crédit a-t-elle été rejetée?

declare, to declare v déclarer p24

I have nothing to declare. Je n'ai rien à déclarer.

deep adj profond(e)

delay n le retard m

How long is the delay? De combien est le retard?

delighted adj ravi(e)

democracy n la démocratie f

dent, to dent v cabosser p24

He / She dented the car. Il / Elle a cabossé la voiture.

dentist n le / la dentiste m f

denture n la prothèse dentaire f

denture plate la plaque de prothèse dentaire

departure(s) n les départs m pl

designer n le / la styliste m f

dessert n le dessert m

dessert menu la carte des desserts

destination n la destination f

diabetic adj diabétique

dial, to dial (phone number) v composer p24

to dial direct composer directement le numéro

diaper n la couche f

Where can I change a diaper? Où puis-je langer mon enfant?

diarrhea n la diarrhée f

dictionary n le dictionnaire m

different (other) adj différent(e)

difficult adj difficile

dinner n le dîner m

directory assistance (phone) n les renseignements m pl

disability n le handicap m

disappear, to disappear v *disparaître* p25

disco n *la disco* f

disconnected adj *coupé(e)*

Operator, I was disconnected. *Opératrice, j'ai été coupé(e).*

discount n *la réduction (store)* f / *le tarif reduit (ticket)* m

Do I qualify for a ____ discount? *Ai-je droit à une réduction pour ____?*

children's *enfants*

senior *personnes âgées*

student *étudiants*

dish (meal) n *le plat* m

dive, to dive v *plonger* p24

scuba diving *la plongée sous-marine*

divorced adj *divorcé(e)*

dizzy (to be) adj *avoir des vertiges*

do, to do v *faire* p33

doctor n *le médecin* m f

doctor's office n *le cabinet du médecin* m

dog n *le chien* m / *la chienne* f

guide dog *le chien guide*

door n *la porte* f

double adj *à deux* / *double*

double bed *lit à deux*

to have double vision *voir double*

down adj *déprimé(e)*

download, to download v *télécharger* p24

downtown n *le centre-ville* m

dozen n *la douzaine* f

drain n *le tuyau d'évacuation* m

drama n *le drame* m

drawing n *le dessin* m

dress (garment) n *la robe* f

dress code n *la tenue de rigueur* f / *le code vestimentaire* m

What's the dress code? *Quel est le code vestimentaire?*

dress, to dress v *s'habiller* p24, 39

dressing (salad) n *la sauce* f

dried adj *séché(e)*

drink n *la boisson* f

I'd like a drink. *Je voudrais quelque chose à boire.*

drink, to drink v *boire* p31

drip, to drip v *fuire* p25

drive, to drive v *conduire* p25

driver n *le conducteur* m / *la conductrice* f

driving range n *le terrain d'exercice* m

drum n *la batterie* f / *le tambour* m

dry adj *sec* m / *sèche* f

This towel isn't dry. *Cette serviette n'est pas sèche.*

dry, to dry v *sécher* p24

I need to dry my clothes. *J'ai besoin de sécher mes vêtements.*

dry cleaner n *le pressing* m

dry cleaning n *le nettoyage à sec* m

duck n le canard m
duty-free adj hors-taxe
duty-free shop n la boutique hors-taxe f
DVD n le DVD m

Do the rooms have DVD players? Les chambres ont-elles des lecteurs de DVD?
Where can I rent DVDs or videos? Où puis-je louer des DVD ou des cassettes vidéo?

E

early adv tôt
It's early. Il est tôt.
eat, to eat v manger / déjeuner (lunch) / dîner p24
to eat out sortir dîner
economy n l'économie f
editor n le rédacteur m / la rédactrice f
educator n l'éducateur m / l'éducatrice f
eight adj huit
eighteen adj dix-huit
eighth adj huitième m
eighty adj quatre-vingt
election n l'élection f
electrical hookup n le raccordement m
elevator n l'ascenseur m
eleven adj onze
e-mail n le courriel m

May I have your e-mail address? Puis-je avoir votre adresse courriel?

e-mail message le message courriel
e-mail, to send e-mail v envoyer un courriel p24
embarrassed adj embarrassé(e)
embassy n l'ambassade f
emergency n l'urgence f
emergency brake n le frein à main m
emergency exit n la sortie de secours f
employee n l'employé(e) m f
employer n l'employeur m / l'employeuse f
engine n le moteur m
engineer n l'ingénieur m f
England n l'Angleterre f
English n adj anglais(e)

Do you speak English? Parlez-vous anglais?

enjoy, to enjoy v aimer p24
enter, to enter v entrer p24
enthusiastic adj enthousiaste
entrance, entry n l'entrée f

Do not enter. Entrée interdite.

environment n l'environnement m
escalator n l'escalier roulant m
espresso n le café m
exchange rate n le taux de change m

What is the exchange rate for U.S. / Canadian dollars? Quel est le taux de change du dollar américain / canadien?

excuse, to excuse (pardon) v excuser / pardonner **p24**

> **Excuse me.** Excusez-moi.

exhausted adj épuisé(e)

exhibit n l'exposition f

exit n la sortie f

exit, to exit v sortir **p36**

> **not an exit** ne pas sortir par cette issue

expensive adj cher m / chère f

explain, to explain v expliquer **p24**

express adj express

> **express check-in** l'enregistrement express

extra (additional) adj supplémentaire

extra-large adj très grand(e)

eye n l'œil m / les yeux m pl

eyebrow n le sourcil m

eyeglasses n les lunettes f pl

eyelash n le cil m

F

fabric n le tissu m / la matière f

face n le visage f

faint, to faint v perdre connaissance **p25**

fall (season) n l'automne m

fall, to fall v (se) tomber **p24, 38**

family n la famille f

fan n le ventilateur m

far adv loin

> **How far is it to _____?**
> Combien y a-t-il jusqu'à _____?

fare n le prix m

fast adj adv rapide / vite

fat adj gros m / grosse f

father n le père m

faucet n le lavabo m (bathroom) / l'évier m (kitchen)

fault n / **at fault** adj la faute f / fautif m / fautive f

> **I'm at fault.** C'est moi le fautif / la fautive.

> **It was his / her fault.** C'est sa faute.

fax n la télécopie m

February n le février m

fee n le prix m

female adj féminin(e)

fiancé(e) n le / la fiancé(e) m f

fifteen adj quinze

fifth adj cinquième

fifty adj cinquante

find, to find v trouver **p24**

fine (for traffic violation) n l'amende f

fine adv bien

> **I'm fine.** Je vais bien.

first adj premier m / première f

Fire! Au feu!

fishing pole n la canne à pêche f

fitness center n le club de remise en forme f

fit, to fit (clothes) v aller **p30**

> **This doesn't fit.** Cela ne va pas.

> **Does this look like it fits?** Est-ce que ça a l'air d'aller?

fitting room n la cabine d'essayage f

five adj cinq

flight n le vol m

Where do domestic flights
arrive / depart? Où se
trouve la zone d'arrivée /
de départ des lignes
intérieures?

Where do international
flights arrive / depart? Où
se trouve la zone d'arrivée
/ de départ des vols internationaux?

What time does this flight
leave? À quelle heure part
ce vol?

flight attendant le steward
m / l'hôtesse de l'air f

floor (level) n l'étage m

ground floor le rez-de-
chaussée

first floor le premier étage

flower n la fleur f

flush (gambling) n le flush m

flush, to flush v tirer la
chasse d'eau **p24**

This toilet won't flush. La
chasse d'eau de ces toi-
lettes ne marche pas.

flute n la flûte f

food n la nourriture f / les aliments m pl

foot n le pied m

forehead n le front m

format n le format m

formula n la préparation lactée **(baby)** f / la formule
(math) f

Do you sell infants' for-
mula? Est-ce que vous
vendez des préparations
lactées pour nourrisson?

forty adj quarante

forward adv en avant

four adj quatre

fourteen adj quatorze

fourth adj le quart m / la
quatrième f

one-fourth un quart

fragile adj fragile

freckle n la tache de rousseur f

free adj gratuit(e) **(complimentary)** / libre **(having
freedom)** / disponible
(available, open)

French n adj français(e)

fresh adj frais m / fraîche f

Friday n le vendredi m

friend n l'ami(e) m f

front adv de devant

front desk n la reception f

front door n la porte d'entrée f

fruit n le fruit m

fruit juice n le jus de fruit m

full adj / to be full (after a
meal) v ne plus avoir faim

Full house! Complet!

fuse n la bougie **(car)** f / le
fusible **(home)** m

G

gallon n le gallon m

garlic n l'ail m

gasoline n l'essence f

gas gauge la jauge d'essence

I'm out of gas. Je suis en panne d'essence.

gate (at airport) n la porte f

German n adj allemand(e)

gift n le cadeau m

gin n le gin m

girl n la fille f

girlfriend n la petite amie f

give, to give v donner p24

glass n le verre m

Do you have it by the glass? Est-ce qu'il est possible de le commander au verre?

I'd like a glass, please. Je voudrais un verre, s'il vous plaît.

glasses (spectacles) n les lunettes f pl

I need new glasses. J'ai besoin de nouvelles lunettes.

glove n le gant m

go, to go v aller p30

goal (sport) n le but m

goalie n le gardien de but m

goat n la chèvre f

gold n l'or (metal)

golden adj doré (color)

golf n le golf m

golf, to golf v jouer au golf p24

good adj bon m / bonne f

goodbye n au revoir

goose n l'oie m

grade school n l'école primaire f

gram n le gramme m

grandfather n le grand-père m

grandmother n la grand-mère f

grandparents n les grands-parents m pl

grape n le raisin m

gray adj gris(e)

Great! adj Super!

Greek n adj grec m / grecque f

green (golf) n le vert m

green (color) adj vert(e)

groceries n les provisions f pl

group n le groupe m

grow, to grow (get larger) v grandir p24

Where did you grow up? Où avez-vous grandi?

guard n le garde m / l'agent m

security guard l'agent de sécurité

guest n l'hôte m / l'hôtesse f

guide (tour) n le / la guide m f

guide (publication) n le guide m

guide, to guide v guider p24

guided tour n l'excursion guidée f

guitar n la guitare f

gym n la gymnastique f

gynecologist n le / la gynécologue m f

H

hair n le cheveu m / les cheveux m pl

haircut n la coupe f

I need a haircut. *J'ai besoin d'une coupe.*

How much is a haircut? *Combien coûte une coupe?*

hairdresser n le coiffeur m / la coiffeuse f

hair dryer n le séchoir m

half n la moitié n

half adj demi(e)

one half *une moitié*

hallway n le couloir (building) m / l'entrée (house) / le hall d'entrée m

hand n la main f

handicapped-accessible adj accessible aux personnes à mobilité réduite

handle, to handle v manip-uler p24

handsome adj beau m / belle f

hangout (hot spot) n lieu de rencontre m

hang out, to hang out (to relax) v traîner / passer du temps p24

hang up (end a phone call) v raccrocher p24

happy adj heureux m / heureuse f

hard adj dur(e)

hat n le chapeau m

have, to have v avoir p25

hazel adj noisette

headache n le mal de tête m

headlight n le feu (avant) m

headphones n le casque m s

hear, to hear v entendre p25

hearing-impaired adj malen-tendant(e)

heart n le cœur m

heart attack n la crise car-diaque f

hectare n l'hectare m

hello n bonjour / salut (infor-mal) / allô (telephone)

Help! Au secours!

help, to help v aider p24

hen n la poule f

her adj sa / son m / ses m f pl

herb n l'herbe f

here adv ici

high adj haut(e)

highlights (hair) n les mèches f pl

highway n l'autoroute f

hike, to hike v faire de la marche p33

him pron lui

Hindu n adj hindou(e) adj

hip-hop n le hip-hop m

his adj son m / sa f / ses m f p

historical adj historique

history n l'histoire f

hobby n le passe-temps m

hold, to hold v tenir (some-thing) p24 / attendre (pause) p25 / rester en ligne (on telephone) p24 / conserver (gambling) p24

to hold hands *se tenir par la main*

Would you hold this for me? *Pouvez-vous tenir cela pour moi?*

Hold on a minute! *Attendez une minute!*

I'll hold. *Je reste en ligne.*

holiday n *les vacances f pl*

home n *le domicile m*

homemaker n *l'homme m / la femme f au foyer*

horn (automobile) n *le klaxon m*

horse n *le cheval m*

hostel n *l'auberge f*

hot adj *chaud(e)*

hot chocolate n *le chocolat chaud m*

hotel n *l'hôtel m*

Do you have a list of local hotels? *Avez-vous une liste des hôtels de la région?*

hour n *l'heure f*

hours (at museum) n *les heures d'ouverture f pl*

how adv *comment* **(manner)** */* *combien* **(amount)**

humid adj *humide*

hundred n adj *cent*

hurry, to hurry v *être pressé(e)* **p27** */ se dépêcher* **p24, 38**

I'm in a hurry. *Je me suis pressé(e).*

Hurry, please! *Dépêchez-vous, s'il vous plaît!*

hurt, to hurt v *avoir mal* **p25** */ faire mal* **p33**

Ouch! That hurts! *Aïe! Ça fait mal!*

My head hurts. *J'ai mal à la tête.*

husband n *le mari m*

I

I pron *je*

ice n *la glace f / le glaçon m (ice cube)*

with ice cubes *avec des glaçons*

identification n *la pièce d'identité f*

inch n *le pouce m*

include, to include v *comprendre* **p25**

Is breakfast included? *Le petit-déjeuner est-il compris?*

India n *l'Inde f*

Indian n adj *indien m / indienne f*

indigestion n *l'indigestion f*

inexpensive adj *pas cher m / pas chère f*

infant n *le petit enfant m*

Are infants allowed? *Les enfants en bas âge sont-ils acceptés?*

information n *l'information f / les renseignements m pl*

information booth n *le stand d'information*

injury n *la blessure f*

insect repellent n l'insectifuge m

inside prep dans / à l'intérieur de

insult, to insult v insulter **p24**

insurance n l'assurance f

intercourse (sexual) n les rapports sexuels m pl

interest rate n le taux d'intérêt m

intermission n l'entracte m

Internet n l'Internet m

high-speed Internet l'Internet à haut débit

Do you have Internet access? Offrez-vous un accès à Internet?

Where can I find an Internet café? Où puis-je trouver un cybercafé?

interpreter n l'interprète m f

I need an interpreter. J'ai besoin d'un interprète.

introduce, to introduce v présenter **p24**

I'd like to introduce you to ___. Laissez-moi vous présenter ___.

Ireland n l'Irlande f

Irish n adj irlandais(e)

is v est See être **(to be) p27.**

Italian n adj italien m / italienne f

J

jacket n le blouson m / la veste f

January n le janvier m

Japanese n adj japonais(e)

jasmine n le jasmin m

jazz n le jazz m

Jewish adj juif m / juive f

jogging n le jogging m

jog, to go jogging v faire du jogging **p33**

juice n le jus m

June n le juin m

July n le juillet m

K

keep, to keep v / **to mind (children)** v garder **p24**

kilo n le kilo m

kilometer n le kilomètre m

kind (type) n la sorte f

kind (nice) adj gentil m / gentille f

What kind of car is it? Quelle sorte de voiture est-ce?

You're very kind! C'est très gentil de votre part!

kiss n le baiser m

kiss, to kiss v donner un baiser (à) **p24**

kitchen n la cuisine f

know, to know v savoir **(a fact) p35** / connaître **(a person or place) p31**

kosher adj kasher

L

lactose-intolerant adj
*allergique aux produits
laitiers*

land, to land v *atterrir* **p24**

language n *la langue* f

laptop n *l'ordinateur
portable* m

large adj *grand(e)*

last, to last v *durer* **p24**

last adj *dernier* m / *dernière* f

late adj *en retard*

Please don't be late. *Ne
soyez pas en retard, s'il
vous plaît.*

later adv *plus tard*

See you later. *À bientôt.*

laundry n *la lessive* f

lavender adj *bleu lavande*

law n *la loi* f

lawyer n *l'avocat(e)* m f

least adv *le moins*

leather n *le cuir* m

leave, to leave (depart) v
partir **p34**

left n *la gauche* f

on the left *à gauche*

leg n *la jambe* f

less adj *moins*

license n *le permis* m

driver's license *le permis de
conduire*

life preserver n *le gilet* m / *la
bouée de sauvetage* f

light n *la lumière* **(lamp)** f / *le
voyant* **(car)** m / *le feu* **(for
cigarette)** m

May I offer you a light?
Puis-je vous offrir du feu?

lighter (cigarette) n *le briquet* m

like, to like v *vouloir* **(want)**
p37 / *aimer* **(take pleasure
in)** **p24**

I would like ____. *Je
voudrais ____.*

limousine n *la limousine* f

liqueur n *la liqueur* f

liquor n *les boissons
alcoolisées* f

liter n *le litre* m

little adj *petit(e)*

live, to live v *vivre* **p25** /
habiter **(place)** **p24**

Where do you live? *Où
habitez-vous?*

living n *la vie* f

**What do you do for a liv-
ing?** *Que faites-vous dans
la vie?*

local adj *local(e)*

lock n *le verrou* **(on door)** m /
le cadenas **(on locker)** m

lock, to lock v *verrouiller* **p24**

I'm locked out. *Je me suis
enfermé(e) dehors.*

locker (storage) n *le local de
stockage* m

locker room n *le vestiaire* m

long adv *longtemps*

For how long? *Pendant
combien de temps?*

long adj *long* m / *longue* f

look, to look v regarder
(observe) p24 / aller (clothing) p30
I'm just looking. Je ne fais
que regarder.
Look here! Regarde ça!
How does this look? Ça me
va comment?
look for, to look for (search)
v chercher p24
I'm looking for a porter. Je
cherche un porteur.
loose adj flottant(e)
lose, to lose v perdre p25
I lost my passport / wallet.
J'ai perdu mon passeport /
porte-monnaie.
I'm lost. Je suis perdu(e).
lost adj perdu(e)
loud adj fort(e)
loudly adv fort
Please speak more loudly.
Parlez plus fort, s'il vous
plaît.
lounge n le salon m / le bar m
lounge, to lounge v se
prélasser p24, 38
love n l'amour m
love, to love v aimer p24
to love (family) aimer
to love (a friend) bien aimer
to love (a lover) aimer
to make love faire l'amour
low adj bas m / basse f
lunch n le déjeuner m

luggage n le bagage m
**Where do I report lost lug-
gage?** Où puis-je déclarer
la perte d'un bagage?
**Where is the lost luggage
claim?** Où se trouve la
zone de récupération des
bagages?

M

machine n la machine f
made of adj en / fait à partir
de
magazine n le magazine m
maid (hotel) n la femme de
chambre f
maiden adj de jeune fille
That's my maiden name.
C'est mon nom de jeune
fille.
mail n le courrier m
registered mail courrier
recommandé
make, to make v faire p33
makeup n le maquillage m
make up, to make up v se
réconcilier (apologize)
p24, 38 / se maquiller
(apply cosmetics) p24, 38
male (man) n l'homme m
male adj masculin
mall n le centre commercial m
manager n le directeur m / la
directrice f
manual (instruction booklet)
n le guide d'utilisation m

many adj beaucoup de

map n la carte f / le plan (subway) m

March (month) n le mars m

market n le marché m

  flea market le marché aux puces

  open-air market le marché en plein air

married adj marié(e)

marry, to marry v (s')épouser p24, 39

massage, to massage v masser p24

match n le match (sport) m / l'allumette (fire) f

  book of matches la boîte d'allumettes

match, to match v aller avec p30

May (month) n le mai m

may (permission) v pouvoir p34

  May I _____? Puis-je _____?

meal n le repas m

meat n la viande f

medication n le médicament m

medium (size) adj moyen(ne)

medium rare (meat) adj saignant(e)

medium well (meat) adj rouge

member n le / la membre mf

menu n le menu m

  May I see a menu? Puis-je avoir un menu?

metal detector n le détecteur de métaux m

meter n le mètre m

Mexican n adj mexicain(e)

middle prep au milieu de

midnight n minuit

mile n le mile m

military n l'armée f / le militaire m

milk n le lait m

  milk shake le milk-shake / le lait frappé

milliliter n le millilitre m

millimeter n le millimètre m

minute n la minute f

  in a minute dans une minute

miss, to miss v manquer (a flight) p24

missing adj manquant(e)

mistake n l'erreur f

moderately priced adj pas trop cher m / chère f

mole (facial feature) n le grain de beauté m

Monday n le lundi m

money n l'argent m / les fonds m

  money transfer le transfer de fonds

month n le mois m

morning n le matin m

  in the morning le matin

mosque n la mosquée f

mother n la mère f

motorcycle n la moto f

mountain n la montagne f

mountain climbing l'escalade f

mouse n la souris f

moustache n la moustache

mouth n la bouche f

move, to move (change homes) v déménager **p24**

movie n le film m

moving walkway n le trottoir roulant m

much adv beaucoup

mugged adj agressé(e)

museum n le musée m

music n la musique

live music la musique live

musician n le musicien m / la musicienne f

muslim adj musulman(e)

mystery (novel) n le roman policier m

N

name n le nom m

My name is ___. Je m'appelle ___.

What's your name? Comment vous appelez-vous?

first name le prénom

last name le nom de famille

napkin n la serviette f

narrow adj étroit(e)

nationality n la nationalité f

nausea n la nausée f

near adj proche

nearby adv près d'ici

neat (tidy) adj bien rangé(e)

need, to need v avoir besoin de **p25**

neighbor n le / la voisin(e) m f

nephew n le neveu m

network n le réseau m

new adj nouveau m / nouvelle f

news (current events) n les actualités f pl

newspaper n le journal m

newsstand n le kiosque à journaux m

New Zealand n la Nouvelle-Zélande f

New Zealander adj néo-zélandais(e)

next adj prochain(e)

next prep à côté de

the next station la prochaine station

next adv puis **(then)** / après **(later)**

nice adj gentil m / gentille f

niece n la nièce f

night n la nuit f

at night pendant la nuit

per night par nuit

nine adj neuf

nineteen adj dix-neuf

ninety adj quatre-vingt-dix

ninety-one adj quatre-vingt-onze

ninth adj neuvième

No. Non.

no (not any) adv pas de

noisy adj bruyant(e)

none pron aucun(e)

nonsmoking adj non fumeur

noon n le midi m

nose n le nez m

novel n le roman m

November n le novembre m

now adv maintenant

number n le numéro m / le chiffre (digit, figure)

Which room number? Quel numéro de chambre?

May I have your phone number? Puis-je avoir votre numéro de téléphone?

nurse n l'infirmier m / l'infirmière f

nurse, to nurse (breastfeed) v allaiter p24

Do you have a place where I can nurse? Y a-t-il un endroit où je puisse allaiter?

nursery n la crèche f

Do you have a nursery or playground? Avez-vous une crèche ou une aire de jeu?

nut la noix f

O

o'clock adv heures

October n l'octobre m

offer, to offer v offrir p24

officer n l'officier m / l'agent m

oil n l'huile f

Ok. D'accord.

Are you okay? Ça va?

old adj vieux m / vieille f / âgé(e) (person)

I'm six years old. J'ai six ans. See for numbers.

olive n l'olive f

one adj un(e)

one way (traffic sign) adj sens unique m

open (business) adj ouvert(e)

Are you open? Êtes-vous ouvert?

open v ouvrir p33

opera n l'opéra m

opera house n l'opéra m

operator (phone) n l'opérateur m / l'opératrice f

optometrist n l'optométriste

orange adj orange (color)

orange juice n le jus d'orange m

order, to order v ordonner / demander / commander (a meal) p24

organic adj biologique

Ouch! Aïe!

outside adv dehors

overcooked adj trop cuit(e)

overheat, to overheat v (car)chauffer p24

The car is overheating. La voiture chauffe.

overflow, to overflow v déborder p24

oxygen tank n la bouteille d'oxygène f

P

package n le colis m

pacifier n la tétine f

page, to page (someone) v faire appeler p33

paint, to paint v peindre p25

painting n la peinture f

pale adj pâle

paper n le papier m

parade n le défilé m

parent n le parent m

park n le parc m

parking n le parking m / le stationnement m

　no parking stationnement interdit

park, to park v se garer p24, 38

　parking fee le prix du stationnement

　parking garage le parking couvert

partner n le / la partenaire m f

party n la soirée (event) f / le parti (political)

pass, to pass (gambling) v passer p24

　I'll pass / double. Je passe.

passenger n le passager m / la passagère f

passport n le passeport m

　I've lost my passport. J'ai perdu mon passeport.

password n le mot de passe m

pay, to pay v payer p24

peanut n la cacahuète f

pedestrian n le piéton m / la piétonne f

pediatrician n le / la pédiatre m f

　Can you recommend a pediatrician? Pouvez-vous me recommander un(e) pédiatre?

permit n le permis f

　Do we need a permit? Avons-nous besoin d'un permis?

permit, to permit v permettre p25

phone n le téléphone m

　Do you have a phone directory? Avez-vous un annuaire (téléphonique)?

　May I have your phone number? Puis-je avoir votre numéro de téléphone?

　Where can I find a public phone? Où puis-je trouver un téléphone public?

　phone operator l'opérateur / l'opératrice téléphonique

　Do you sell prepaid phones? Vendez-vous des téléphones portables prépayées?

phone call n l'appel m

　I need to make a collect phone call. Je dois faire un appel en PCV.

　an international phone call un appel à l'étranger

photocopy, to photocopy v photocopier p24

ENGLISH—FRENCH

piano n le piano m

pillow n l'oreiller m

down pillow l'oreiller en duvet d'oie

pink adj rose

pint n la pinte f / la bière (pint of beer) f

pizza n la pizza f

place, to place v mettre p25

plastic n le plastique m

play n la pièce de théâtre f

play, to play v jouer (à) (de) (game, instrument) p24

playground n l'aire de jeu f

Do you have a playground or nursery? Avez-vous une aire de jeu ou une crèche?

please (polite entreaty) adv s'il vous plaît

please, to be pleasing to v plaire p25 / faire plaisir (à) p33

pleasure n le plaisir m

It's a pleasure. C'est un plaisir.

plug n la prise (electrical outlet) f

plug in, to plug in v brancher p24

point, to point v montrer p24

Would you point me in the direction of ___? Pouvez-vous me montrer dans quelle direction se trouve ___?

police n la police f

police station n le bureau de police m

pool n la piscine (swimming) f / le billard (game) m

pop music n la musique pop f

popular adj populaire

port n le porto (beverage) m / le port (ship) m

porter n le porteur m

portrait n le portrait m

postcard n la carte postale f

post office n le bureau de poste m

Where is the nearest post office? Où se trouve le bureau de poste le plus proche?

poultry n la volaille f

pound n la livre f

prefer, to prefer v préférer p24

pregnant adj enceinte

prescription n l'ordonnance f

price n le prix m

print, to print v imprimer p24

private berth / cabin n la couchette particulière f / le compartiment privé m

problem n le problème m

process, to process (transaction) v traiter p24

product n le produit m

professional adj professionnel m / professionnelle f

program n le programme m / le spectacle m

May I have a program? Puis-je avoir un programme?

Protestant n adj le / la protestant(e)
publisher n l'éditeur m / l'éditrice **(person)** f / la maison d'édition **(publishing house)** f
pull, to pull v tirer **p24**
pump n la pompe f
purple adj violet
purse n le sac à main m
push, to push v pousser **p24**
put, to put v miser **p24**

Q

quarter adj le quart m
  one-quarter un quart
Quebec n le Québec m
Quebecois n adj québécois(e)
quiet adj calme

R

rabbit n le lapin m
radio n la radio f
  satellite radio la radio par satellite
rain, to rain v pleuvoir
  Is it supposed to rain? Est-ce qu'il va pleuvoir?
  It's rainy. Le temps est pluvieux.
ramp, wheelchair n la rampe d'accès f
rape n le viol m
  I was raped. Je suis violé(e).
rare (meat) adj bleue
rate (car rental, hotel) n le tarif m

What's the rate per day? Quel est le tarif par jour?
What's the rate per week? Quel est le tarif hebdomadaire?
rate plan (cell phone) n le forfait m
  Do you have a rate plan? Offrez-vous des forfaits?
rather adv mieux
read, to read v lire **p25**
really adv vraiment
receipt n le reçu m
receive, to receive v recevoir **p37 (like VOIR)**
recommend, to recommend v recommender **p24**
red adj rouge
redhead n le roux m / la rousse f
refill n la même boisson **(beverage)** f / le renouvellement d'une ordonnance **(prescription)** m
reggae n le reggae m
relative n le membre de la famille m
remove, to remove v ôter **p24**
rent, to rent v louer **p24**
  I'd like to rent a car. Je voudrais louer une voiture.
repeat, to repeat v repeater **p24**
  Would you please repeat that? Pourriez-vous répéter ce que vous venez de dire, s'il vous plaît?

reservation n la réservation f

I'd like to make a reservation for ___ people. Je voudrais faire une réservation pour ___ personnes.

restaurant n le restaurant m

Where can I find a good restaurant? Où puis-je trouver un bon restaurant?

restroom n les toilettes f pl / les WC m pl

Do you have a public restroom? Avez-vous des toilettes publiques?

return, to return v retourner p24

ride, to ride v conduire p25

right adj droit(e)

It is on the right. C'est à droite.

Turn right at the corner. Tournez à droite au coin de la rue.

rights n les droits m pl

civil rights les droits civiques

river n la fleuve f / la rivière f

road n la route f / la rue (street) f

road closed (sign) n route fermée f

rob, to rob v voler p24

I've been robbed. J'ai été victime d'un vol.

rock and roll n le rock m

rock climbing n la varappe f

rocks (iced beverage) adj avec des glaçons

I'd like it on the rocks, please. Avec des glaçons, s'il vous plaît.

romantic adj romantique

room (hotel) n la chambre f

room service le service en chambre

rooster n le coq m

rope n la corde f

rose n la rose f

royal flush n la quinte royale f

rum n le rhum m

run, to run v courir p24

S

sad adj triste

safe (for valuables) n le coffre-fort m

Do the rooms have safes? Les chambres sont-elles équipées de coffres-forts?

safe (secure) adj sûr(e) / sans danger

Is this area safe? Ce quartier est-il sûr?

sail n la voile f / la navigation f

sail, to sail v appareiller p24

When do we sail? À quelle heure le navire appareille-t-il?

salad n la salade f

salesperson n le / la représentant(e) commercial(e)

salt *n* le sel *m*

Is that low-salt? *Est-ce à
faible teneur en sel?*

satellite *n* le satellite *m*

satellite radio *la radio par
satellite*

Saturday *n* le samedi *m*

sauce *n* la sauce *f*

say, to say *v* dire **p32**

scan, to scan (document) *v*
scanner **p24**

schedule (of events) *n* le programme *m*

school *n* l'école *f*

high school *le lycée*

law school *l'université de
droit*

scooter *n* le scooter *m*

score *n* le score *m*

Scottish *n adj* écossais(e)

scratched *adj* rayé(e)

scuba dive, to scuba dive *v*
faire de la plongée sous-
marine **p33**

sculpture *n* la sculpture *f*

seafood *n* les poissons et
fruits de mer

search *n* la fouille *f*

search, to search *v* chercher
p24

seasick (to be) *adj* avoir le
mal de mer

I am seasick. *J'ai le mal de
mer.*

seasickness pill *n* le cachet
contre le mal de mer *m*

seat *n* la place *f* / le siège *m*

child seat *le siège pour
enfant*

second *adj* second(e)

security *n* la sécurité *f*

security guard *l'agent de
sécurité*

sedan *n* la berline *f*

see, to see *v* voir **p37**

May I see it? *Puis-je le / la
voir de plus près?*

self-serve *adj* en libre-service *m*

sell, to sell *v* vendre **p25**

seltzer *n* l'eau de Seltz *f*

send, to send *v* envoyer **p24**

separated (marital status)
adj séparé(e)

September *n* le septembre *m*

serve, to serve *v* server **p24**

service *n* le service *m* / l'office (religious) *m*

out of service *hors service*

service charge *n* frais de
traitement *m*

seven *adj* sept

seventy *adj* soixante-dix

seventeen *adj* dix-sept

seventh *adj* septième

sew, to sew *v* coudre **p25**

sex (gender) *n* le sexe *m*

sex, to have intercourse *v*
avoir des rapports sexuels
p25

sheet *n* le drap (bed) *m* / la
feuille (paper) *f*

shellfish *n* les fruits de mer *m*

ship *n* *le navire m*

ship, to ship *v* *expediter* **p24**

> **How much to ship this to
> ____?** *Combien cela coûte-
> t-il pour expédier cela en
> ____?*

shipwreck *n* *le naufrage m*

shirt *n* *la chemise* **(man's)** *f /
le blouson* **(woman's)** *m*

shoe *n* *la chaussure f*

shop *n* *la boutique f*

shop, to shop *v* *faire des
achats / chercher* **(to look
for)** */ faire des courses* **p33**

> **I'm shopping for ____
> clothes.** *Je cherche des
> vêtements pour ____*
> **men's** *hommes.*
> **women's** *femmes.*
> **children's** *enfants.*

short *adj* *court(e)*

shorts *n* *les shorts m*

shot (liquor) *n* *le verre m*

shout, to shout *v* *crier* **p24**

show (performance) *n* *le
spectacle m*

> **What time is the show?** *À
> quelle heure est le specta-
> cle?*

show, to show *v* *montrer* **p24**

> **Would you show me?**
> *Pouvez-vous me montrer?*

shower *n* *la douche f*

> **Does it have a shower?** *Est-
> ce qu'il y a une douche?*

shower, to shower *v* *se
doucher* **p24, 38**

shrimp *n* *la crevette f*

shuttle bus *n* *la navette f*

sick *adj* *malade*

> **I feel sick.** *Je ne me sens pas
> bien.*

side *adv* *à part*

sidewalk *n* *le trottoir m*

sightseeing *n* *l'excursion m*

> **sightseeing bus** *n* *le car
> d'excursion m*

sign, to sign *v* *signer* **p24**

> **Where do I sign?** *Où dois-je
> signer?*

silver *adj* *argent*

sing, to sing *v* *chanter* **p24**

single *n adj* *le / la célibataire*
(unmarried) */ seul(e)*
(alone, only)

> **Are you single?** *Êtes-vous
> célibataire?*

single bed *le lit à une place*

sink *n* *le lavabo* **(bathroom)**
m / l'évier **(kitchen)** *m*

sister *n* *la sœur f*

sit, to sit *v* *s'asseoir* **p39**

six *adj* *six*

sixteen *adj* *seize*

sixty *adj* *soixante*

size (clothing, shoes) *n* *la
taille f*

skin *n* *la peau f*

sleeping berth *n* *la couchette f*

sleeping car *n* *le wagon-lits m*

slow *adj* *lent(e)*

slow, to slow *v* *ralentir* **p24**

> **Slow down!** *Ralentissez! /
> Veuillez ralentir!*

slowly adv lentement

Please speak more slowly.
Parlez plus lentement, s'il
vous plaît.

slum n les bas quartiers m pl

small adj petit(e)

smell, to smell v sentir p24

smoke, to smoke v fumer p24

smoking adj (pour) fumeurs

smoking area la zone
fumeurs

no smoking interdit de fumer

snack n le snack m

Snake eyes! Paire d'as!

snorkel, to snorkel v faire de la
plongée avec un tuba p33

soap n le savon m

sock n la chaussette f

soda n la boisson gazeuse f /
le coca (cola) m

diet soda la boisson
gazeuse allégée

soft adj doux m / douce f

software n le logiciel m

sold out adj complet m /
complète f

some adj du m / de la f / des
m f pl

someone n quelqu'un (definite) / on (indefinite)

something n quelque chose f

son n le fils m

song n la chanson f

sorry adj désolé(e)

I'm sorry. Je suis désolé(e).

soup n la soupe f

spa n le spa m

Spain n l'Espagne f

Spanish n adj espagnol(e)

spare tire n la roue de secours f

sparrow n le moineau m

speak, to speak v parler p24

Do you speak English?
Parlez-vous anglais?

Please speak louder. Parler
plus fort, s'il vous plaît.

Please speak more slowly.
Parler plus lentement, s'il
vous plaît.

special (featured meal) n le
plat du jour m

specify, to specify v spécifier
p24

speed limit n la limite de
vitesse f

**What's the speed limit in
town?** Quelle est la limite
de vitesse en ville?

speedometer n l'indicateur
de vitesse m

spell, to spell v peeler p24

Would you spell that, please?
Pourriez-vous épeler ce mot,
s'il vous plaît?

spices n les épices f pl

spill, to spill v renverser p24

split (gambling) v partager
p24

sports n les sports m pl

spring (season) n le printemps m

stadium n le stade m

staff (employees) n le personnel m / les employés m pl

stamp (postage) n le timbre m

stair n l'escalier m

Where are the stairs? Où sont les escaliers?

stand, to stand v se tenir debout p24, 38

start, to start v commencer **(begin)** / démarrer **(a car)** p24

state n l'état m

station n la station f

Where is the nearest gas station? Où se trouve la station essence la plus proche?

Where is _____ Où se trouve _____

the bus station? la station de bus?

the subway station? la station de métro?

the train station? la gare?

stay, to stay v rester p24

We'll be staying for _____ nights. Nous resterons _____ nuits. See for numbers.

steakhouse n le grill m

steal, to steal v voler p24

stolen adj volé(e)

stop n l'arrêt m ,

Is this my stop? Est-ce mon arrêt?

I missed my stop. J'ai manqué mon arrêt.

stop, to stop v (s')arrêter p24, 39

Please stop. Arrêtez-vous, s'il vous plaît.

STOP (traffic sign) STOP

Stop, thief! Au voleur! Arrêtez-le!

store n le magasin m

straight (gambling) n la quinte f

straight adj droit(e) / raide **(hair)** / sec **(drink)**

straight ahead adv tout droit

street n la rue f

across the street de l'autre côté de la rue

down the street en bas de la rue

Which street? Quelle rue?

How many more streets? Dans combien de rues?

stressed adj stressé(e)

striped adj à rayures f pl

stroller n la poussette f

Do you rent baby strollers? Est-ce que vous louez des poussettes?

suburb n la banlieue f

subway n le métro m

subway line la ligne de métro

subway station la station de métro

Which subway do I take for _____? Quelle ligne de métro dois-je prendre pour aller à _____?

subtitle n le sous-titre m

suitcase n la valise f

suite n la suite f

summer n l'été m

sun n le soleil m

sunburn n le coup de soleil m

I have a bad sunburn. J'ai un mauvais coup de soleil.

Sunday n le dimanche m

sunglasses n les lunettes de soleil f

sunny adj ensoleillé(e)

It's sunny out. Il fait du soleil.

sunroof n le toit ouvrant m

sunscreen n la crème solaire f

Do you have sunscreen SPF ___? Avez-vous une crème solaire indice ___? See for numbers.

supermarket n le supermarché m

surf, to surf v surfer p24

surfboard n la planche de surf f

suspiciously adv d'une manière étrange

swallow, to swallow v avaler p24

sweater n le pull m

swim, to swim v nager p24

Can one swim here? Peut-on nager ici?

swimsuit n le maillot de bain m

swim trunks n le caleçon de bain m

Swiss n adj suisse

Switzerland n la Suisse f

symphony n l'orchestre symphonique m

T

table n la table f

table for two la table pour deux

tailor n le tailleur m

Can you recommend a good tailor? Pourriez-vous me recommander un bon tailleur?

take, to take v prendre p35 / emmener p24

Take me to the station. Emmenez-moi à la gare, s'il vous plaît.

How much to take me to ___? Quel est le prix de la course d'ici à ___?

takeout menu n le menu des plats à emporter m

talk, to talk v parler p24

tall adj grand(e)

taste n le goût m

taste, to taste v goûter / déguster p24

tax n la taxe f

value-added tax (VAT) la taxe sur la valeur ajoutée (TVA)

taxi n le taxi m

Taxi! Taxi!

Would you call me a taxi? Pouvez-vous m'appeler un taxi?

tea n le thé m

herbal tea la tisane

team n l'équipe f

techno n la musique techno f

television n la télévision f

temple n le temple m

ten adj dix

tennis n le tennis m

  tennis court le court de tennis

tent n la tente f

tenth adj dixième

terminal n le terminal m

Thank you. Merci.

that (nearby) pron celui-ci m / celle-ci f

that (far away) pron celui-là m / celle-là f

theater n le théâtre m

them pron pl eux m / elles f

then adv alors (so, in that case) / puis (next)

there adv là

  Is / Are there ___? Est-ce qu'il y a ___?

  over there là-bas

these adj ces

thick adj épais m / épaisse f

thin adj fin(e)

third adj troisième

thirteen adj treize

thirteenth adj treizième

thirty adj trente

this adj ce m / cette f

those adj ces

thousand adj mille

three adj trois

Thursday n le jeudi m

ticket n le billet m

  ticket counter le guichet

  one-way ticket un aller simple,

  round-trip ticket un aller-retour,

tight adj serré(e)

time n l'heure f

  Is it on time? Est-il / Est-elle à l'heure?

  At what time? À quelle heure?

  What time is it? Quelle heure est-il?

timetable n l'horaire m

tip (gratuity) le pourboire m

  tip included service compris

tire n le pneu m

  I have a flat tire. J'ai un pneu crevé.

tired adj fatigué(e)

today n adv aujourd'hui

toilet n les toilettes f pl / la cuvette des toilettes f

  The toilet is overflowing. La cuvette des toilettes déborde.

  The toilet is backed up. Les toilettes sont bouchées.

toilet paper n le papier de toilette m

  You're out of toilet paper. Il n'y a plus de papier toilette.

toiletries n le nécessaire de toilette m

toll n le péage m

tomorrow n adv demain

ton n la tonne f

too adv trop (excessively) / aussi (also)

tooth *n* la dent *f*
I lost my tooth. J'ai perdu une dent.
toothache *n* le mal de dents *m*
I have a toothache. J'ai mal à une dent.
total *adv* en tout
What is the total? Ça fait combien en tout?
tour *n* l'excursion *f*
Are guided / audio tours available? Y a-t-il des excursions guidées / audio-guidées?
towel *n* la serviette *f*
May we have more towels? Pouvons-nous avoir plus de serviettes?
toy *n* le jouet *m*
toy store le magasin de jouets
Do you have any toys for the children? Avez-vous des jouets pour enfants?
traffic *n* la circulation *f*
How's traffic? Comment est la circulation?
traffic rules le code de la route
trail *n* le sentier *m* p171
Are there trails? Y a-t-il des sentiers?
train *n* le train *m*
express train le train express
local train la ligne régionale
Does the train go to ____? Le train va-t-il à ____?
Where is the train station? Où se trouve la gare?

train, to train *v* entraîner **p24**
transfer, to transfer *v* transférer **p24**
I need to transfer funds. J'ai besoin de transférer des fonds.
wire transfer le virement
transmission *n* la transmission *f*
automatic transmission la transmission automatique
standard transmission la transmission standard
travel, to travel *v* voyager **p24**
travelers' check *n* le chèque de voyage *m*
Do you cash travelers' checks? Encaissez-vous les chèques de voyage?
trim, to trim *v* couper (hair) **p24**
trip *n* le voyage *m*
triple *adj* triple
trumpet *n* la trompette *f*
trunk *n* le coffre *m*
try, to try *v* essayer **p24**
Tuesday *n* le mardi *m*
turkey *n* la dinde *f*
turn, to turn *v* tourner **p24**
to turn left / right tourner à gauche / à droite
to turn off / turn on éteindre / allumer
turn signal *n* le clignotant *m*
twelve *adj* douze
twelfth *adj* douzième
twenty *adj* vingt
twentieth *adj* vingtième
two *adj* deux

U

umbrella n le parapluie m

uncle n l'oncle m

undercooked adj pas assez cuit(e)

understand, to understand v comprendre **p25**

I don't understand. Je ne comprends pas.

Do you understand? Vous comprenez?

underwear n le sous-vêtement m

United States n les États-Unis m

university n l'université f

up adv vers le haut

update, to update v mettre à jour **p25**

upgrade n la mise à niveau f

upload, to upload v télécharger **p24**

upscale adj huppé(e)

us pron nous

USB port n le port USB m

use, to use v utiliser **p24**

V

vacation n les vacances f

on vacation en vacances

to go on vacation partir en vacances

vacancy n les chambres libres f pl

no vacancy complet

van n le fourgon m

VCR n le magnétoscope m

Do the rooms have VCRs? Les chambres sont-elles équipées de magnétoscope?

vegetable n le légume m

vegetarian n végétarien m / végétarienne f

vending machine n le distributeur m

version n la version f

very adj très

video n la vidéocassette f

Where can I rent videos or DVDs? Où puis-je louer des cassettes vidéo ou des DVD?

view n la vue f

beach view la vue sur mer

city view la vue sur ville

vineyard n le vignoble m

vinyl adj en vinyle m

violin n le violon m

visa n le visa m

Do I need a visa? Ai-je besoin d'un visa?

vision n la vision f

visit, to visit v visiter **(a place) p24** / rendre visite à **(person) p25**

visually-impaired adj malvoyant(e)

vodka n la vodka f

volume n le volume m

Please turn up / turn down the volume. Veuillez augmenter / baisser le volume.

vote, to vote v voter

voucher n le bon m / le coupon m

meal voucher le coupon-repas

room voucher le coupon d'hébergement

W

wait, to wait v attendre **p25**
 Please wait. Attendez, s'il
  vous plaît!
waiter n le serveur m / la
 serveuse f
waiting area n la salle d'attente f
wake-up call n le réveil téléphonique m
wallet n le portefeuille m
 I lost my wallet. J'ai perdu
  mon portefeuille.
 Someone stole my wallet.
  On a volé mon portefeuille.
walk, to walk v marcher **p24**
 / aller à pied **p28, 30**
walker (ambulatory device)
 n le déambulatoire m
walkway n le trottoir m
want, to want v vouloir **p37**
war n la guerre f
warm adj chaud(e)
watch, to watch v regarder
 p24
water n l'eau f
 Is the water drinkable?
  L'eau est-elle potable?
 **Do you have sparkling
  water?** Avez-vous de l'eau
  pétillante?
wave n la vague **(water)**
waxing n l'épilation à la cire f
weapon n l'arme f
wear, to wear v porter **p24**
weather forecast n les prévisions météorologiques f pl

Wednesday n le mercredi m
week n la semaine f
 this week cette semaine
 last week la semaine dernière
 next week la semaine
  prochaine
weigh v peser **p24**
 I weigh ____. Je pèse ___.
 It weighs ____. Cela pèse
  ___. See for numbers.
weights n les altères f pl
welcome adv bienvenu(e)
 You're welcome. Vous êtes
  le bienvenu / la bienvenue.
well adv bien
 well done (meat) bien cuite
 well done (task) bon travail
 I don't feel well. Je ne me
  sens pas bien.
western adj western **(movie)**
whale n la baleine f
what adv quel m / quelle f
 What sort of ____? Quelle
  sorte de ____?
 What time is it? Quelle
  heure est-il?
wheelchair n la chaise
 roulante f
 wheelchair access l'accès
  aux handicapés
 wheelchair ramp la rampe
  d'accès pour handicapés
 power wheelchair le fauteuil roulant motorisé
wheeled (luggage) adj à
 roulettes
when adv quand

where *adv* où
  Where is it? *Où est-ce?*
which *adj* lequel *m* / laquelle *f* / lesquels *m pl* / lesquelles *f pl*
  Which one? *Lequel /
  Laquelle?*
  Which is it? *Lequel /
  Laquelle est-ce?*
white *adj* blanc *m* / blanche *f*
who *pron* qui
whose *pron* à qui
wide *adj* large
widow / widower *n* la veuve *f* / le veuf *m*
wife *n* la femme *f*
Wi-Fi *n* la Wi-Fi *f*
window *n* la fenêtre *f*
  drop-off window le guichet de dépôt
  pickup window le guichet de récupération
windshield *n* le pare-brise *m*
windshield wiper *n* l'essuie-glace *m*
windsurf, to windsurf *v* faire de la planche à voile **p33**
windy *adj* du vent
wine *n* le vin *m*
winery *n* le vignoble *m*
winter *n* l'hiver *m*
wiper *n* l'essuie-glace *m*
with *prep* avec
withdraw *v* retirer **p24**
  I need to withdraw money. *J'ai besoin de retirer de l'argent.*

withdrawal *n* le retrait *m*
without *prep* sans
woman *n* la femme *f*
work, to work *v* travailler **(job) p24** / marcher **(function) p24**
  This doesn't work. *Cela ne marche pas.*
workout *n* l'entraînement *m*
worse *adj* pire
worst *adj* le pire
write, to write *v* écrire **p32**
  Would you write that down for me? *Pourriez-vous m'écrire cela?*
writer *n* l'écrivain

X
x-ray machine *n* l'appareil de radiographie *m*

Y
yellow *adj* jaune
yes *adv* oui
yesterday *n* hier *m*
  the day before yesterday *avant-hier*
yield sign *n* panneau de priorité *m*
you *pron* tu *s* / vous *pl*
  you (s. informal) *tu*
  you (s. formal) *vous*
  you (pl. informal) *vous*
  you (pl. formal) *vous*
your, yours *adj* ton *m* / ta *f* / tes *pl*
young *adj* jeune

Z
zoo *n* le zoo *m*

A

l'abeille *f* bee *n*

abîmé(e) damaged *adj*

accepter to accept *v* **p24**

accessible aux personnes à mobilité réduite handi-capped-accessible *adj* p

l'accident *m* accident *n*

D'accord. Okay. *adv*

acheter to buy *v* **p24**

l'acné *f* acne *n*

actuel actual *adj*

l'adaptateur *m* adapter plug *n*

l'addition *f* check (tab) *n*

l'adresse *f* address *n*

l'aéroport *m* airport *n* p

l'affaire *f s* deal *n*

les affaires *f pl* business *n*

> **Voici ma carte de visite.** Here's my business card.

affréter to charter *v* **p24**

afro afro *n adj*

afro-américain(e) *m f* African-American *n adj*

l'âge *m* age *n*

> **Quel âge avez-vous?** What's your age?

l'agence *f* agency *n* p

> **l'agence de location de voitures** car rental agency

l'agent *m* guard *n*

agnostique agnostic *adj*

agressé(e) mugged *adj*

l'aide *f* help *n*

aider to help *v* **p24**

Aïe! Ouch! *exclamation*

l'ail *m* garlic *n*

aimer to like, to enjoy / to love *v* **p24**

> **faire l'amour** to make love

l'aire de jeu *f* playground *n*

l'alcool *m* alcohol *n*

allaiter to nurse *v* **p24**

allemand(e) German *n adj*

aller to go / to look (appear) / to fit (clothes) / to go with (match) *v* **p30**

l'aller simple *m* one-way ticket *n*

l'aller-retour *m* round-trip ticket *n*

l'allergie *f* allergy *n*

allergique allergic *adj* See for common allergens.

allumer to turn on *v* **p24**

l'allumette *f* match *n*

> **la boîte d'allumettes** book of matches

alors then *adv* / yet *adv* / so *adv*

l'altitude *f* altitude *n*

l'ambassade *f* embassy *n*

l'ambulance *f* ambulance *n*

l'amende *f* fine (for traffic violation) *n*

américain(e) American *n adj*

l'ami(e) *m f* friend *n*

l'amour *m* love *n*

l'amphithéâtre *m* colisseum *n*

anglais(e) English *n adj*

l'Angleterre *f* England *n*

l'animal *m* animal *n*

annuler to cancel *v* **p24**

Le vol ____ a été annulé. *Flight ____ has been canceled.*

l'antibiotique *m* antibiotic *n*

l'antihistaminique *m* antihistamine *n*

anxieux *m* / **anxieuse** *f* anxious *adj*

le août *m* August *n*

l'appareil de radiographie *m* x-ray machine *n*

appareiller to sail away *v* **p24**

l'appel *m* phone call *n*

un appel en PCV collect phone call

l'appel à l'étranger international phone call

appeler to call (on the phone) / to call (shout) *v* **p24**

l'après-midi *m* afternoon *n*

l'argent *m* money *n* / silver *n*

l'arme *f* weapon *n*

l'armée *f* military, army *n*

l'arrêt *m* stop *n p*

l'arrêt de bus bus stop

arrêter to stop *v* **p24, 39**

Arrêtez-vous, s'il vous plaît. *Please stop.*

Je veux que vous vous arrêtiez. *I need you to stop.*

STOP STOP (traffic sign)

l'arrivée *f* / **les arrivées** *f pl* arrival(s) *n p*

arriver to arrive *v* **p24**

l'art *m* art *n*

exposition d'art exhibit of art

d'art art *adj*

le musée d'art art museum

l'artisan(e) *m f* craftsperson *n*

l'artiste *m f* artist *n*

l'ascenseur *m* elevator *n*

asiatique Asian *n adj*

l'aspirine *f* aspirin *n*

s'asseoir to sit *v* **p39**

l'assistance assistance, help *n*

assister to assist, to help *v* **p24**

l'assurance *f* insurance *n*

la tierce collision collision insurance

l'assurance responsabilité civile liability insurance

l'asthme *m* asthma *n*

athée atheist *adj*

attendre to wait / to hold (telephone) *v* **p25**

Attendez, s'il vous plaît! *Please wait.*

Attendez une minute! *Hold on a minute!*

l'attente *f* wait *n*

atterrir to land *v* **p24**

l'aube *f* dawn *n*

l'auberge *f* hostel *n p*

aucun(e) none *n*

au-dessus de above *prep*

audio audio *adj p*

l'assistance audio audio assistance

aujourd'hui today *n*

aussi too (also) *adv*

l'Australie *f* Australia *n*

australien *m* / **australienne** *f* Australian *n adj*

l'autobiographie *f* autobiography *n*

l'autobus *m* bus *n*

l'automne m autumn (fall) n
l'autoroute f highway n
autre another adj
de l'autre côté de across adv

de l'autre côté de la rue / en face across the street
avaler to swallow v **p24**
l'avance f advance (money) n
à l'avance in advance adv
en avant forward adj
avec with prep

avec des glaçons on the rocks (beverage)
Avec des glaçons ou sec? On the rocks or straight?
aveugle blind adj
l'avocat(e) m f lawyer n
avoir to have v **p25**
avoir besoin de to need v **p25**
avoir des rapports sexuels to have intercourse v **p25**
avoir mal to hurt v **p25**

Aïe! Ça fait mal! Ouch! That hurts!
l'avril m April n

B

le / la baby-sitter m f babysitter n

Les baby-sitters parlent anglais. The babysitters speak English.
les bagage(s) m pl baggage, luggage n

bagages perdus lost baggage
récupération des bagages baggage claim p

se baigner to bathe v **p24, 38**
la baignoire f bathtub n
le bain m bath n
le baiser m kiss n
baiser vulgar to fuck v **p24**
le balai d'essuie-glace m wiper blade n
le balcon m balcony n p
le ballon m / **la balle** f ball (sport) n
la banlieue f suburb n
la banque f bank n
bancaire bank, banking adj

le compte bancaire bank account
la carte bancaire bank card
le bar m bar, lounge n
la barbe f beard n
bas m / **basse** f low adj
les bas quartiers m slum(s) n
le bateau m boat n p
la batterie f battery (car) n
le tambour m drum n
beau m / **belle** f handsome, beautiful adj
beaucoup much n
beaucoup de many adj
le bébé m baby n
beige beige adj
belge Belgian n adj
la Belgique f Belgium n
le berceau m crib n
la berline f sedan n p
le beurre m butter n
le biberon m baby bottle n
bien fine / well adv

Je vais bien. I'm fine.

Je ne me sens pas bien. *I don't feel well.*

bienvenu(e) *welcome adv*

Vous êtes le / la bienvenu(e). *You're welcome.*

la **bière** *f beer n*

la **bière pression** *draft beer*

bilingue *bilingual adj*

le **billard** *m pool (game) n*

le **billet** *m ticket n / bill (currency) n*

le **distributeur automatique** *f ATM / cash machine n*

DAB (distributeur automatique de billets) *ATM*

la **biographie** *f biography n*

biologique *organic adj*

biracial *biracial adj*

blanc *m /* **blanche** *f white adj*

la **blessure** *f injury n*

bleu(e) *blue adj*

bleue *rare (meat) adv*

bleu lavande *lavender adj*

blond(e) *blond(e) adj*

bloquer *to block v* **p24**

le **blouson** *m jacket n*

le **bœuf** *m beef (meat) n*

boire *to drink v* **p31**

la **boisson** *f drink n*

la **boisson gratuite** *complimentary drink*

Voulez-vous quelque chose à boire? *Would you like something to drink?*

les **boissons alcoolisées** *f liquor n*

la **boisson gazeuse** *f soda n*

la **boisson gazeuse allégée** *diet soda*

la **boîte de nuit** *f nightclub n*

la **bombe** *f bomb n*

le **bon** *m voucher n* **p**

bon *m /* **bonne** *f good / correct adj*

Bonjour. *Good morning.*

Bon après-midi. *Good afternoon.*

Bonsoir. *Good evening.*

Bonne nuit. *Good night.*

Bonjour. *Hello. (morning and daytime)*

le **bord** *m board n*

à **bord** *on board*

la **bosse** *f dent n*

la **bouche** *f mouth n*

la **boucle** *f curl n*

bouclé(e) *curly adj*

bouddhiste *m f Buddhist adj*

bouger *to move v* **p24**

la **bougie** *f fuse (car) / candle n*

la **bouteille** *f bottle n*

la **bouteille de vin** *wine bottle*

la **bouteille d'oxygène** *oxygen tank*

la **boutique** *f shop n*

la **boutique hors-taxe** *duty-free shop* **p**

le **braille américain** *m braille, American n*

brancher *to plug v* **p24**

le **bras** *m arm n*

le **bridge** *m bridge (dental) n*

le **briquet** *m lighter (cigarette) n*

bronzé(e) *tanned adj*
brûler *to burn v* **p24**
brûn *brown (hair) adj*
la brune *f brunette n*
bruyant(e) *noisy adj*
le budget *m budget n*
budgéter *to budget v* **p24**
le buffet *m buffet n*
le bureau de police *m police station n*
le bureau de poste *m post office n*
le but (sport) *m goal (sport) n*

C

la cabine d'essayage *f changing room, fitting room n*
le cabinet du médecin *m doctor's office n*
cabosser *to dent v* **p24**
   Il / Elle a cabossé la voiture. *He / She dented the car.*
la cacahuète *f peanut n*
en cachemire *cashmere adj*
le cachet contre le mal de mer *m seasickness pill n*
le cadeau *m /* **les cadeaux** *m pl gift n* **p**
le café *m coffee / café n*
   le café glacé *iced coffee*
   le café au lait *latte*
le caleçon de bain *m swim trunks n*
calme *quiet adj*
camper *to camp v* **p24**
de camper *camping adj*
le camping-car *m camper n*
le Canada *m Canada n*

canadien *m /* **canadienne** *f Canadian n adj*
le canard *m duck n*
la canne à pêche *f fishing pole n*
le cappucino *m cappuccino n*
le car *m bus (coach) n*
   le car d'excursion *m sightseeing bus n*
la carie *f cavity (tooth) n*
la carte *f card n*
   Voici ma carte de visite. *Here's my business card.*
la carte *f map n*
   la carte de crédit *credit card*
   la carte d'embarquement *boarding pass* **p**
   la carte postale *postcard*
le casier *m locker n*
le casino *m casino n*
(se) casser *to break v* **p24, 38**
la cassure *f break n*
le casque *m headphones n*
catholique *Catholic adj*
le CD *m CD n*
ce *m /* **cette** *f this adj*
la ceinture *f belt (clothing) n*
célébrer *to celebrate v* **p24**
célibataire *single (unmarried)*
   Êtes-vous célibataire? *Are you single?*
celui-ci *m /* **celle-ci** *f that (nearby) adj*
celui-là *m /* **celle-là** *f that (far away) adj*
cent *hundred adj* **p**
centaine *f hundred n* **p**

le **centimètre** m *centimeter* n

le **centre commercial** m *mall* n

le **centre-ville** m *downtown* n

ces *these / those* adj

la **chaise roulante** f *wheelchair* n

  l'**accès aux handicapés** *wheelchair access*

  la **rampe d'accès pour handicapés** *wheelchair ramp*

  le **fauteuil roulant motorisé** *power wheelchair*

la **chambre** f *room* n

  le **service en chambre** *room service*

  la **chambre d'hôte** *bed-and-breakfast (B & B)*

  chambres libres *vacancy*

  complet *no vacancy*

le **change** m *currency exchange* n

changer *to change* v **p24**

la **chanson** f *song* n

chanter *to sing* v **p24**

le **chapeau** m *hat* n

charter *charter* adj

le **chat** m / la **chatte** f *cat* n

chaud(e) *hot / warm* adj

chauffer *to overheat* v **p24**

la **chaussette** f *sock* n

la **chaussure** f *shoe* n

la **chemise** f *shirt* n

le **chemisier** m *blouse* n

le **chèque** m *check* n

  le **chèque de voyage** *travelers' check*

cher m / **chère** f *expensive* adj

pas cher m / **pas chère** f *cheap*

chercher *to look for, to search* v **p24**

le **cheval** m *horse* n

le **cheveu** m / les **cheveux** m pl *hair* n

la **chèvre** f *goat* n

le **chien** m / la **chienne** f *dog* n

  le **chien accompagnant** *service dog* p

la **Chine** f *China* n

chinois(e) *Chinese* n adj

le **chiropracticien** m / la **chiropracticienne** f *chiropractor* n

le **chocolat chaud** m *hot chocolate* n

chrétien m / **chrétienne** f *Christian* adj

le **cigare** m *cigar* n

la **cigarette** f *cigarette* n

le **cil** m *eyelash* n

le **cinéma** m *cinema* n

cinq *five* adj p

cinquante *fifty* adj p

le / la **cinquième** *fifth* adj

la **circulation** f *traffic* n

la **citronnade** f *lemonade* n

clair(e) *clear* adj

la **clarinette** f *clarinet* n

la **classe** f *class* n p

  la **classe affaires** *business class*

  la **classe économique** *economy class*

  la **première classe** *first class*

la **climatisation** f *air conditioning* n p

le **clos** *vineyard / orchard* n

le club de remise en forme f
fitness center n

le cochon m *pig* n

le code vestimentaire m
dress (general attire) n

le cœur m *heart* n

le coffre (à bagages) m *trunk
(luggage, car)* n p

coffre-fort m *safe (for storing
valuables)* n

le cognac m *cognac* n

le coiffeur m / **la coiffeuse** f
hairdresser n

le coin m *corner* n

le colis m *package* n

collectionner *to collect* v p24

colorer *to color* v p24

commander *to order (a meal)*
v p24

commencer *to start, to com-
mence* v p24

comment / combien *how* adv

  Comment allez-vous? *How
are you?*

  **Combien de temps cela va-
t-il prendre?** *How long will
it take?*

  **Combien est-ce que cela
coûte?** *How much does
this cost?*

commencer *to begin* v p24

compenser *to make up (com-
pensate)* v p24

complet *full house* n

complet m / **complète** f *sold
out* adj

composer *to dial (a phone
number)* v p24

**composer directement le
numéro** *to dial direct*

comprendre *to understand* v
p25

  Vous comprenez? *Do you
understand?*

compris(e) *included*

le compte m *account* n

le comptoir m *counter (in
bar)* n

le concert m *concert* n

le conducteur m / **la conductrice** f *driver* n

conduire *to drive / to ride* v p25

confirmer *to confirm* v p24

  **Vous n'avez pas confirmé
votre réservation.** *You
didn't confirm your reservation.*

la confirmation f *confirmation* n

confus(e) *confused* adj

la congestion f *congestion
(sinus)* n

connaître *to know (someone)* v p31

constipé(e) *constipated* adj

continuer *to continue* v p24

le coquillage m *shellfish* n

la corde f *rope, twine* n

corriger *to correct* v p24

à côté (de) *next (to)* prep

le coton m *cotton* n

la couche f *diaper* n

  la couche jetable *disposable
diaper*

la couchette particulière f
private berth / cabin n

coudre *to sew* v **p25**

la couleur *f color* n

le coup de soleil *m sunburn* n

la coupe (de cheveux) *f haircut* n

coupé(e) *disconnected* adj

couper *to cut / to trim (hair)* v **p24**

le coupon *m voucher* n p
  le coupon-repas *meal voucher*
  le coupon d'hébergement *room voucher*

courir *to run* v **p24**

la couronne *f crown (dental)* n

le courriel *m e-mail* n
  Puis-je avoir votre adresse courriel? *May I have your e-mail address?*

le courrier *m mail* n
  courrier par avion *air mail*
  courrier en recommandé avec accusé de réception *certified mail*
  courrier exprès *express mail*
  courrier première classe *first class mail*
  courrier recommandé *registered mail*

le court *m court (sport)* n

court(e) *short* adj

courtois(e) *courteous* adj

coûter *to cost* v **p24**

le / la cousin(e) *m f cousin* n

la couverture *f blanket* n p

la crèche *f nursery* n

la crème *f cream* n

la crème solaire *f sunscreen* n

la crème solaire indice ____ *sunscreen SPF ____*

la crevette *f shrimp* n

crier *to shout* v **p24**

la crise cardiaque *f heart attack* n

le cuir *m leather* n p

la cuisine *f kitchen* n

cuisiner *to cook* v **p24**

très cuite *charred (meat)* adj

trop cuit(e) *overcooked* adj

cuivre *copper (color)* adj

le culte *m service (religious)* n

le cybercafé *Internet café, cybercafé* n

D

le danger *m danger* n

la danse *f dance* n

danser *to dance* v **p24**

dans *in, inside* prep

le déambulatoire *m walker (ambulatory device)* n

déborder *to overflow* v **p24**

décapotable *convertible (car)* adj

le décembre *m December* n

déclarer *to declare* v **p24**
  Vous n'avez rien à déclarer? *You don't have anything to declare?*

le déguisement *m costume* n

la dégustation *f tasting, sampling* n

déguster *to taste* v **p24**

dehors *outside* n

le déjeuner *m lunch* n

déjeuner *to eat (lunch) v p24*
demain *tomorrow adv*
demander / poser *to ask v p24*
démarrer *to start (car) v p24*
déménager *to move (house-hold) v p24*
demi(e) *half adj*
la démocratie *f democracy n*
la dent *f tooth n*
le / la dentiste *m f dentist n*
les départs *m departure(s) n*
se dépêcher *to hurry v p24, 38*
déprimé(e) *down, depressed adj*
dernier *m /* **dernière** *f last adv*
derrière *behind prep p*
désolé(e) *sorry adj*
  Je suis désolé(e), je ne comprends pas. *I'm sorry, I don't understand.*
le dessert *m dessert n*
  la carte des desserts *dessert menu*
le dessin *m drawing n*
en dessous de *below prep*
la destination *f destination n*
le détecteur de métaux *m metal detector n*
deux *two adj*
à deux / double *double adj*
  à deux lits *double room*
devant *front prep*
diabétique *diabetic adj*
la diarrhée *f diarrhea n*
le dictionnaire *m dictionary n*
différent(e) *different (other) adj*

difficile *difficult adj*
le dimanche *m Sunday n*
la dinde *f turkey n*
le dîner *m dinner n*
dîner *to eat v p24*
  sortir dîner *to eat out*
dire *to say v p32*
le directeur *m /* **la directrice** *f manager n*
la disco, la discothèque *f disco / nightclub n*
disparaître *disappear v p25*
disponible *available adj*
le distributeur *m vending machine n*
divorcé(e) *divorced adj*
dix *ten adj p*
dix-huit *eighteen adj p*
dix-neuf *nineteen adj p*
dix-sept *seventeen adj p*
dixième *tenth adj*
le docteur *m /* **la docteresse** *f doctor n*
le dollar *m dollar n*
le domicile *m home n*
donner *to give / to deal (cards) v p24*
doré(e) *golden adj*
le dos *m back (body) n*
la douane *f customs n p*
la douche *f shower n p*
se doucher *to shower v p24, 38*
doux *m /* **douce** *f soft adj*
la douzaine *f dozen n*
douze *twelve adj p*
douzième *twelfth adj*
le drame *m drama n*

le drap *m* sheet (bed linen) *n*

la droite *f* right *n* p

les droits civiques civil rights

droit(e) / raide straight *adj* / right *adj*

tout droit straight ahead

C'est à droite. It is on the right.

Tournez à droite au coin de la rue. Turn right at the corner.

dur(e) hard *adj*

durer to last *v* p24

le DVD *m* DVD *n* p

E

l'eau *f* water *n*

l'eau chaude hot water

l'eau froide cold water

l'eau courante *f* current (water) *n*

l'eau de Javel *f* bleach *n*

l'eau de Seltz *f* seltzer *n*

l'eau-de-vie de pommes *f* brandy *n*

échouer to beach *v* p24

l'école *f* school *n*

l'économie *f* economy *n* p

l'Écosse *f* Scotland *n*

écossais(e) Scottish *n* adj

écrire to write *v* p32

Pourriez-vous m'écrire cela? Would you write that down for me?

l'écrivain *m* *f* writer *n*

l'éditeur *m* / l'éditrice *f* editor *n*

l'éducateur *m* / l'éducatrice *f* educator *n*

l'église *f* church *n*

l'égratignure *f* scratch *n*

l'élection *f* election *n*

emballer to bag *v* p24

embarquer to board *v* p24

embarrassé(e) embarrassed *adj*

l'embouteillage *m* congestion (traffic) *n*

l'employé(e) *m* *f* employee *n*

l'employeur *m* / l'employeuse *f* employer *n*

encaisser to cash *v* p24

en-cas *m* snack *n*

enceinte pregnant *adj*

enchanté(e) charmed *adj*

l'enfant *m* infant / child *n*

enlever to clear, delete, remove *v* p24

l'enregistrement *m* check-in *n*

l'enregistrement électronique electronic check-in

ensoleillé(e) sunny *adj*

l'entaille *f* cut (wound) *n*

entendre to hear *v* p25

enthousiaste enthusiastic *adj*

l'entracte *m* intermission *n*

l'entraînement *m* workout *n*

entraîner to train *v* p24

l'entrée *f* entrance / cover charge (in bar) *n*

entrée interdite do not enter

l'entreprise *f* business *n*

entrer to enter *v* p24

l'enveloppe *f* envelope *n*

l'environnement *m* environment *n*

envoyer to send *v* p24

épais *m* / **épaisse** *f* thick*adj*

épeler to spell*v* **p24**

> **Pourriez-vous épeler ce mot, s'il vous plaît?** *Can you spell this word, please?*

les épices *f* spice*n*

l'épilation à la cire *f* waxing*n*

> **l'épilation ____ à la cire ____** waxing
> **du maillot** bikini
> **des sourcils** eyebrow
> **des jambes** leg

(s')épouser to marry, to get married*v* **p24, 39**

épuisé(e) exhausted*adj*

l'équipe *f* team*n*

l'erreur *f* mistake *n*

l'escalade *f* climbing*n*

escalader to climb*v* **p24**

l'escalier *m* stair*n*

l'escalier roulant *m* escalator*n*

l'Espagne *f* Spain*n*

espagnol(e) Spanish*n adj*

les espèces *f* cash*n*

> **espèces uniquement** cash only

essayer to try*v* **p24**

l'essence *f* gas*n*

l'essuie-glace *m* windshield wiper*n*

est is*v* See **être** (to be)**p27**.

l'étage *m* floor*n*

> **le premier étage** first floor

l'état *m* condition / state*n*

l'été *m* summer*n*

éteindre to turn off*v* **p25**

êtes are*v* See **être** (to be)**p27**.

être to be*v* **p27**

étroit(e) narrow*adj*

eux *m pl* / **elles** *f pl* them*pron*

s'évanouir to faint*v* **p24, 39**

l'évier *m* sink (kitchen)*n*

l'excursion *m* sightseeing / tour*n*

> **les excursions guidées** guided tours
> **les excursions audio guidées** audio tours

excuser to excuse (pardon)*v* **p24**

> **Excusez-moi.** *Excuse me.*

expédier to ship*v* **p24**

expliquer to explain*v* **p24**

l'exposition *f* exhibit*n*

F

fâché(e) angry*adj*

facturer to bill*v* **p24**

faire to do, to make*v* **p33**

fait à partir de made of*adj*

la famille *f* family*n*

fatigué(e) tired*adj*

la faute *f* fault*n*

le fautif *m* / **la fautive** *f* at fault*adj*

> **C'est moi le fautif / la fautive.** *I'm at fault.*
> **C'est sa faute.** *It is his / her fault.*

féminin(e) female*adj*

la femme *f* woman / wife*n*

la femme au foyer *f* homemaker*n*

la femme de chambre *f* maid (hotel)*n*

la fenêtre *f* window*n*

fermé(e) *closed adj*

fermer *to close v* **p24**

le festival *m festival n*

le festival de rue *street festival*

Au feu! *m Fire! n*

le feu *m light n*

Puis-je vous offrir du feu?
May I offer you a light?

février *m February n*

le fiancé *m* / **la fiancée** *f*
fiancé(e) n

la fille *f girl, daughter n*

le film *m movie n*

le fils *m son n*

fin(e) *thin adj*

finir *to finish v* **p24**

la fissure *f crack (in glass
object) n*

la fleur *f flower n*

flottant(e) *loose adj*

le flush *m flush (gambling) n*

la flûte *f flute / small baguette n*

les fonds *m pl money (in an
account) / stocks, securities n*

le forfait *m rate plan n*

le format *m format n*

fort(e) *loud adj*

fort *loudly adv*

Parlez plus fort, s'il vous plaît.
Please speak more loudly.

la fouille *f search n p*

le fourgon *m van n p*

fragile *fragile adj*

frais *m* / **fraîche** *f fresh adj*

frais de traitement *m service
charge n*

la France *f France n*

français(e) *French n adj*

le frein *m brake n*

le frein à main *emergency
brake*

freiner *to brake v* **p24**

le frère *m brother n*

froid(e) *cold adj*

le fromage *m cheese n*

le front *m forehead n*

le fruit *m fruit n*

les fruits de mer *seafood n*

fumer *to smoke v* **p24**

les fumeurs *m pl smokers n*

la zone fumeurs *smoking area*

interdit de fumer *no smoking*

fuire *to drip v* **p25**

le fusible *m fuse (home) n*

G

le gallon *m gallon n*

le gant *m glove n*

le garçon *m boy n*

le garde *m guard n*

garder *to keep v* **p24**

se garer *to park v* **p24, 38**

la gauche *f left n p*

à gauche *on the left*

gentil *m* / **gentille** *f kind
(nice) adj*

le gilet *m* / **la bouée** *f de
sauvetage* *life preserver n*

le gin *m gin n*

la glace *f ice / ice cream n*

avec des glaçons *with ice
cubes / on the rocks*

la machine à glaçons *ice
machine*

le golf *m golf n*

le terrain de golf *golf course*
le club de golf *golf club*
le goût *m taste* n
goûter *to taste* v **p24**
le grain de beauté *m mole (facial feature)* n
le gramme *m gram* n
grand(e) *big / tall* adj
très grand(e) *extra-large* adj
la grand-mère *f grandmother* n
le grand-père *m grandfather* n
les grands-parents *m f pl grandparents* n
grandir *to grow (get larger)* v **p24**

Où avez-vous grandi? *Where did you grow up?*

gratter *to scratch* v **p24**
gratuit(e) *complimentary, free* adj
graver *to burn (CD)* v **p24**
grec *m / grecque f Greek* adj
le grill *m steakhouse* n
gris(e) *gray* adj
gros *m / grosse f fat* adj
le groupe *m band (musical ensemble) / group* n
la guerre *f war* n
le guichet *m ticket counter, box office* n
le / la guide *m f guide (of tours)* n
le guide *m guide (publication)* n
le guide d'utilisation *m manual (instruction booklet)* n
guider *to guide* v **p24**

la guitare *f guitar* n
la gymnastique *f gym* n
le / la gynécologue *m f gynecologist* n

H

s'habiller *to dress* v **p24, 39**

Vous devriez vous habiller pour cet événement. *You should dress up for that affair.*

habiter *to live* v **p24**
le hall d'entrée *m hallway* n
le handicap *m handicap, disability* n
haut(e) *high* adj p
l'hectare *m hectare* n
l'herbe *f herb* n
l'heure *f hour / time* n
les heures d'ouverture *f pl hours (of operation)* n
heureux *m / heureuse f happy* adj
hier *yesterday* adv p

avant-hier *the day before yesterday*

hindou(e) *Hindu* adj
hip-hop *hip-hop* n
l'histoire *f history* n
historique *historical* adj
l'hiver *m winter* n
l'homme *m / la femme f au foyer homemaker* n
l'homme *m / la personne de sexe masculin f man* n / *male* n
l'horaire *m timetable* n
hors-taxe *duty-free* adj

l'hôte *m* / l'hôtesse *f* guest *n*

l'hôtel *m* hotel *n* p

l'huile *f* oil *n*

huit eight *adj*

huitième eighth *adj*

humide humid *adj*

huppé(e) upscale *adj*

I

ici here *n* p

n'importe lequel *m* / laquelle *f* any *adj*

n'importe quoi *m f* anything *n*

n'importe où anywhere *adv*

imprimer to print *v* **p24**

l'Inde *f* India

indien *m* / indienne *f* Indian *n adj*

l'indicateur de vitesse *m* speedometer *n*

l'indigestion *f* indigestion *n*

l'infirmier *m* / l'infirmière *f* nurse *n*

l'Information *f* information *n*

l'ingénieur *mf* engineer *n*

l'inscription *f* membership *n*

l'insecte *m* bug *n85*

l'insectifuge *m* insect repellent *n*

l'institution de crédit *f* credit bureau *n*

insulter to insult *v* **p24**

à l'intérieur de inside *prep*

l'Internet *m* Internet *n*

l'Internet à haut débit high-speed Internet

l'interprète *m f* interpreter *n*

l'Irlande *f* Ireland *n*

irlandais(e) Irish *n adj*

l'Italie *f* Italy *n*

italien *m* / italienne *f* Italian *n adj*

J

la jambe *f* leg *n*

le janvier *m* January *n14*

le Japon *m* Japan *n*

japonais(e) Japanese *n adj*

jaune yellow *adj*

le jazz *m* jazz *n*

je I *pron*

le jeudi *m* Thursday *n*

jeune young *adj*

de jeune fille maiden *adj*

J'ai gardé mon nom de jeune fille. I kept my maiden name.

le jogging *m* jogging *n*

jouer to play *v* **p24**

le jouet *m* toy *n*

le magasin de jouets toy store

le jour *m* day *n*

le journal *m* / les journaux *m pl* newspaper *n*

juif *m* / juive *f* Jewish *adj*

le juillet *m* July *n*

le juin *m* June *n*

le jus *m* juice *n*

le jus de fruit fruit juice

la justice *f* / le tribunal *m* court (legal) *n*

K

kasher kosher *adj*

le kilo *m* kilo *n*

le kilomètre *m* kilometer *n*

le kiosque à journaux *m* newsstand *n*

la kitchenette *f* kitchenette *n*

le klaxon *m* horn *n*

L

là there *adv* p

là-bas over there

le lait *m* milk *n*

le milk-shake / le lait frappé milkshake

la langue *f* language *n*

le lapin *m* rabbit *n*

large wide *adj*

(à) large bande *f* broadband *n*

le lavabo *m* sink (bathroom) *n*

la leçon *f* lesson *n*

le lecteur de CD *m* CD player *n*

le légume *m* vegetable *n*

lent(e) slow *adj*

lentement slow(ly) *adv*

Parlez plus lentement, s'il vous plaît. Please speak more slowly.

les lentilles de contact *f* contact lens *n*

lequel *m* / **laquelle** *f* / **lesquels** *m pl* / **lesquelles** *f pl* which *adj*

Lequel? *m* / **Laquelle?** *f* Which one?

Lequel *m* / **Laquelle** *f* est-ce? Which is it?

la lessive *f* laundry *n*

la libération de la chambre *f* check-out *n*

l'heure de libération de la chambre check-out time

la librairie *f* bookstore *n*

en libre-service self-serve *adj*

le lieu de rencontre *m* hang-out (hot spot) *n*

la limite de vitesse *f* speed limit *n*

la limousine *f* limo *n*

la liqueur *f* liqueur *n*97

lire to read *v* p25

le lit *m* bed *n*75

le très grand lit king-sized bed

le canapé-lit pull-out bed

le grand lit queen-sized bed

le lit à une place single bed

le litre *m* liter *n*

le livre *m* book *n*

la livre *f* pound *n*

local(e) / locaux *pl* local *adj*

la loge *f* box (seat) *n*

le logiciel *m* software *n*

la loi *f* law *n*

loin far *adj* p

long *m* / **longue** *f* long *adj*

longtemps long *adv*

louer to rent *v* p24

lui him *pron*

la lumière *f* light (lamp) *n*

lumineux *m* / **lumineuse** *f* bright *adj*

le lundi *m* Monday *n*

les lunettes *f pl* glasses (spectacles) *n*

les lunettes protectrices safety glasses

les lunettes de soleil sunglasses

M

la **machine** f machine n

le **magasin** m store n

le **magazine** m magazine n

le **magnétoscope** m VCR n

le **mai** m May (month) n

le **maillot de bain** m swimsuit n

la **main** f hand n

mais but conjunction

maintenant now adv p

malade sick adj

le **mal de tête** m headache n

le **mal des transports** m car sickness n

malentendant(e) hearing-impaired adj73

malvoyant(e) visually-impaired adj p

manger to eat v p24

d'une manière étrange suspiciously adv

manipuler to handle v p24

manquant(e) missing adj

manquer to miss / to lack v p24

le **manteau** m coat n

le **maquillage** m makeup n

se **maquiller** to make up (apply cosmetics) v p24, 38

le / la **marchand(e) ambulant(e)** m f street vendor n

la **marche** f walk n

le **marché** m market n

le **marché aux puces** flea market

le **marché en plein air** open-air market

marcher to walk v p24

le **mardi** m Tuesday n

le **mari** m husband n

marié(e) married adj

marron brown adj

le **mars** m March (month) n

masculin male adj

le **massage dorsal** m back rub n

masser to massage v p24

le **match (sport)** m match (sport) n

la **matière** f subject matter, content / fabric n

le **matin** m morning n

les **mèches** f highlights (hair) n

le / la **médecin** m f doctor n

le **médicament** m medication n

meilleur(e) best adj

le / la **membre** m f member n

même same adj

le **menu** m menu n

le **menu des plats à emporter** m takeout menu

Merci. Thank you.

le **mercredi** m Wednesday n

la **mère** f mother n

le **mètre** m meter n

le **métro** m subway n p

la **ligne de métro** subway line

mettre to place / to charge (money) v p25

mettre à jour to update v p25

le **Mexique** m Mexico n

mexicain(e) Mexican n adj

le **midi** m noon n adv

mieux best / better / rather adj

le **mile** m mile n

au milieu de in the middle prep

le / la militaire *m f military n*
mille *thousand adj*
le millilitre *m milliliter n*
le millimètre *m millimeter n*
mince *damn expletive / slender adj*
le minuit *m midnight n*
la minute *f minute n*
la mise *f / le pari m bet n*
   Je veux connaître votre mise. *I'll see your bet.*
la mise à niveau *f upgrade n*
miser *to put / to bet v p24*
moins *less adv / least adv*
le mois *m month n*
la moitié *f half n*
   une moitié *one half*
la monnaie *f change (money) n*
   Vous voudrais de la monnaie? *Would you like change back?*
la montagne *f mountain n*
le montant *m amount n*
monter *to climb / to get in (a vehicle) v p24*
montrer *to show / to point v p24*
mordoré(e) *bronze adj*
la mosquée *f mosque n*
le mot de passe *m password n*
le moteur *m engine n*
la moto *f motorcycle n p*
le mousqueton *m carabiner n*
la moustache *f moustache n*
moyen(ne) *medium (size) adj*
le musée *m museum n*
le musicien *m / la musicienne f musician n*

la musique *music n*
musulman(e) *Muslim adj*

N

nager *to swim v p24*
   défense de nager *no swimming*
la nationalité *f nationality n*
le naufrage *m shipwreck n*
la nausée *f nausea n*
la navette *f shuttle bus n*
le navire *m ship, boat n p*
le nécessaire de toilette *m toiletries n*
néo-zélandais(e) *New Zealander n adj*
le nettoyage à sec *m dry cleaning n*
nettoyer *to clean v p24*
neuf *nine adj p*
neuvième *ninth adj*
le neveu *m / les neveux m pl nephew n*
le nez *m nose n*
la nièce *f niece n*
le noir *m dark n*
noir(e) *black adj*
noisette *hazel adj*
la noix *f nut n*
le nom *m name n*
   Quel est ton nom? *What's your (sur)name?*
   le nom de famille *last name*
non fumeur *nonsmoking adj*
   zone non fumeurs *non-smoking area*
   voiture non fumeurs *non-smoking car*

chambre non fumeurs *non-smoking room*

la nourriture *f food* n

nous *us* pron

nouveau *m* / **nouvelle** *f new* adj

la Nouvelle-Zélande *f New Zealand* n

le novembre *m November* n

nuageux *cloudy* adj

la nuit *f night* n

par nuit *per night* p

le numéro *m number* n p

Puis-j'avoir votre numéro de téléphone? *May I have your phone number?*

O

occupé(e) *busy, occupied* adj

l'octobre *m October*

l'œil *m* / **les yeux** *m pl eye(s)* n

l'officier *m officer* n

offrir *to offer* v **p24**

l'oie *m goose* n

l'oiseau *m bird* n

l'olive *f olive* n

l'once *m ounce* n

l'oncle *m uncle* n

onze *eleven* adj p

l'opéra *m opera* / *opera house* n

l'opérateur *m* / **l'opératrice** *f operator (phone)* n

l'optométriste *m f optometrist* n

l'or *m gold* n adj

l'orange *f orange* n adj

l'orchestre symphonique *m symphony* n

l'ordinateur *m computer* n

l'ordinateur portable *m laptop* n

l'ordonnance *f prescription* n

l'oreiller *m pillow* n

l'orgue *m organ* n

orthodoxe *orthodox* adj

ôter *to remove* v **p24**

où *where* adv

oui *yes* adv

ouvert(e) *open* adj

Nous ne sommes plus ouvert. *We're not open anymore.*

P

le pain *m bread* n

pâle *pale* adj

panneau de priorité *m yield sign* n

le pansement (adhésif) *m band-aid* n

le papier *m paper* n

le papier de toilette *m toilet paper* n

le parapluie *m umbrella* n

le parc *m park* n

le pare-brise *m windshield* n

le parent *m parent* n

parier (sur) *to bet (on), to gamble (on)* v **p24**

le parking *m parking* n

parler *to speak, talk* v **p24**

Parlez-vous français? *Do you speak French?*

Pourriez-vous parler plus fort, s'il vous plaît? *Would you speak louder, please?*

partager *to divide* / *to split (gambling)* v **p24**

le / la **partenaire** *m f partner n*

le **parti** *m party n*

participer (à) *to attend v* **p24**

partir *to leave, depart v* **p25**

pas de *no adv*

le **passager** *m /* la **passagère** *f passenger n*

le **passe-temps** *m hobby n*

le **passeport** *m passport n*

le **pâté de maisons** *m block (residential) n*

le **patron** *m /* la **patronne** *f boss n*

payer *to pay v* **p24**

en PCV *collect adv*

Veuillez faire votre appel en PCV. *Please make your call collect.*

le **péage** *m toll n*

la **peau** *f skin n*

le / la **pédiatre** *mf pediatrician n*

peindre *to paint v* **p25**

la **peinture** *f painting n*

perdre *to lose v* **p25**

perdu(e) *lost adj*

le **père** *m father n*

permettre *to permit v* **p25**

le **permis** *m license, permit n*

le **permis de conduire** *driver's license*

le **personnel** *m staff, employees n*

peser *to weigh* **p24**

Combien de kilos pèsez-vous? *How much do you weigh (in kilos)?*

petit(e) *little, small adj*

le **petit ami** *m /* la **petite amie** *f boyfriend / girlfriend n*

le **petit déjeuner** *m breakfast n*

On ne sert plus le petit déjeuner. *Breakfast is no longer being served.*

le **petit gâteau** *m cookie n*

un **peu** *m bit (small amount) n*

un **peu de** *some adj*

le **phare** *m headlight n*

le **piano** *m piano n*

la **pièce** *f coin / room (of house) / play (theater) n*

la **pièce d'identité** *f identification n p*

le **pied** *m foot n*

à pied *walking, on foot adj*

le **piéton** *m /* la **piétonne** *f pedestrian n*

la **pile** *f battery (for flashlight) n*

la **pillule contraceptive** *f birth control pill n*

la **pinte** *f pint n*

pire *worse / worst adj adv*

la **piscine** *f swimming pool n*

la **piste de décollage** *f runway n*

la **pizza** *f pizza n*

la **place** *f seat n / plaza, square n*

la **plage** *f beach n*

le **plaisir** *m pleasure n*

le **plastique** *m plastic n*

le **plat** *m dish n*

le **plat du jour** *special (featured meal)*

plein *adj busy (restaurant) adj*

pleuvoir *to rain v* **p24**

plonger *to dive v* **p24**

pluvieux m / **pluvieuse** f rainy adj

le pneu tire n

la poignée f handle n

la police f police n

le pont m bridge (across a river) n

populaire popular adj

le port m port (for ship mooring) n

le port USB m USB port n

la porte f door n / gate (airport) n

le portefeuille m wallet n

porter to wear v **p24**

le porteur m porter n p

le porto m port (beverage) n

poser une question to ask a question v **p24**

le pouce m inch n

le poulet m chicken n

le pourboire m tip (gratuity) n

pousser to push v **p24**

la poussette f stroller n

pouvoir can (able to) v / may v **p34**

Puis-je _____? May I _____?

préférer to prefer v **p24**

se prélasser to lounge v **p24, 38**

premier m / **première** f first adj

prendre to take v **p35**

Cette place est-elle prise? Is this seat taken?

la préparation lactée f formula n

préparé(e) adj prepared adj

près de close (near) prep

présenter to introduce v **p24**

Laissez-moi vous présenter à _____. I'd like to introduce you to _____.

le préservatif m condom n

pas sans préservatif not without a condom

le pressing m dry cleaner n

les prévisions météorologiques f pl weather forecast n

le printemps m spring (season) n

la prise f plug n

privé(e) private adj

le prix m fee n / price n

le prix d'entrée m admission fee n

le prix du traject m fare n

le problème m problem n

prochain(e) next adj p

proche near adj p

le produit m product n

professionnel m / **professionnelle** f professional adj

profond(e) deep adj

le programme m schedule n / program n

propre clean adj

protestant(e) Protestant adj

la prothèse dentaire f denture n

les provisions f pl groceries n

puis next, then adv

le pull m sweater n

Q

Quand when adv

quarante forty n adj p

le quart *m quart n / fourth n / quarter n adj*

quatorze *fourteen adj p*

quatre *four adj p*

quatre-vingt *eighty adj7*

quatre-vingt-dix *ninety adj*

quatre-vingt-onze *ninety-one adj*

quatrième *fourth adj*

le Québec *m Quebec n*

québécois(e) *Quebecois n adj*

quel *m /* **quelle** *f what adv*

quelque chose *f something*

quelqu'un *m someone pron*

qui *who adv*

à qui *whose adj*

la quinte *f straight (gambling) n*

la quinte royale *f royal flush n*

quinze *fifteen adj7*

Quoi de neuf? *What's up?*

R

le raccordement *m electrical hookup n*

raccrocher *hang up (end a phone call) v* **p24**

la radio *f radio n p*

le raisin *m grape n*

ralentir *to slow v* **p24**

Ralentissez! *Slow down!*

ramasser *to collect v* **p24**

la rampe d'accès *f ramp (wheelchair) n*

rapide *fast adj*

les rapports sexuels *m pl intercourse (sexual) n*

ravi(e) *delighted adj*

rayé(e) *scratched adj*

le rayon *m aisle (in store) n*

à rayures *striped adj*

recevoir *to receive v* **p24**

recharger *to charge (a battery) v* **p24**

le récif *m reef (coral) n*

la réclamation *f claim n*

Voulez-vous faire une réclamation? *Do you want to file a claim?*

recommander *to recommend v* **p24**

se réconcilier *to make up (apologize) v* **p24, 38**

le reçu *m receipt n*

le rédacteur *m /* **la rédactrice** *f editor n*

la réduction *f discount n*

la réduction pour enfants *children's discount*

la réduction pour personnes âgées *senior discount*

la réduction étudiante *student discount*

regarder *to look (observe) / to watch v* **p24**

le reggae *m reggae n*

régler la note *to check out (of hotel) v* **p24**

rejeté(e) *declined adj*

Votre carte de crédit a été rejetée. *Your credit card was declined.*

le rendez-vous *m appointment n*

rendre visite à *to pay a visit to v* **p25**

renoncer à to wave v **p24**
le renouvellement m refill (prescription) n
les renseignements m pl information / directory assistance (phone) n
rentrer to return (to a place, usually home) v **p24**
renverser to spill v **p24**
le repas m meal n
répéter to repeat v **p24**

Pourriez-vous répéter ce que vous venez de dire, s'il vous plaît? Would you please repeat that?

répondre to answer v **p25**
la réponse f answer n
le / la représentant(e) commercial(e) m f salesperson n
le réseau m / **les réseaux** m pl network n
la réservation f reservation n
le restaurant m restaurant n
rester to stay v **p24**

Combien de nuits est-ce que vous resterez? For how many nights will you be staying?

rester en ligne to hold (telephone) v **p24**
en retard late adj
le retard m delay n **p**
retirer withdraw v **p24**
retourner to return v **p24**
le retrait m withdrawal n
le réveil m alarm clock n
le réveil téléphonique m wake-up call n

Au revoir! Goodbye!
le rhum m rum n
le rhume m cold (illness) n
la rivière f river n
le robinet m faucet n
le rock m rock and roll n
la roue de secours f spare tire n
le roman m novel n
romantique romantic adj
la rose f rose n
rose pink adj
rouge red / medium well (meat) adv
à roulettes wheeled adj p
la route f road n
route fermée f road closed (sign) n
le roux m / **la rousse** f redhead n
la rue f street n

de l'autre côté de la rue across the street
en bas de la rue down the street

S

sa f his, her adj
le sac bag n
le sac à main m purse n p
le sac de vol m carry-on bag n
le sac vomitoire m airsickness bag n p
saignant(e) medium rare (meat) / bloody adj
la salade f salad n
la salle d'attente f waiting area n
la salle de dégustation f tasting room n

le salon m lounge, bar n

le samedi m Saturday n

sans without prep

la sauce f dressing (salad) n / sauce n

savoir to know (something) v p35

le savon m soap n

scanner to scan (document) v p24

le scooter m scooter n p

le score m score n

la sculpture f sculpture n

se oneself, himself, herself pron

sec m / **sèche** f dry adj

séché(e) dried adj

sécher to dry v p24

le séchoir m hair dryer n

second(e) second n adj

Au secours! Help!

la sécurité f security n

  le contrôle de sécurité security checkpoint

  l'agent de sécurité security guard

seize sixteen adj p

le sel m salt n

  Ce plat est à faible teneur en sel. This is a low-salt dish.

la semaine f week n

  cette semaine this week

  la semaine dernière last week

  la semaine prochaine next week

sens unique m one way adj

le sentier m trail n

sentir to smell v p24

séparé(e) separated (marital status) adj

sept seven adj p

le septembre m September n

septième seventh adj

serré(e) tight adj

le serveur m / **la serveuse** f waiter n

le service m service n

  hors service out of service

la serviette f napkin / towel / briefcase n p,

servir to serve v p24

ses mf pl his, her adj

seul(e) single (one) adj

le sexe m sex (gender) n

les shorts m shorts n

le siège auto m car seat (child's safety seat) n p

signer to sign v p24

  Signez ici, s'il vous plaît. Sign here, please.

s'il te plaît s please (informal)

s'il vous plaît please (formal)

six six adj p

la sœur f sister n

la soie f silk n

soixante sixty adj p

soixante-dix seventy adj p

le solde m balance (bank account) / sale (discount) n

le soleil m sun n

sombre dark adj

sommes are v See **être** (to be) p27

son m / **sa** f / **ses** m f his, her adj

sont are v See **être** (to be) p27

la sorte *f kind (type) n*

la sortie *f exit n*

la sortie de secours *f emergency exit n*

sortir *to exit / to go out v* **p36**

ne pas sortir par cette issue *not an exit*

sortir en boîte *to go clubbing v* **p36**

la soupe *f soup n*

le sourcil *m eyebrow n*

sourd(e) *deaf adj*

le sous-titre *m subtitle n*

le sous-vêtement *m underwear n*

le spa *m spa n p*

spécifier *to specify v* **p24**

le spectacle *m show (performance) n*

les sports *m sports n*

le stade *m stadium n*

le stand d'information *m information booth n*

la station *f station n*

la station essence *gas station*

la station de bus *bus station*

la station de métro *subway station p*

stationner *to park (a vehicle) v* **p24**

stationnement interdit *no parking*

stressé(e) *stressed adj*

le / la styliste *m f designer n*

la substitution *f substitution n*

la Suisse *f Switzerland n*

suisse *Swiss n adj*

la suite *f suite n p*

la suite avec terrasse *f penthouse n*

super *great adj*

superficiel *shallow adj*

le supermarché *m supermarket n* **105**

supplémentaire *extra (additional) adj*

sur *on, over prep*

sûr(e) *safe (secure) adj*

Ce quartier n'est pas sûr. *This area isn't safe.*

surfer *to surf v* **p24**

T

ta *f / ton m / tes m f pl your, yours pron*

la table *f table n*

la taille *f size (clothing, shoes) n*

le tailleur *m tailor n*

la tante *f aunt n*

plus tard *adv later adv p*

le tarif *m rate (car rental, hotel) n*

le tarif par jour *daily rate*

le tarif hebdomadaire *weekly rate*

le taux de change *m exchange rate n*

le taux d'intérêt *m interest rate n*

la taxe *f tax n*

la taxe sur la valeur ajoutée (TVA) *value-added tax (VAT)*

le taxi *m taxi n*

télécharger *to download / to upload v* **p24**

la télécopie *m fax n*

le téléphone *m phone n*

Nous n'avons pas de télé-phone public. *We don't have a public phone.*

le téléphone portable *m cell phone n*

téléphonique *phone adj*

la carte téléphonique *phone card*

l'annuaire téléphonique *phone directory*

la télévision *f television n*

la télévision par câble *cable television*

la télévision par satellite *satellite television*

le temple *m temple n*

tenir *to hold v* **p24**

se tenir *to behave v* **p24, 38**

se tenir debout *to stand v* **p24, 38**

le tennis *m tennis n*

la tente *f tent n*

la tenue de rigueur *f* / **le code vestimentaire** *m dress (general attire) n*

le terminal *m terminal (air-port) n*

le terrain de camping *m campsite n*

le terrain d'exercice *m driving range n*

la terrasse *f terrace / side-walk seating n*

Voulez-vous dîner sur ter-rasse? *Would you like to be seated outdoors?*

tes *m f pl* / **ton** *m* / **ta** *f your, yours pron*

la tétine *f pacifier n*

le thé *m tea n*

le théâtre *m theater n*

le timbre *m stamp (postage) n*

le tire-bouchon *m corkscrew, bottle opener n*

tirer *to pull v* **p24**

tirer la chasse d'eau *to flush v* **p24**

le tissu *m fabric n*

la toile *f canvas n* **57**

la toilette *f s toilet (fixture) n*

les toilettes *f pl bathroom n*

les toilettes pour hommes *men's restroom*

les toilettes pour femmes *women's restroom*

les toilettes publiques *public restroom*

le toit ouvrant *m sunroof n*

tomber *to fall v* **p24**

ton *m* / **ta** *f* / **tes** *mf pl your, yours adj*

la tonne *f ton n*

tôt *early adj*

tourner *to turn v* **p24**

tourner à gauche / **à droite** *to turn left / right*

tousser *to cough v* **p24**

tout *all n*

en tout *total adv*

Ça fait ___ euros en tout. *It comes to ___ euros.*

tout *m* / **toute** *f* / **tous** *m pl* / **toutes** *f pl all adj*

la toux *f cough n*

le train *m train n*

un horaire des trains *train schedule*

traîner *(passer du temps)* to hang out (to relax) *v* **p24**

traiter *to process (a transaction)* *v* **p24**

la transaction *f transaction n*

transférer *to transfer v* **p24**

le transfert *m transfer n*

la transmission *f transmission n*

la transmission automatique *automatic transmission*

la transmission standard *standard transmission*

travailler *to work v* **p24**

en travers de *across prep*

treize *thirteen adj*

treizième *thirteenth adj*

trente *thirty adj*

très *very adj*

la tresse *f braid n*

le tribunal *m court (legal) n*

le tribunal des infractions à la circulation *traffic court*

triple *triple adj*

triste *sad adj*

trois *three adj*

troisième *third adj*

la trompette *f trumpet n*

trop *too (excessively) adv*

le trottoir *m sidewalk n / walkway n*

trouble *blurry adj*

trouver *to find v* **p24**

tu *you (singular, informal) pron*

le tuyau d'évacuation *m drain n*

U

un(e) *one adj*

l'université *f university / college n*

l'urgence *f emergency n*

utiliser *to use v* **p24**

V

les vacances *f pl holidays n / vacation n*

la vache *f cow n*

la valise *f suitcase n*

la varappe *f rock climbing n*

végétarien *m /* **végétarienne** *f vegetarian adj*

vendre *to sell v* **p25**

le vendredi *m Friday n*

le ventilateur *m fan n*

vérifier *to check v* **p24**

le verre *m glass n / shot (liquor) n*

Ce vin se sert au verre ou à la carafe. *This wine is served by the glass or by the carafe.*

le verrou *m lock (on door) n*

verrouiller *to lock v* **p24**

vers le haut *up adv*

la version *f version n*

le vert *m green (golf) n*

vert(e) *green adj*

des vertiges (avoir) *dizzy (to be) adj*

la veste *f jacket n*

la veuve *f /* **le veuf** *m widow, widower n*

viande *f meat n*
la vidéocassette *f video n*
la vie *f living n / life n*
Que faites-vous dans la vie?
What do you do for a living?
vieux *m / vieille f old adj*
la vigne *f vine n*
le vignoble *m vinyard, winery n*
la ville *f city n*
le vin *m wine n*
la carte des vins *wine list*
le vin sec *dry wine*
le vin doux *sweet wine*
le vin rosé *blush wine*
le vin mousseux *sparkling wine*
vingt *twenty adj*
vingtième *twentieth adj*
le vinyle *m vinyl n*
violer *to rape v p24, 199*
violet *purple adj*
le violon *m violin n*
le visa *m visa n*
le visage *f face n*
la vision *f vision n*
visiter *to visit v p24*
vite *fast adv*
vivre *to live v p25*
la vodka *f vodka n97*
la voile *f sail n*
voir *to see v p37*
le voisin *m / la voisine f neighbor n*
la voiture *f car n*
agence de location de voitures *car rental agency*

le vol *m flight n*
Vous allez changer de vol.
You have a connecting flight.
la zone d'arrivée des vols internationaux *international arrivals*
la zone de départ des vols internationaux *international departures*
la volaille *f poultry n*
volé(e) *stolen adj*
voler *to rob, to steal v p24*
le volume *m volume n*
voter *to vote v p24*
vouloir *to want, to desire v p37*
le voyage *m trip n*
voyager *to travel v p24*
le voyant *m light (car) n*
le voyant de contrôle *check engine light*
le voyant du niveau d'huile *oil light*
vraiment *really adj*
la vue *f view n*

W

le wagon-lits *f sleeping car n*
les WC *f pl restrooms n*
la Wi-Fi *f Wi-Fi n*

Z

le zoo *m zoo n*